Upholding the Law
by
'Special'
Appointment

D. J. Rodgerson

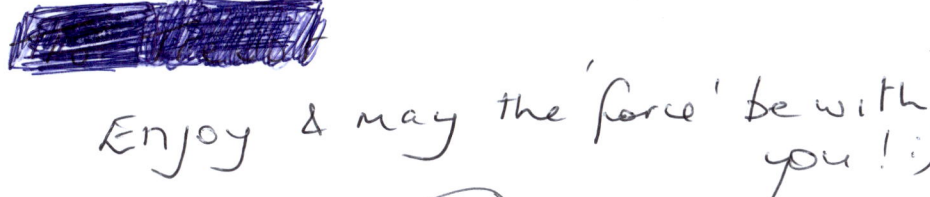

Enjoy & may the 'force' be with you! :)

Published in 2024 by
ELSP

Origination by Ex Libris Press
www.ex-librisbooks.co.uk

Typeset in 10.5/14 point Minion Pro

Printed by CPI Antony Rowe
Chippenham, Wiltshire

ISBN 9781912020010

CONTENTS

Preface		5
Prologue		7
1	Rude Awakening	9
2	Duty Bound	15
3	Lost & Found	23
4	Never a Dull Moment	33
5	More Eye Openers	40
6	Crossroads Reached	51
7	Gap Years	56
8	Back in the Fold	70
9	A New Dawn	77
10	In at the Deep End	82
11	Variety – the Spice of Life	95
12	Twists of Fate	110
13	'Minding the Shop'	116
14	When Duty Calls	126
15	Clowning About	141
16	'Lol'	149
17	Lack of Domestic Bliss	162
18	Wayward Driving	178
19	Stake-Outs	190
20	Caught 'Bang to Rights'	204
21	Public Order	215
22	Danger Zone	234
23	Hellbent on Criminal Intent	244
24	'Mispers'	263
25	End of the Line	268
	Epilogue	275
	Acknowledgements	278

Preface

THIS MEMOIR FOCUSES on all the different experiences I encountered during 22 years on the beat, initially chronicling my career as a police cadet and then thematically charting my time as a special constable. The emphasis is predominantly on the quirky, comical or extremely scary and challenging aspects of police work, as opposed to the more routine tasks associated with performing the duties of a police cadet or voluntary copper – although, personally, I always enjoyed the many aspects of community policing that formed an intrinsic and essential part of the overall service.

Within the context of the various tales, I've tried to capture the very human element of police work by referencing the relationships you develop with colleagues, members of the community and even those people linked to the criminal fraternity. Integral to this frank account of policing is the camaraderie and lifelong friendships that feature as a result of working closely with colleagues, often in circumstances that can be exceptionally stressful and traumatic, or indeed very sad on occasion. I hope the book constantly reminds readers that behind every uniform is a fellow human being, who is simply trying to do a job that can be very testing – a job that requires every officer to demonstrate a vast array of skills and personal qualities whilst upholding the law, including common sense, integrity and compassion. A sharp wit can also sometimes help! Understandably it is a role that puts those performing such duties very much in the firing line, not only in terms of dealing with a variety of complex incidents, ranging from serious crimes to human tragedies, but also in regard to facing constant scrutiny and, in some instances, unfair criticism. Not surprisingly, a copper's emotions can fluctuate from boredom to excitement, or even extreme terror in the blink of an eye, and it should be evident from these tales that those engaged in policing frequently display immense courage as they to respond to incidents and deal with them accordingly, no matter how challenging.

All the stories contained within the book are based on actual events, or true accounts relayed to me by other police officers but, to preserve anonymity, I have used pseudonyms, including for myself. Place names and titles of organisations have also been left out, changed or obscured, and certain operational details omitted or altered where necessary to ensure I do not give away any trade secrets, embarrass anyone or inadvertently reveal information that could be deemed sensitive or confidential under the 'Official Secrets Act'.

To ensure it is an authentic account of how things were in the 1970's, 80's and 90's, I have included some quotes from that era. Readers should therefore note that a few of the phrases and terms contained in the book, which were once the norm, but in contemporary times are understandably considered to be inappropriate, have been retained in order to maintain accuracy and reflect the type of language, vocabulary, rhetoric and typically crass or risqué humour used back then.

Prologue

ONE DAY BACK IN THE SPRING OF 1973, a friend of mine unexpectedly announced he'd applied to join the Police Cadets. Although police work interested me, and I'd been an avid watcher of police-related TV programmes such as 'Dixon of Dock Green' and 'Z Cars' during my childhood, I'd never given joining the force any serious consideration. However, for some reason, my friend's announcement struck a chord and prompted me to follow in his footsteps. At the age of 17, I therefore found myself submitting an application to my local police force, a rural Constabulary located in the West Country.

It was very much an impromptu decision, influenced by my friend's news, and it certainly wasn't based on a vocational calling or, for that matter, a great deal of in-depth thought. Ironically, my friend's application was rejected, while I was offered the chance to join; so, just after my 18th birthday, I embarked on my first spell in the police force and went off to start my basic training.

Looking back, I did feel a bit guilty at being accepted, when he hadn't. However, I soon realised there was little room for sentiment, and I had to focus on my training if I was going to succeed and meet the many challenges that lay ahead. Besides, my friend hadn't helped himself with his answer to a question posed during the preliminary vetting and sifting process:

'So, if you encountered a fight in the street what would you do?'

To which he'd replied, 'Well, naturally, I'd run away and call the police'

I did have a particularly inauspicious start to my own police career. The day before I joined up I went ice-skating with my mates, broke my nose falling head-first on the rink, and ended up looking more like a battered street-fighting lout than a budding police officer.

1 Rude Awakening

So, there I was in the summer of 1973 about to dive headlong into a new adventure. I was one of just six 18-year-olds, out of an intake of 30 new male recruits who'd been enlisted as police cadets that year. All-male because back then women were excluded from joining the cadets – although I'm glad to say that discrimination ended within a few years of my appointment. Those of us in the older age category were classed as 'seniors' and split into a separate group; whilst junior recruits aged 16 to 17 were formed into their own section. During the four-week introductory period however, the age groups were combined.

Basic training was daunting. Trainers went out of their way to be intimidating to test our strength of character, and gauge whether we had the potential to cope when exposed to the most challenging facets of police work. As fledglings, our first few weeks mostly involved us being talked at, often in derogatory or crude terms – shock tactics that were designed to push us to our limits and prepare us for the type of abuse we would experience on the streets. Our reaction to their unrelenting bombastic approach, and the abusive comments aimed at us during training, doubtless enabled our trainers to judge if we would be able to stay calm in such circumstances, and take the heat when put under pressure.

In spite of my rather prim and proper upbringing, it wasn't so much the crude comments that I found shocking. It was more the fact we were constantly being referred to as a bunch of immature wimps and having our masculinity questioned – along with our ability to adequately perform basic human functions; such as being able to aim straight when going to the toilet. The speech given by the training centre's chief warden during our induction remains etched on my memory. Without a hint of humour in his voice, he announced that he could arrange a 'todger' transplant for anyone who was unable to accurately use the toilet facilities during their ablutions! Following this threat, I of course heeded his warning as I was keen to hang onto my existing vital body part.

In a stern tone the warden also outlined the establishment's rules in no uncertain terms:

'Right, you horrible lot, let me remind you that this is a residential training centre for potential police officers and not a hotel for bawdy and virile young men on a stag night! You will not be sowing your seeds whilst you are in residence and, under no circumstances, are members of the fairer sex permitted in your rooms. Break that rule and you'll be out of here pronto – do I make myself clear?'

Hopefully things are different now, but for anyone taken aback or surprised by the warden's choice of words, please remember it was 1973; a time when blokeish humour and sexist language were more prevalent and generally tolerated.

Anyway, once I realised the sarcasm and unflattering remarks were simply an implicit part of the initiation process, I soon became immune to them. Besides, unlike the junior cadets, who would have to endure such mockery for months to come, we 'seniors' didn't have to put up with it for long – because we were excused from participating in most of the basic training activities so we could prepare for our imminent posting to Division. We were, however, required to take part in the daily early morning drill sessions for the first month of our induction. Mind you, they could be amusing events because one of the guys would usually mess up and make a fool of himself during inspection. Memorably, these included a fellow cadet turning up with perfect creases in his trousers – the only trouble was they ran down the sides rather than front and back, so it looked like he was wearing a pair of clown's trousers with flares running from his crotch to his ankles!

Incidents like this must have made our drill sergeant wonder if some of us would make the grade, and whether he had any chance of shaping us into a fine body of young men in just a matter of weeks. We were a ragged bunch of misfits whose marching skills lacked rhythm – and, with little co-ordination, we initially looked like an ensemble of inept performers. However, much to his amazement, by the time we'd reached the end of our preliminary training we'd become a troupe of well-disciplined trainee police officers and did him proud at our final parade.

In some ways, the six-week induction was reminiscent of my senior school days and made me feel like I'd started to regress – especially the juvenile behaviour. Much of it, however, was informative and great fun. It gave me a useful insight into what would lie ahead – and, whilst I didn't know it at the time, it was a breeze compared to what was to come once I took the plunge and experienced life on the beat for the first time with my tutor constable. And, perhaps most importantly, my time at the training establishment had of course taught me to concentrate on aiming straight when taking a wee – something I'd taken on board, just in case the warden hadn't been joking when he made his transplant comment!

My first posting was to a seaside resort with a parochial population of around 50,000 inhabitants. An influx of holiday revellers during the peak holiday season doubled this number, stretching our resources to the limit. Although the extent and nature of the workload varied considerably between the summer and winter months, there were rarely slack periods. The town attracted a lot of retirees and could appear to be a rather sleepy place to live during winter, but from a policing perspective this was deceptive. Sadly, winter often saw a sharp rise in the number of sudden deaths amongst older members of the community and, as these required police attendance, we were always busy – even outside the summer holiday period.

During my first few months on Division, my on-the-job training was interspersed with spells away at an Outward Bound school and a Cheshire home. These activities were seen as extensions of police training, aimed at taking recruits out of their comfort zones by introducing them to new challenges. This was all part of the character-building process, and it certainly had the desired impact in my case. I'd never participated in activities such as rock climbing, caving or surf canoeing – nor taken early morning dips in the sea in the midst of winter! Neither had I worked closely with severely disabled people or anyone with a terminal illness. It was a sobering experience that helped me face up to some of the harsh realities of life, and realise how fortunate I was to be in good health.

I was supposed to spend a month at the Cheshire home but, due to a fire in the staff residential block, this was curtailed. In some ways, I was relieved; I'd had a fairly sheltered upbringing and working at the home was an eye-opener. The impact was still significant though as it made me appreciate there is always someone worse off than yourself. I'd like to think it also made me more caring and a better person. Good police officers need to be confident and assertive, but to also be capable of empathy and compassion.

I did complete the full month at the Outward Bound school, and have mainly positive memories of my time on the course, especially the comradeship. Naïvely, I thought a month away at outward bound would be like being paid to go on vacation; until my travelling companion put me right during our journey to the venue in central Wales. He was clearly more enlightened than me about what lay ahead, as I soon I found out it was more like a boot camp than a holiday camp!

I was naïve in more ways than one and, whilst we were awaiting a connection at Shrewsbury station, I remember I again showed my youthful ignorance. There were two young ladies in their late teens sitting next to us on the platform who started fooling around play fighting. They had their legs intertwined and my travelling companion said they were flirting and being provocative for our benefit. He was probably right but, in my blissfully innocent world, it had never crossed my mind they were flaunting their femininity to get our attention. Back then girls were still a complete mystery to me (perhaps because I'd attended an all-male senior school), and it didn't even register they might be remotely interested in us and seeking a reaction to their lascivious antics.

Our arrival at the Outward Bound facility was late, due to a delay in our connection at Shrewsbury, so we were sent straight to our digs to join members of our group who had already prepared for bed. It was simply deemed tough luck we'd missed supper, and we'd have to wait for breakfast to satisfy our hunger pangs. That's when it finally dawned on me that my colleague had been spot on when he'd said it wouldn't be like Butlin's, and we weren't going to be viewed as honoured guests.

The conditions seemed harsh and reminded me of a prisoner of war camp I'd seen in a movie. However, once I'd recovered from the indignity of being treated like a confined inmate at Colditz, I soon got stuck in and largely enjoyed the challenges we faced. It wasn't all plain sailing; at times I was tested to my limit and certain activities were terrifying.

Unfortunately, several fellow course members suffered accidents, a few of them serious and one, tragically, was life-changing. When we were surf canoeing in rough seas, an army cadet capsized and got trapped under the water. Canoeists had been paired up with nominated observers before setting off, so these individuals could go to their aid if they got into difficulty, but it was a couple of minutes before this poor chap's guardian reached him, and by then he'd stopped breathing. Even though he was resuscitated, he suffered some brain damage and, sadly, this resulted in him being medically discharged from the army due to him developing epilepsy.

Surf canoeing in rough seas was more dangerous than I'd imagined; even our instructor almost came close to capsizing, when he and I nearly collided whilst riding the crest of a particularly big wave. Somehow, we both ended up surfing the same wave, which we'd been told was a big 'no, no' because of the collision risk. Luckily, he just about managed to veer away as I was about to crash into him, so that my canoe only made a glancing blow with the stern of his vessel. Initially, he thought the near miss was solely my fault but, we were equally blameworthy as we'd simply not spotted each other on setting off. It wasn't until we'd gathered speed and almost collided that either of us realised our mistake.

In addition to the brain injury suffered by the army cadet, our contingent also had its fair share of broken bones, with one lad breaking his arm, another his leg, and a third his ankle. Perhaps the most avoidable of these accidents was the last one. We were undertaking a woodland clearance exercise on National Trust land in conjunction with students from another Outward Bound school located nearby, which catered exclusively for young women – at the time, I believe it was the only one in the country that did so. I'm not sure whether being in the presence of female students distracted us lads but, while wielding his axe, one of the guys somehow managed to miss his target, and embedded his chopper into the ankle of the chap next to me. The blow caused massive tissue damage and we suspected his ankle had been broken.

We were miles from civilisation when this occurred, without any means of transport as our instructor had been called away on an errand, so we faced a tricky situation. On the plus side, we did have a first aid kit with us and were able to administer basic medical assistance. Some members of our group wanted to remove the injured lad's boot but, fortuitously, those of us who'd recently done our first aid training persuaded them otherwise as we knew that the boot might be preventing major blood loss, and removing it could worsen his condition. Instead we put on a tourniquet, and applied further pressure by placing a bandage around his ankle on the outside of the boot, in an effort to minimise the bleeding as much as possible. There was a danger he could go into severe shock – or even respiratory arrest if he lost too much blood and deteriorated rapidly.

This happened well before the advent of mobile phones, so deciding on our next course of action presented us with a dilemma. Should we stabilise him as best we could, by immobilising his damaged limb with a splint and keeping it raised – and then await the return of our instructor, while one of us went to seek help? Or should we try getting him to the nearest inhabited area, so he could be transported to hospital? The idea of making a stretcher to carry him to safety was mooted but, since the only materials at our disposal were wood and the clothes we were wearing, this wasn't a feasible option. We soon realised that moving him without a stretcher would make the bleeding worse, so that idea was discounted. Ultimately, staying put proved to be the right decision, as our instructor returned about ten minutes later and we were able to transport our stricken colleague to the nearest hospital, some 20 miles away, where he was duly patched up. Luckily the axe hadn't severed any major arteries, but he had suffered significant damage to his tendons, a broken ankle (as we'd feared) and a deep laceration, which required 15 stitches; so, regrettably, his time on the programme came to a premature end.

Worryingly, we nearly lost another group member two days later when we were out on exercise in the Welsh mountains and had to cross a fast-flowing stream, which was swollen following torrential rain. Rather than go on a five-mile detour, our instructor decided we could just about jump across this obstacle, as long as we took the necessary precautions. A safety rope was attached to the waist of the group member who volunteered to go first – a strapping lad who was by far the biggest guy on the course. However, when he took his running leap across the stream, he lost his balance on landing the other side and toppled back into the torrent. To compound the problem, his safety rope slipped down his body as we tried to haul him out of the water. Everybody held their breath in this grim situation. It appeared he was going to be swept away in the rushing water, and possibly drowned but, just as we thought we were going to lose him, the rope suddenly tightened around his ankles and we were able to drag him out. Other than being wet and bedraggled he was unharmed and, amazingly, he didn't seem unduly fazed by what had happened or the danger he had faced. To everyone's surprise and admiration, he nonchalantly changed into his emergency set of dry clothes and insisted on having another go. His second attempt was successful, and once he was across it made things easier for others to make this perilous leap, because he was able to pull them towards him as they landed on the opposite bank. This was just one of many incidents that tested our resilience and ability to deal with adversity when put into risky and potentially dangerous situations.

The most daunting experience I personally endured on the course arose when I was selected to go first during an abseiling exercise when we were exploring some old slate mines. This entailed plummeting approximately 100 feet through a narrow mine shaft in the pitch dark, with just a small lamp on my safety helmet to guide me as I abseiled down the sheer drop and navigated my way over the craggy rocks. I remember my fellow outward bounders giving me 'helpful encouragement' before I set off on my descent, by advising me to watch out for the bladder bats that urinate on you as you bounce off the rock face, and also the nest of vipers that reside at the bottom of the shaft and would be there to greet me! My most striking recollection of this event is how lonely and claustrophobic I felt when I reached the bottom and, indeed, how relieved I was once the next person down had joined me in the very confined space at the base of the shaft.

Despite going through a lot of mentally and physically taxing times during my month on outward bound, I somehow managed to complete the course unscathed and I proudly received my badge of honour and instructor's award at the passing out ceremony. Looking back, it is understandable that the sort of activities we participated in would be fraught with problems and lead to some mishaps, considering our programme took place during an era that pre-dated routine risk assessments. However, whilst the trials and tribulations that beset our intake weren't inconsequential, they were nothing like as horrifying in comparison to the tragedy that had occurred on the preceding course, when a participant had sadly died as the result of a fall during a horse-riding trek. Following this accident, horse-riding had been removed from the programme, so I should perhaps be grateful that I was spared from exhibiting my very dubious prowess in equestrian sports. I have no riding skills whatsoever, and a particularly poor sense of balance when on horseback – or any beast for that matter, as demonstrated the previous summer when I'd even managed to fall off the back of a donkey during a ride on the beach!

2 Duty Bound

THE MULTITUDE OF CHALLENGES I FACED during my initial training had technically prepared me for police work, and some of the traumatic experiences and unpleasant sights I would encounter once out on the streets, but there is nothing quite like the real thing to drive home just what a cruel and sad place the world can sometimes be. Being of tender age, and having led a sheltered and privileged existence up to that point, suddenly witnessing the more morbid and disturbing aspects of everyday life was a shock to the system. However, there was nothing too shocking or challenging about the situation I faced when I reported for my first duty at my appointed station – an early turn that ran from 0600hrs to 1400hrs. I soon discovered that when working this shift pattern, my most important task would be collecting the freshly baked doughnuts from the local bakery! Having to perform such a simple and menial task took me by surprise, and it masked the truth about what I would encounter over the next couple of weeks. Within a matter of days I found myself being introduced to proper police work, and having to confront some truly harrowing scenes.

During my third tour of duty I witnessed my first murder scene. It was a dreadful sight. A father had blasted his seven-year-old son with a shotgun, inflicting catastrophic, unsurvivable injuries, before unsuccessfully attempting to take his own life. CJ, my initial tutor constable, and I weren't the first officers to get to the devastating scene, but upon arriving we had to help secure the murder site and preserve any vital evidence for our CID and forensic colleagues. Once we'd completed this task, and the Home Office pathologist had finished his medical examination, we were then assigned to escort duties, and had to go with the vehicle transporting the boy's body to the mortuary. There we had to liaise with the coroner's officer, oversee the transfer of the body and observe its receipt by the mortuary attendant. Neither I, nor CJ, who'd only just completed his two-year probationary period, had any further involvement with the murder investigation, but it was considered to be an open and shut case. At the ensuing trial the father's plea of guilty to manslaughter on the grounds of diminished responsibility was accepted by the prosecution. He was sentenced to be held in a secure psychiatric hospital for an unspecified period. I suspect this outcome was of little comfort to the lad's mother or other family members.

This particular tragedy was definitely the saddest thing I'd ever had to deal with up to that point in my life, and the memory of this atrocity has stayed with me ever since. Facing up to the fact this innocent young boy's life had been cut short at the hands of his own father, using such violent means, certainly took its toll, and it was naturally a while before I came to terms with what had happened. Being able to do so was principally down to my first section sergeant, who was not only very supportive, but also something of a mentor to me during my early days as a cadet. I was grateful to him for recommending a couple of key coping mechanisms for dealing with traumatic episodes. Firstly, he informed me that you should not dwell on such incidents or allow anything so ghastly to dominate your thoughts, as doing so is likely to eat you up in the long-term and cause you to lose focus. Secondly, he advised that you should never spend time trying to search your mind for rational explanations when anything of this nature occurs; he stressed it would be futile because there are rarely any logical or reasonable answers to find. These were both salutary lessons that went on to serve me well throughout my service and in many other facets of my life. Adopting his suggested philosophical approach did help keep the demons at bay, and stop such memories from coming back to torment me.

During those early days of my service, I also recall my wise and pragmatic sergeant gave me other suitable words of advice. He recommended I apply a cathartic approach to dealing with my emotions rather than bottle things up. This wasn't something I totally understood back then, but over the years I came to fully appreciate what he meant – and taking on board this suggestion has served me well. He also explained that as you become accustomed to policing, and more acclimatised to witnessing the brutal, cruel and bleak side of life, along with the worst of humanity, it's easy to become cynical about human nature and start tarring everyone with the same negative brush. My canny sergeant therefore emphasised the importance of keeping things in perspective, and appreciating the vast majority of people are law-abiding, decent citizens, who deserve to be treated with respect – and shown humility and kindness unless they have given you a good reason not to do so. Lastly, he reminded me that in this country we police by consent and always need to keep the public onside.

Over the next few weeks I attended my first serious road accident, two sudden deaths and a post-mortem (PM). The last of these was a horrendous experience because, when I walked into the mortuary lab, there were about a dozen dead bodies laid out on their slabs awaiting dissection. It was a grotesque scene, and I had to rapidly put out of my mind that these were recently living, breathing people with loved ones who'd be grieving their loss, and instead concentrate on the task in hand and its scientific purpose. That's a tough call. The sight itself is bad enough, but you then have to deal with the repulsive smell that hits you once they cut into the cadaver and remove the organs, particularly when they access the gut.

Following my first observation of a PM, I tried hard to obliterate it from my mind and follow the advice I'd been given by my section sergeant – but, when I returned to my lodgings that evening and was presented with a plate full of braised steak for my tea, the graphic memory of that grisly scene came rushing back and I had to decline the offering!

When I reflected on the many gruesome things I'd encountered during my first few weeks on the beat, I soon realised my introduction to the most dramatic aspects of police work had begun in earnest. These lurid experiences certainly left a lasting impression. To this day I still have vivid memories, in spite of the many years that have elapsed since I first witnessed those gory events early in my service. Naturally, I came across many similarly grim and unpleasant situations while serving as a special, but it is always those initial ones that come to mind when I reminisce about my two spells in the police force – probably because they had a huge impact in terms of enlightening me about the more upsetting and macabre side of life.

From these initial tales it will be clear that early in my career as a police cadet I had to confront some truly horrible scenes; however, the first time I was permitted to venture out on my own whilst on duty it wasn't to attend anything too distressing. I'd been in the role for about six weeks when I was thrust headfirst into dealing single-handedly with my first tricky situation – in more ways than one! Thrust is probably the wrong word because I actually volunteered for my first solo outing. A young mother had locked herself out of her house, leaving her two-year-old son alone inside – meaning there was no time to lose and an urgent response was needed. It wasn't the norm for cadets to be allowed to attend an incident on their own, but I was entrusted with doing so as all other local officers were already committed at a serious traffic collision, along with colleagues from the fire brigade.

As I made my way to the address where the infant was trapped I felt very conspicuous. Other than during my initial driving induction, this was the first time I'd driven a marked police vehicle. I soon reached my destination, where the panicking young mother greeted me as her saviour – although I was far from convinced I would be able to meet this expectation. She quickly explained what had happened, and told me her husband was the only other key-holder and wouldn't be back until late evening because he was out of town. As there would be a significant delay before either a locksmith or the fire brigade could attend, my only option soon became clear – I would have to somehow gain entry to the property.

Without the right equipment, forcing entry through a door would be impractical, so I knew I'd have to get in via a window. A quick inspection revealed none had been left open – so, after consulting with the frantic householder, we agreed I should break a pane of glass to get access without further delay. I chose the small upstairs toilet window to keep the resultant repair costs to a minimum; then, having borrowed a ladder from a neighbour, I somewhat ironically set about my task of breaking and entering.

Once I'd smashed the glass, and cleared the broken shards and other debris out of the way, I knew it would probably be touch and go as to whether I would fit through the small window frame, but I was determined to give it my best shot. From my precarious position on the ladder, I managed to squeeze the upper part of my torso, up to my waist, into the gap I'd created. However, forcing the rest of my body through the small opening, without getting my backside wedged or falling headfirst into the toilet bowl, proved to be more of a challenge. To those watching below, I must have been an undignified sight to behold, and nothing like the image of the professional police officer that I strove to become. Somehow though, I finally managed to ease my way into the house, by which time I had become very dishevelled and just a little disorientated. My appearance hadn't been improved by the fact I'd accidentally caught and pulled the handle to the toilet flush as I'd descended towards the small WC, just at the point when my head had been adjacent to the lavatory bowl – and had ended up soaking my face and hair in the water normally meant for flushing away toilet deposits!

I soon located the bemused toddler, who must have been wondering why this unkempt stranger was in his home. He appeared completely unperturbed by my presence and oblivious to what all the fuss was about. Once I'd duly re-united him with his delighted and relieved mother, I was able to head back to the station knowing it was mission accomplished. It wasn't my finest hour in uniform, and not exactly the duty I had in mind when the opportunity arose for me to start proving myself as a worthy prospective police officer, but at least I had my first grateful, highly satisfied customer.

Not long after that initial rescue act, I was seemingly attempting another 'forced entry'; this time when I was called upon to clamber into a house via a bedroom window, which had at least been left slightly ajar. A concerned citizen had alerted police that his elderly female neighbour hadn't been seen for over a week. I was working with Tommy, my second tutor constable and a former army veteran who'd been in the police for five years, when we were despatched to this elderly person's residence to check on her welfare, and determine if there was any justified cause for concern.

After arriving, and establishing this elderly lady was well into her eighties and hadn't been seen throughout the festive period, we rapidly concluded we would need to investigate further. Firstly, we tried banging on the door and calling loudly through the letterbox to identify ourselves as the police, but this proved to be of no avail. Secondly, we made enquiries to establish whether our 'missing' subject had any local relatives, friends or other neighbours that possessed a key to her property, or knew if she'd gone away for Xmas. Again, this turned out to be a fruitless exercise. Having explored and exhausted these options, Tommy decided we would have to gain entry to her house to check if she was there and, most essentially, whether she was ok.

In view of the open window on the first floor, he reckoned it was something we could achieve ourselves without enlisting additional help, providing we could get hold of a ladder – and, since the concerned neighbour was more than happy to oblige in that regard, we were soon able to set about our task.

The wooden ladder he provided had seen better days – therefore, in his wisdom, Tommy promptly volunteered me for the dubious privilege of climbing to the first-floor bedroom window to effect entry. This seemed fair enough considering my smaller and lighter frame; so that was how my second attempt at breaking and entering came about soon after my first brazen and shameful effort to be a gamekeeper turned poacher. And when I set forth on my journey up the ladder to gain access, I wondered whether I was going to get further opportunities to hone my skills in the art of breaking into locked properties over the coming months, and if this would become my speciality in the force.

Once I'd climbed the rickety old ladder, and started clambering through the bedroom window, I immediately realised something was amiss. I was hit by the most abnormal stench – so bad it took my breath away and caused me to wretch. Although I'd not come across exactly the same unpleasant odour before, I instinctively knew from the similar smell I'd endured during my first autopsy, that this foul aroma was coming from a putrefying corpse. Sure enough, on the floor by the other side of the bed, I found a badly decomposing body. Even based on my limited experience of such matters, I knew it had clearly been there for several days, if not weeks. The rate of decomposition had probably been expedited due to the central heating having been on full blast – which was hardly surprising as we'd been in the midst of a harsh winter when this dear old lady had sadly passed away.

Whilst we completed the tasks associated with dealing with a sudden death,

I learned a valuable lesson – how to partially mask the unbearable odour that emanates from a decomposing body and dominates the atmosphere in a confined space. Tommy taught me that frying some coffee beans or granules on a stove or open fire will create a wafting aroma, which will slowly take the edge off the overwhelmingly repugnant smell once it circulates around the house. However, I also found out the putrid taste you get at the back of your throat from being in an enclosed area with a decaying body lingers for several hours before it starts to dissipate!

No evidence was discovered to suggest this senior citizen's lamentable death had occurred as a result of anything sinister, and a subsequent PM showed she had died of natural causes. Nonetheless, I found it disturbing that her body had lain undiscovered in the house throughout the whole Xmas period following her untimely death, with nobody missing her sufficiently to think something untoward might have happened. On the other hand, it was heartening to know that her kindly neighbour had shown an interest in her welfare soon after his return from his own festive break, and then taken the trouble to report his concerns to the police.

Certainly, this harrowing experience once more brought home the harsh realities of life or, perhaps more pertinently, death. I chalked it up as another critical eye-opener, which formed a key part of my personal development as I hardened to the role of a trainee police constable. At the time, it fleetingly crossed my mind that maybe I'd had to confront more than my fair share of morbid scenarios for someone with limited time in policing, and I'd now get a welcome break from this element of the job. Deep down though, I knew that was wishful thinking and there'd be many more to come as my career progressed. Such thoughts about any changes in fortune did indeed prove to be overly optimistic because it wasn't long before I again had to contend with the unmistakable acrid smell of rotting flesh.

This time it was the corpse of a gentleman of no fixed abode, who'd expired whilst taking refuge in a derelict building. I won't go into graphic detail about the state of this homeless person's emaciated body but, since he'd clearly been deceased for some time, it was a ghastly mess. From his position it appeared that he'd curled up in the corner of a downstairs room to tack a nap, and then departed from this life whilst in slumber. I couldn't help but wonder if his passing had been a blessing for him as it looked as though he'd been homeless for many years, and that a torrid lifetime of living rough on the streets had undoubtedly taken its toll. Subsequently, I found out his death had been due to an overdose, and a witness at the inquest indicated the deceased had led a wretched life and, after recently hitting rock bottom, had been threatening to end his existence. It therefore also crossed my mind that perhaps this tormented soul had nothing and nobody to live for – and how dreadful it is when someone reaches such despair they believe the only way out is to end it all.

During my next encounter with a suspected suicide, when I was once more under the watchful supervision of Tommy, I learned an alarming fact for someone as innocent as I was back then. A young man's death had come about as a consequence of his own actions, but my worldly-wise colleague was certain he hadn't intended to take his own life, and that his untimely passing had been accidental. The lifeless body of the victim had been discovered by a farmer hanging in a secluded outbuilding located on his smallholding – nearby to where the deceased lad lived – and he'd understandably reported the death as a probable suicide. However, due to the deceased's state of partial undress and some other telltale signs, it was clear to Tommy this young man's demise had likely occurred during an act of sexual gratification, which had gone horribly wrong.

Tommy told me that coming across this type of tragic situation is unusual, but not entirely unique. He explained it is not unknown for those of male gender to occasionally place some form of tourniquet around their neck to simulate the affects of hanging whilst pleasuring themselves – because doing so can starve the brain of oxygen and, allegedly, give the individual a real high in terms of the climax they will experience whilst performing such an act. This was horrific news to me. Clearly, the risk posed to any individual engaging in such activity is considerable – which was all too apparent in the case of our victim, who had likely lost his life unintentionally.

Once Tommy had enlightened me about the shocking facts and giveaway signs relating to the probable cause of death in this instance, I then needed to find out how we treated this matter when we informed the deceased's loved ones of his sad passing, and also when we submitted our report to the coroner. I was hoping we wouldn't have to reveal any of the sordid details, and might be able to mask the truth for the sake of doing the greater good, but I sensed that wouldn't be possible.

Tommy shared with me that dealing with anything of this nature creates something of a dilemma because, instinctively, you have the desire to protect a victim's loved ones by sparing them from the harsh truth. You naturally don't want to add to the immense pain they will already be suffering when they learn of their loss, by then having to explicitly tell them about the actual reasons the person died. However, he stated we are required to tell the truth no matter how unbearable that might be, and must always stick to the facts – whether it is passing on a death message or presenting evidence to the coroner. Besides, as Tommy further iterated, the only alternative would be to infer the victim had committed suicide, which could be just as painful for his loved ones if they ended up thinking they should have done something to prevent it, or blaming themselves in some way. It therefore struck me that any attempt to cushion the blow out of human kindness could easily be misconstrued, and wouldn't necessarily make the outcome any more palatable – so, all the more reason why the truth has to prevail.

3 Lost & Found

I'M GLAD TO REPORT THAT THE NEXT TIME I was working with Tommy I spent my whole tour of duty dealing with the living. We were on mobile patrol together, working a late shift, when we came across two young girls trying to hitch a lift on the main road leading north out of town. Concerned for their welfare, we pulled over to check where they were heading and give them suitable words of advice about the dangers of hitch-hiking. They were made-up for a night out on the town, and when we'd first seen them Tommy and I had assumed they were probably in their mid-teens. Once we'd observed them more closely though, it had become evident they could well be much younger than we'd first thought, and we were staggered when we discovered their actual ages. It emerged they were trying to get a lift into the nearest city about 20 miles away, where they were planning to go to a night-club. At first they tried to convince us they were 16, but following some careful interrogation, one of the girls then admitted she was only 13. Her companion was more reticent about telling us her genuine age, and it took further gentle persuasion before she came clean. I was astonished when she finally told us she was just 11-years-old!

Initially, they were both blasé about their intentions, and didn't seem bothered that their foolhardy actions had put them at risk. However, the older one did start to see the error of her ways – and become more subdued – after we'd outlined the dangers they could have faced. As we had a duty of care, we took them into our protection so we could return them to their respective parents. We headed to the younger girl's home first. During the journey, I was expecting her to show some remorse for her behaviour but she wasn't in the least bit contrite, and seemed to find the whole matter amusing as she spent most of the trip giggling away. When we arrived at her home we handed her over to her father, who appeared unconcerned, disinterested and dismissive when we explained what had happened. Based on his attitude, it was understandable why his daughter had seen the matter as something of a joke.

It was a different story when we headed off to the older girl's home. After we'd dropped off her mate, any bravado she had displayed rapidly evaporated and she became sheepish. She lived in a village outside of the main town and, as we neared her house, she became increasingly worried about how her father would react to her antics that evening. By the time we arrived at her home address she was almost hysterical and wouldn't get out of the police car, so Tommy decided he would speak to her parents in the first instance, whilst I remained in the vehicle with their daughter and tried to calm her down.

The young girl and her middle-class family lived in a lovely bungalow and, on the outside, everything about the setting looked idyllic and very rosy. While Tommy was alerting her parents to the situation, I did all I could to pacify the girl and tried hard to give her some re-assurance. Despite this, she still seemed genuinely petrified and kept pleading with me not to leave her there as her father would be furious, and she would face a severe punishment. From her account, it sounded like her dad ruled the family in an autocratic fashion, and used a firm hand to ensure his children conformed to his thinking and obeyed his rules. It became clear she was frightened of him, and terrified she would be in for a good hiding after we were gone. Naturally, this bothered me considerably. I decided I would have a quiet word with Tommy before we handed her back to her parents, to raise my concerns that I was fearful she was going to get a beating.

Although the parents had come across to Tommy as though they had a nurturing attitude towards their daughter, he was also uneasy about returning her to their custody once I'd outlined my concerns. Based on the fears expressed by the poor girl, Tommy felt there was a strong possibility that the public persona presented by the father of him being a warm, friendly and gentle man could well be a façade and, behind the scenes, he would show his true colours of being a strong disciplinarian. However, Tommy explained that we were powerless to intervene at that stage because, without any solid evidence that a criminal act had occurred, or the young girl was in serious danger, we didn't have authority under current laws to justify taking her into care. The best we could therefore do was bring our concerns to the attention of Social Services – even though we knew their hands would also largely be tied by the rules that governed us all at that point in time, when the rights of parents (and adults in general) seemed to take precedence over those of children.

As we drove away – potentially leaving the sobbing girl to her likely fate – I appreciated there was little else we could've done in the circumstances. However, I was desperately disappointed that we were effectively impotent in this situation, and couldn't do anything to prevent her father from probably inflicting pain in a way that now seems barbaric to us – as, back then, administering corporal punishment was regrettably still legal, and widely accepted as the norm amongst many people within our society. Consequently, it was customary for children to frequently be chastised in this way by some parents, and indeed in many schools, including those that were state-funded until it was banned in such establishments in 1986.

Despite knowing this, I was still left feeling deflated and frustrated immediately afterwards. As her protectors, it seemed like we'd been unable to fulfil our role, and therefore had failed her, even though I accepted we had no alternative but to hand her back to her parents. Recognising that you can't save everyone was another harsh realisation for me to assimilate and digest as I became more attuned to the world of policing.

A missing person enquiry was next on the agenda for Tommy and me, when we were once again paired up for a series of night duties. A call had been received from a young woman reporting that her 19-year-old flatmate and best friend Amy was missing, so we were asked to make some initial enquiries and determine whether a major search would be necessary. Upon our arrival at the flat the girls shared, we were greeted by the friend of the missing person, who was named Kate and also aged 19. It was already late evening so Kate was dressed for bed, and I recall that her skimpy night attire was quite revealing, which didn't seem to bother Tommy. However, with me being so innocent it made me blush – although I tried to hide my embarrassment as Kate explained the circumstances surrounding her friend's disappearance.

According to Kate, her flatmate Amy had become upset the previous night during a friendly but intense discussion about relationships, which had been fuelled by alcohol. The focus of their chat had been about Amy feeling rejected as she tried to come to terms with a couple of recent break-ups following short-term relationships. During the course of their heart-to-heart, Amy had also revealed that being dumped on two consecutive occasions made her feel like she was a failure. In Kate's view, this seemed to really bother Amy, and she thought her friend could be feeling depressed – and had probably gone to bed with this matter playing on her mind.

Once we'd listened to Kate's explanation, and knew the reason why her friend's mental state might be a cause for concern and account for her mystery disappearance, Tommy decided what action needed to be instigated. It was now clear Amy had last been seen late the previous night, at the point she'd gone to bed following her emotionally charged chat with Kate, and that her disappearance was out of character. Tommy, therefore, reached the opinion we needed to undertake some urgent enquiries to establish her whereabouts and make sure she was safe. He felt she may be vulnerable and at risk of self-harm, due to her fragile state of mind; however, he was reluctant to set in motion a large-scale missing person investigation until we'd carried out some initial checks and searched the local area. For this we needed to enlist some further help from Kate. She supplied us with a recent photograph of Amy and details of places she might go to unwind or reflect when she was feeling down. We also obtained details of Amy's previous abode, a large house that was currently unoccupied and waiting to be renovated – as Kate thought this might be a place of sanctuary for her friend, especially if she was seeking a refuge away from everyone.

Although we had the photo of Amy, Tommy decided it would be helpful if we took Kate with us on our search around town, as she would immediately recognise her friend if we came across her. He also felt she'd be able to offer her comfort in the event she was in distress; making an approach less intrusive or threatening for her. So, as the time approached midnight on that shift, the three of us set off on our quest to find Amy – but, not before we'd conducted a quick search of her room and other parts of the communal dwelling. We needed put our minds at rest that she wasn't somewhere in the property keeping a low profile, and also double check for any signs that could indicate where she'd gone. Whilst we did this, Kate wrote a note for Amy explaining why she'd gone out to look for her, and requesting she call the police immediately in the event she returned home.

We first headed to Amy's former home to check if there was any sign of her at that address or somewhere in the vicinity. Upon our arrival, Tommy thought it best if we maximised our scope for searching the area as quickly as possible by splitting up. I was therefore dropped off at the house where Amy used to reside so I could check out the property for any signs of life. Meanwhile, Tommy and Kate cruised the streets in the local area and did a recce of the nearby park, including a derelict outhouse in the grounds often frequented by homeless people.

The mansion where Amy had previously resided in a bed-sit was a detached three-storey building, which had now fallen into disrepair. All the tenants at this accommodation had been evicted several months ago, due to the poor state of the property, and it had been boarded up, so I wasn't quite sure how I was going to gain access. I managed to do so after spotting that the rear door had been partially kicked in, leaving just enough room for a person to crawl through the resulting gap. Once I'd ventured inside I diligently carried out my search, checking each room for any sign of Amy by torchlight as the electricity had been disconnected. The poor condition of the floorboards meant I had to tread carefully, especially when searching the first floor. My focus was therefore on where I was putting my feet as I entered the bathroom, rather than whether I was going to come across our missing young lady. So, when I suddenly caught sight of something that looked very much like a body lain out in the bath, I was totally taken aback and my heart nearly missed a beat! It took me several seconds to recover my composure, and realise it wasn't a body at all that I'd spotted in the shadow of my flickering torchlight but, in fact, a set of clothes that somebody had laid out to soak.

It turned out the washing in the bath belonged to a squatter, who I subsequently found lurking on the next floor. I'm not sure which of us was most startled when we stumbled upon one another during my search, as doing so caused us both to take a sharp intake of breath. This squatter told me he'd moved into the empty house to take advantage of its limited facilities now it was unoccupied, and he'd never come across Amy.

With my house search complete, and my heart still pounding a little faster, I radioed Tommy to report there was no sign of Amy at the house, and then rejoined him and Kate so we could jointly resume our mission to locate her. As we continued our mobile hunt around town, I relayed to Tommy and Kate what had happened at the vacant house – but, when I got to the bit about the clothes in the bath and my discovery of the resident squatter, I tried to make light of these incidents and conveniently forgot to mention I'd nearly jumped out of my skin. After all, with Kate accompanying us, I felt I didn't want to let the side down and needed to impress her by being macho. Being older and wiser now, however, I'm happy to admit these encounters frightened the life out of me.

Shortly after I'd finished the story about my 'heroic' house search we got good news. Amy was back home safe and well and we could cease our search. Apparently, she'd returned after a day out and, upon finding Kate's note, had immediately contacted the police to notify them she was fine. Later we found out Amy had taken time off work due to feeling a bit down and, on the spur of the moment, had ended up spending the day with the male tenant from the flat above. He'd offered to take her out somewhere to cheer her up and, not realising they wouldn't be back till late, she hadn't thought to leave a message telling Kate where she'd gone.

It didn't matter that Kate reporting her friend missing was in effect a false alarm. We told her it's always better to be safe than sorry, and stressed she had every reason to be concerned about her friend's welfare. Having a positive outcome was all that mattered, and far better than any of the other possible outcomes you might get when dealing with a missing person.

This episode taught me that dealing with missing persons, or 'mispers' as they are referred to in the trade, along with attending domestics, takes up a disproportionate amount of time compared to fighting street crime. Regardless of this, they are understandably always given a high priority.

Once Amy had been found, I thought that was the end of the matter, but next day at our briefing session, Tommy brought up the events of the previous night and told our section colleagues all about our missing person enquiry. Much to my embarrassment, he suggested Kate would be an ideal girlfriend for me. He then told me that when we'd dropped Kate off at her home he'd forgotten to give back the photo of Amy that she'd loaned us, and I could pop around to return it to her – as this would give me a reason to visit her again and, more to the point, the opportunity to ask her out. Apart from thinking Kate was out of my league, I also wondered if taking a personal interest in someone we'd dealt with on duty would be frowned upon and deemed unprofessional. However, all my fellow section colleagues were onside with Tommy's idea and insistent it would be fine. They said there'd be nothing wrong in asking her out because she wasn't a vulnerable victim who'd been the subject of our enquiry. Despite this assurance, I still felt uncomfortable about taking up the challenge – but, with everyone egging me on, I knew I had little choice. I would lose face if I didn't do so, even though I was concerned it might be a set-up, had limited experience of the dating scene and little confidence when it came to asking girls out.

The following evening, prior to my night shift, I therefore reluctantly visited Kate's flat to return the photo, and also with the intention of inviting her out, providing my courage didn't desert me. As I approached the door to the flat, I was shaking in my boots even more than I had during the search of the derelict house, and I was in two minds whether to go through with it. If I hadn't felt compelled to act in response to the relentless encouragement I'd received from my work colleagues, I would have cut and run there and then. After I'd plucked up enough courage to ring the bell, the door was eventually answered, not by Kate, but her 'missing' friend Amy. I recognised her straightaway from her photograph.

Amy coming to the door put me in a bit of a stew as I hadn't rehearsed for this situation. I wondered how on earth I was going to get to speak to Kate, without making it obvious I also had another motive for my visit. It turned out I needn't have worried because, once I'd introduced myself to Amy and explained I was there to return her photo, she seemed delighted to meet me and immediately invited me in for a coffee and a chat. I therefore didn't have to ask her any surreptitious questions on the doorstep to ascertain whether Kate was home, which could have given the game away about the additional reason for my visit.

She made me feel so welcome I felt like a long-lost friend and, during our ensuing conversation, I soon learned that Kate was actually out on a meal date – with the same male co-tenant that had taken Amy out the previous day, when she had supposedly gone missing. On hearing this, I instantly thought their co-tenant must be something of a modern-day Casanova, until Amy then pointed out the three of them were just good friends. She told me going out on meal dates was a common occurrence, and they usually went as a threesome.

Encountering Amy as a result of my visit gave me peace of mind because she came across as very level-headed, which of course wasn't the image of her that I'd perceived in my head, based on the concerns I'd had for her wellbeing when I thought she'd gone missing. It was a delight getting the opportunity to find out what she was really like in person, especially as she proved to be extremely warm and friendly.

When I'd first arrived, and Kate hadn't answered the door, I'd experienced mixed emotions, feeling both relief and disappointment at the same time, but as it happened my visit couldn't have gone any better. Not only did I get to meet Amy, which, in itself, was something of a bonus, but I also got an invitation to join herself, Kate, Mike (the other co-tenant) and some of their friends for drinks one evening. Needless to say I jumped at the chance and gratefully accepted the invite.

Consequently, I was back at the flat a few days later for a social gathering, and got my chance to get to know Kate a little better outside of a work-related situation. During our get together, I learned something notable about Kate. Her friends made me aware she was a budding actress, who they believed was bound for stardom, having already received rave reviews from critics after appearing in several theatre productions. Hearing this strengthened my resolve to get to know her better, although, at the same time, it made me even more convinced I wasn't in her league in any romantic sense, and any growing connection would be purely platonic. By acknowledging this would likely be the case, I didn't have any false hopes, and I was able to enjoy the evening getting to know Kate, Amy and their friends without building up my expectations. In the circumstances, I didn't have the nerve to invite Kate out in the traditional sense by requesting the pleasure of her company on a date, but I did hint it would be great to go for coffee sometime and give her my family's home phone number. This way I wasn't making an offer to take her out that could be declined, and I'd be spared the ignominy of rejection.

Following this soirée, a few weeks went by without any contact; then, much to my delight, I got an unexpected call from Kate requesting my assistance. She had been invited to an audition for a part in a television production, and wondered if I would be able to give her a lift to the TV studio later that week. As luck would have it, I had no work or social commitments that clashed with the date of the audition so I leapt at the opportunity to be her driver for the night. Kate's call gave me a glimmer of hope that perhaps she viewed me as potential boyfriend material, but the idea only briefly crossed my mind and I soon discounted this thought because, deep down, I knew there was little possibility of this happening.

Besides, I was far too modest to imagine that any type of relationship was on the cards. I was, however, excited by the thought of spending an evening with Kate. I also felt honoured that she'd chosen me to escort her, even though I knew the real attraction wasn't the prospect of sharing my company, and was more likely due to me having a car and being able to provide her with access to free transport!

Any faint expectations I had of impressing her during my evening as chauffer were partly dashed on the initial leg of our journey, and then soon became a forlorn hope in respect of the second leg. Firstly, my car broke down on the way, and, although I was quickly able to rectify the problem with my old banger, it resulted in her being slightly late for the biggest occasion of her acting career to date. Secondly, the producer of the programme and the director of the show for which she was auditioning, both predatory males who possessed considerably more panache than me, were 'all over her' the minute they met Kate. They immediately made it abundantly clear my taxi service wouldn't be required for the return journey, as one of them would be happy to give her a lift home. As they respectively competed for this privilege, I could tell Kate seemed a bit embarrassed and overwhelmed by their attentions. However, I could appreciate she needed to win favour with them, and understood why she didn't want to decline their insistent offers to drive her home and possibly scupper her chances of a role in a TV production – which would be a huge breakthrough for someone aspiring to succeed in the acting profession.

Finding out I was redundant as her taxi driver felt like a tremendous blow because, other than the minor difficulty we'd experienced with the car during the inbound journey, I'd sensed this element of the trip had gone well and there'd been some positive vibes. It felt like a degree of chemistry was evolving between us, and I'd been looking forward to our trek home together – but it was not to be. However, although she'd dispensed with my services for the return leg, I did get a crumb of comfort from knowing she'd probably done so reluctantly, and appeared to feel both guilty and disappointed at having to reject this part of my kind gesture. Also, my evening transporting Kate during the inbound journey had been worthwhile because it had given me the chance to get to know her better, and further develop our platonic relationship.

The next time I saw Kate it was purely a chance encounter, which occurred about a week after our return leg from the TV centre had been aborted. I was on an early turn and had been sent to recover a stolen bike that had been dumped in the rear yard of a shop. As I was wheeling it back to the police station, I bumped into Kate walking to work. From my reaction, it was probably obvious I was delighted to see her – and as she greeted me with a big smile I think she was equally pleased to see me. We'd not had a chance to catch up since that fateful night of the audition, primarily because I'd been working on a tour of late duties. In part, it was also because I'd been disinclined to ring her up or make another unsolicited visit in case it made me seem overly keen and too pushy.

With our paths having crossed, she instantly explained her motive for ditching me shortly after I'd delivered her safely for her audition, which tallied with the reason I'd already deduced for myself. She seemed genuinely remorseful, but I told her I totally understood her predicament and why she'd felt compelled to abandon ship. However, by means of an apology, she invited me to a theatre production she was appearing in the following weekend – so I came away from our latest brief encounter feeling elated and wondering if karma was at play. Before we parted company, I was also thrilled to learn that she had been awarded a part in the TV show following her audition – and chuffed to know that I now had a friend who may soon become a celebrity, if not a movie star some day! Although I was delighted for her, hearing such news further reinforced my thinking that a platonic relationship with someone on the road to success would prove to be the safer option, as I'm sure anything more could easily have resulted in her becoming my femme fatale.

When I went to watch Kate's virtuoso performance at the theatre, I could soon appreciate why she was viewed as a talented thespian, and the reason she was being sought after as an aspiring actress by those in the theatrical world who knew a lot more than me about such matters. I'm something of a Philistine when it comes to the arts and theatre, and I didn't have a clue what the play was about. Mind you, the storyline was so abstract and obscure I'm not surprised it went over my head, and I think other members of the audience were equally bewildered. Even so, it was still patently clear Kate was something special and definitely the star performer of the show, as she stood out by a country mile in comparison to her fellow actors. Both the producer and the director involved in Kate's audition at the TV studios were also there, presumably to watch their protégé showcase her theatrical talents. They must have been equally impressed because they subsequently expanded the part she would go on to play in their TV show. For me, it was therefore great to be present at an event that effectively became the launch-pad for her extended and successful acting career – despite the fact I had no idea what was going on during the play.

During the next few months I regularly hung out with Kate and her friends but, as her career took off, and there was an incremental growth in the number of male suitors showing an interest in her, I realised I needed to assess whether I'd become surplus to requirements. Although I was a dedicated and avid fan,

I had no desire to be just another one of her male groupies – and, since I didn't have the confidence to try to initiate anything more than friendship back then, I consciously decided to gracefully withdraw from the scene. It was a case of gradually fading away, rather than instantaneously stepping aside, so I retained some limited contact for awhile and continued watching her acting career progress from afar – but those initial encounters were as close as I ever got to developing any sort of meaningful relationship with her.

4 Never a Dull Moment

WITH TOMMY ON LEAVE FOR A COUPLE OF WEEKS, I was once again under the watchful eye of CJ as he chaperoned me during seven consecutive day shifts. On our first morning back together, we were requested to attend the local abattoir, where two lambs had been stabbed to death overnight. Upon our arrival, we were greeted by the manager who informed us that he had discovered the mutilated bodies of the lambs when doing his initial rounds of the day, and had immediately reported the matter to the police because he was sure it was due to foul play. The guy seemed genuinely cut up about the situation, which was ironic considering the animals in question were effectively on death row and due to be slaughtered that morning – albeit humanely – but you could understand his sentiment because they had clearly been viciously stabbed in some sort of macabre frenzy.

There was no sign of forced entry at the slaughterhouse but, since the security measures at the site seemed lax, it would have been easy for someone to have accessed the premises in the night, simply by climbing over the surrounding wall. It also looked like the perpetrator would then have had no difficulty getting into the animal pen to commit this random atrocity – with little chance of being disturbed or heard due to the abattoir being located on the outskirts of town. CJ requested a colleague from the Scenes of Crime team attend, even though we both knew there was little chance of any useful forensic evidence being found, bearing in mind the type of facility. To me, it seemed like one of the station's specialists in crime prevention would be more helpful, as clearly steps needed to be taken to improve security and reduce the chances of this venue becoming a regular target for acts of criminality.

Whilst we awaited the arrival of our forensic colleague, we checked the scene for any obvious clues as to who might have carried out this terrible attack. While doing so, I asked CJ if he had ever come across an incident of animal murder before – but he light-heartedly told me he thought this was more a case of lamb-slaughter! As my early career in the force progressed, I learned that sometimes being able to make light of certain distressing or dreadful situations you encounter is a trait many police officers develop. For some, it apparently helped minimise the adverse affect ordeals can have on mental wellbeing, and enabled them cope when constantly having to deal with the most unpleasant aspects of life – for example witnessing horrendous sights or confronting vile acts. I therefore had to acclimatise to the way many officers typically dealt with such matters in my day.

Once we'd completed our preliminary enquiry at the abattoir, we passed on information about the incident to C.I.D., and they further investigated the crime in an attempt to identify and track down the offender – but, with no significant leads and little to go on, their initial enquiries proved to be fruitless. However, six months later, the culprit responsible for this hideous act was arrested in connection with another unrelated crime. When charged with this other offence, he chose to also come clean about stabbing the lambs, probably because he knew that if he received custodial sentences for both offences they would likely run concurrently; whereas, if he was brought to justice for killing the animals at a later stage, there was always a risk any sentence would be consecutive. In such circumstances, it's not unusual for criminals to have other offences they've committed taken into account (TICs). It's in their interests to do so because, if concrete evidence emerged at a later date connecting them to unsolved crimes, they would likely face additional time in prison – as already outlined.

In regard to the abattoir killer, it surfaced that he'd been working there when the stabbing offence was committed. As part of his defence, he pleaded that he was distraught and mentally impaired at the time, due to relationship issues he was experiencing. He claimed the resultant anguish he was suffering accounted for his violent behaviour, and contributed to him carrying out the motiveless attack on defenceless animals. This mitigating factor didn't wash with the magistrates and, when convicted, he got six months for animal cruelty, the maximum sentence for committing such an offence at that time – to run concurrently with the prison term he also got for theft!

The following week I was on the twilight watch, my favourite shift pattern, working the 1800hrs to 0200hrs stint. This was normally the busiest tour of duty with never a dull moment. It was usual to be double-crewed when on mobile patrols for such shifts, which overlapped firstly with the team covering the late turn and then the group on nights. In the absence of both Tommy and CJ, I was assigned to work with Tony, a happy-go-lucky and chirpy PC with a cheerful disposition, who was an ardent Leo Sayer fan with three years of service under his belt. During our initial shift together, I was treated to a rendition of Leo Sayer numbers, all of them sung passionately, but out of tune in a key I didn't recognise.

My first duty paired with Tony proved to be eventful. Around 2100hrs, a call came over the Panda radio to be on the look out for a suspected stolen vehicle that had failed to stop for one of our colleagues. No further sightings of the car in question were reported for about an hour, and then it was suddenly spotted cruising along the seafront by the crew of a traffic car. The radio crackled into life, advising us the suspect vehicle was heading in our direction, hotly pursued by the traffic car, so we positioned our vehicle across the road in an attempt to block its path. This proved to be of no avail as the car swerved on to the pavement to squeeze by, narrowly missing a collision with our Panda. The cat and mouse chase around town continued for another 30 minutes, until an experienced PC on foot patrol in the town centre spotted it coming at speed towards him. This particular officer didn't suffer fools gladly, and was determined to bring this reckless driver's escapade to a rapid halt – so he stepped out in front of the suspect vehicle as it hurtled towards him and, in traditional police fashion, signalled the driver to stop.

To shocked bystanders, it must have looked like this brave PC's action could prove to be suicidal, and many of them turned away as he attempted to bring events to a conclusion by putting himself in mortal danger. At the last second, the officer must have realised they were right, and there was no chance of the driver heeding his signal to stop. He took evasive action by literally diving out of the way – but not before he'd launched his police issue torch at the speeding car's windscreen as it tried to mow him down, no doubt in a last-ditch effort to get the driver to swerve before he reached the point of no return.

In the cold light of day, the PC reportedly explained he had little recollection of throwing the torch. One could only assume it had been an impulsive and desperate act of self-preservation; presumably because he feared he was in imminent danger of being run over as the car sped towards him. Anyway, as a consequence of the torch smashing the rogue driver's windscreen, the guy at the wheel did indeed brake and swerve at the last second. Doing so took him straight through a shop window!

By the time Tony and I arrived on the scene to assist it was pandemonium. Panic and chaos reigned amongst those bystanders who'd been in the firing line once the vehicle had lost control; understandably so, since they'd narrowly avoided being struck as it had careered towards them. There was also a big crowd of rubberneckers gathering around to get a glimpse of the action. The suspect vehicle was embedded in what remained of the shop front, and the driver, who appeared unharmed, was trapped inside unable to exit through any of the doors. This incident could easily have resulted in utter carnage but, luckily, those pedestrians who'd been in the path of the crashing vehicle had all managed to scatter before it ran into them. So, although several people present were in severe shock, there were no casualties in need of medical attention due to physical injuries.

Once the fire brigade had managed to extricate the driver, he was duly arrested on suspicion of theft of a motor vehicle, dangerous driving and failing to stop, and carted off to hospital for a check-up prior to being 'locked up'. Before things then started to calm down, one onlooker took umbrage at the PC who'd thrown the torch. He started lambasting him for his action, but was given short shrift by the officer and advised of the process for lodging a formal complaint. When he ignored this advice and continued to harangue the officer even more vociferously, he was then warned by our sergeant that he needed to calm down and follow the proper procedure for making a complaint, or he would be arrested for obstruction. This had the desired affect and, once this guy was no longer around to aggravate the situation with his outspoken criticism, we were able to get on with controlling the traffic and dispersing the gathering crowd. While doing so the crash site debris was cleared, the building was made safe, and the smashed-up vehicle was recovered and towed away.

No sooner had we finished dealing with the aftermath of this incident and resumed our mobile patrol, than we were off again on yet another chase. This time we were confronted by a vehicle being driven at a ridiculous speed in a built up area with a 30mph limit. The car in question was a Lotus Élan, and the driver had the audacity to go flying by at around 50mph as he overtook us in our marked police car – so we set off in hot pursuit. Our Panda was no match for such a sports car going hell for leather, and it zoomed away leaving us in its wake – but not before we'd managed to get its number and put out a shout for assistance. Not long after losing the audacious driver, we got a radio call requesting we RV with a traffic unit, which had managed to spot and stop the Lotus Élan just after it had joined the nearby motorway network. We duly obliged, and when we reached our colleagues from Traffic they had already arrested the driver for failing a breathalyser. As the stop had occurred on the motorway's northern carriageway, it was then necessary to take both police vehicles and the owner's seized Lotus on a 12-mile detour back to base.

One of the traffic officers volunteered to drive the Lotus and he invited me to join him on the ride. It was an invitation I soon regretted accepting because, whilst we were on the motorway, he decided to put the car through its paces – and when the speedometer read 140mph at one stage, I honestly thought my life was about to end prematurely! Although my colleague was an excellent driver, he scared the living daylights out of me, and I couldn't believe someone responsible for upholding the law on our roads would drive at that speed. I was just grateful to survive the experience and felt relieved when we got back in one piece to the sanctuary of our police station. By this time, I didn't feel right about us booking the Lotus driver for speeding, even though 'boy racers' had always been one of my pet hates.

Typically, the only thing the speedster appeared concerned about when we met up with him back at the nick was the state of his Lotus Èlan. Disturbingly, he wanted to know whether we'd taken good care of his pride and joy whilst driving it to the police compound. My colleague unashamedly assured him it had been well looked after, and I didn't have the gall to tell him otherwise – especially when the owner informed us the car had a new engine, and wasn't meant to be driven over 50mph for any sustained periods until it had been run-in. In his view, that was the only reason the traffic car had been able to catch him on the motorway.

Ultimately, our drink-driver got a lucky break because the doctor was delayed in getting to the police station to undertake a blood test, and the result subsequently showed the amount of alcohol in his system was just marginally below the permitted limit. Perhaps it was divine justice that the delay in taking the sample probably enabled his alcohol count to drop just under the drink-driving threshold; although he did still get a conviction for speeding after admitting he'd gone well over the 30mph limit whilst passing through the resort.

So far, it might have come across that my work as a police cadet featured mostly doom and gloom but, much of the time, the emphasis was also on helping people or responding to situations that involved fighting crime. Equally, there were instances when we had fun and enjoyed the camaraderie of working together in a close-knit group; sometimes when we were out socialising together and, on rare occasions, when we had quiet interludes during a shift – particularly when we were on nights.

In the early hours, it would generally be less demanding and, if there was nothing much happening due to most people being tucked up in their beds, certain members of my section saw it as an opportunity for relieving any stresses by larking about. And, when there was an unusually quiet interlude, playtime would occasionally involve taking the Panda cars down on to the beach to have 'time trials'. For some reason, senior officers tended to turn a blind eye to such childish capers, even though they were tough disciplinarians back in those days who generally applied the rules in a robust fashion. Unsurprisingly though, such larking about wasn't so easily overlooked after one colleague managed to get his vehicle stuck in the sand with the tide coming in, and had to be towed out of harms way using the Division's Land Rover. Any lax attitude soon evaporated following this near disaster, and no longer was such foolhardy behaviour tolerated or treated so leniently. However, plenty of other ways were still found to enable us to amuse ourselves, and there were pranksters on our section who enjoyed keeping us on our toes with practical jokes – so work was rarely dull even during slack periods.

A particular favourite was exploiting any new PC's unfamiliarity with driving the Hillman Imp Panda cars, which in the mid-1970's made up the bulk of our fleet of police vehicles. The manual choke on these cars was located at the base of the gear stick, meaning a passenger during a double-crewed patrol could easily pull it out momentarily to increase the vehicle's speed. This would cause considerable consternation for the driver, especially as the dastardly deed could be achieved discreetly without the person at the wheel noticing. Normally, the unsuspecting driver wouldn't realise what was going on, especially if the choke was quickly turned back off before they cottoned on to the cause of the fluctuating speed. Sometimes the unwitting colleague would, therefore, end up returning to the station to report the malfunction to the duty sergeant. The novice officer would then be enlightened by the sergeant as to the probable cause! I'm pleased to report that I never fell foul of this trick as my first car had been a Hillman Imp, and some of my friends had already made me well aware of how easy it was for a passenger to get a cheap thrill from interfering with the choke.

Good-humoured banter was also rife – generally harmless and well-meaning – and this helped relieve us from the mentally challenging pressures we were constantly under as a result of regularly dealing with traumatic incidents. It also contributed to an excellent rapport and strong team spirit, providing everyone knew where to draw the line and didn't offend anyone by making inappropriate or insensitive comments.

Back in those days the police service attracted a lot of characters. Tommy, being a former squaddie with a mischievous side to his personality and a wicked sense of humour, definitely fitted into that category. Whenever I was on an early turn, he would often arrive unannounced at my lodgings to give me a lift, and I soon realised the reason for this. Betty, one of my landladies, would always be up at the crack of dawn to make me a cooked breakfast to set me up for the day ahead when I was on this shift, and Tommy, who could be quite a charmer with the older ladies, knew that she would be willing to also make him a bacon-butty. While munching through his early morning snack, he would reveal shocking stories about things that had purportedly happened on duty, which were either fake or considerably embellished. Betty would sit there all agog, totally believing every word as she listened intently to his tales of debauchery. He even had me fooled the first time, when he told her he'd just come from an incident where he'd had to separate two voluptuous ladies fighting naked in the street over a little old man who looked like a dead ringer for Popeye. It wasn't until he described one of the cavorting ladies as a 'Nora Batty' lookalike – and the other as resembling 'Olive' – that I cottoned on it was a total wind-up.

Following this little gem, I recall he then relayed another of his yarns the next time he called around to give me a lift. Betty was once more transfixed when he explained he'd come across a couple getting frisky in a car during a recent night shift. He told her that after shining his torch on the canoodling occupants inside the car, he realised he knew the amorous pair as a married couple from his street, so he'd then said to the chap: 'Sorry sir, I didn't realise you were with your wife.'

To which the husband allegedly replied: 'Nor did I officer, until you shone your torch!'

This time I wasn't the least bit taken in by his fabricated anecdote, as luckily I'd heard this one before during a comedy show, but I think Betty again fell for his tall story big time.

5 More Eye Openers

WORKING WITH TOMMY AND CJ could be a bundle of fun at times, but that didn't in any way undermine their public persona or affect their ability to act professionally. Above all else they were committed and competent police officers. That was most certainly the case when the three of us were together on mobile patrol late one night, and got a call summoning us to attend a worrying but strange incident that had occurred in an outlying village.

Initially we were informed that a male house owner had reported discovering an intruder on his premises. However, whilst we were still en route, we were notified that a concerned neighbour had also phoned in about a disturbance at this same address, and it now appeared we could actually be responding to a violent domestic – so additional backup had been requested. Another police unit, which was single-crewed by a PC called Alan, arrived at the same time as us. In view of the conflicting information we'd received thus far, none of us knew what to expect as we joined forces to deal with the incident. CJ and I went to cover the back of the property, while Tommy and Alan cautiously approached the front door, not knowing what sort of reception awaited them. There was clearly some sort of commotion going on inside the house as we could hear raised voices once we neared the back door, but the ensuing argument suggested the parties involved might well know each other. We soon got a radio message from Tommy advising us Alan and himself had gained entry at the front door and, by the time CJ and I joined them, they already had one male suspect in custody. He was a man of large build in his mid-thirties, who looked like he worked out, and he'd been apprehended after the house owners had stated this chap had broken into their property. Although he'd been arrested on suspicion of breaking and entering, there were no apparent signs of a break-in, and it was therefore clear from the outset that the story we'd been told by the occupants of the house didn't fully stack up.

The husband was very agitated and he took the lead role in firmly telling us the intruder had not only broken into their house, but had also sexually assaulted his wife. This new revelation came out of the blue but, when his wife coyly supported his accusation, our prisoner was further arrested on suspicion of sexual assault – reluctantly because confusion reigned and the couple's explanation seemed questionable. In spite of our concerns that his accusers were possibly being disingenuous, we had little choice but to act on the information we'd been given, especially with the wife corroborating her husband's further allegation. Our initial priority was to restore calm and prevent escalation of an already volatile situation by removing the suspected intruder, who had taken exception to the husband's accusations and become aggressive. We knew we'd then be able to investigate the allegations further in the cool light of day, in order to get to the truth of the matter and discover whether the guy in custody had indeed committed the alleged offences – or if the couple were being deceitful, and deliberately trying to lead us astray for some unknown reason.

Our prisoner resisted getting into the police car and then caused us a bit of hassle as we set off on our journey, so had to be forcibly restrained until we'd driven away from the scene. Once we'd left the village he gradually became more amenable, although he remained obdurate and argumentative for a while. He vehemently protested his innocence during the early part of our trip, and tried giving us a multitude of reasons as to why we should release him. His moaning was incessant and, if having a hyperactive tongue was a crime, there's no doubt he would have been guilty as charged. CJ got so fed up with him bellowing in his ear that he made it clear this wasn't like a union negotiating meeting, whereby he could persuade us to accept his argument or win concessions by constantly pleading his case – and that he would have the opportunity to present his side of the story when he was formally interviewed about the allegations. This had the desired effect and, on realising his futile protestations were falling on deaf ears, he finally shut up; so the remainder of our journey back was peaceful. However, when we arrived back at base and attempted to get him out of the car, he became awkward again.

For some reason, he took a dislike to a fellow officer who'd come to assist us and reacted aggressively to his presence. It was therefore necessary to manhandle him using reasonable force as we escorted him into the station. Similarly, he got stroppy when he was being taken to his cell, and our superintendent forcefully intervened to help us keep him under control. Although our senior colleague didn't cross the line and his actions were justified, I naively thought he was possibly being over-zealous. I wondered if he could have used his powers of persuasion to get our prisoner to accede to his instructions, rather than a heavy-handed approach, which was more likely to provoke a belligerent response. Ultimately though, I soon realised there are times when you have to be assertive to get the upper hand and stay safe.

This was a rare example of me witnessing a police officer getting close to overstepping the mark – and I'm glad to say that during my entire service, spanning some 22 years, I never once saw a colleague actually cross that particular line. There was, however, one further occasion when I observed someone come mighty close to breaching the threshold between using reasonable force and resorting to unnecessary aggression. It happened when an off-duty inspector was out with his family one evening and was threatened by a well-known local yob. Fearing the worst, and seeking to defend his wife and child, it was understandable that the inspector reacted firmly to this provocation – and, but for the timely arrival of several other colleagues, including myself, he might have dished out his own form of restorative justice, rather than rely on the court system. However, I like to think that the fact he recovered his composure, and stopped short of going too far, was as much down to his own self-control kicking back in, as it was to do with our intervention.

Through these types of experiences, I soon learned that the outlook I had during the early stages of my police career was far too idealistic, and there are many circumstances where actions speak louder than words – and sometimes you have to intervene forcefully to maintain control and prevent situations from getting out of hand. Therefore, although I always believed your tongue can be a potent 'tool' in helping to defuse volatile situations, I readily accepted that sometimes anything you say can be academic. For example, talk alone will rarely bear a positive result if tempers are frayed, or when someone's aggressive or violent behaviour is predominantly being fuelled by alcohol, drugs, emotional overcharge or certain states of the mind. Inevitably, such factors can severely impact a person's ability to make reasoned judgements – especially if that individual has a conflicted or distorted view of a given situation – and you have to implement whatever measures are necessary to combat violence and prevent them from doing harm. However, whilst recognising that a police officer's first responsibility is to protect everyone and preserve life, I never lost sight of the fact you should only ever use reasonable force, no matter what amount of provocation you endure. Alongside discovering that interaction can't always keep you out of trouble or resolve every issue, I also rapidly found out that appropriately using your discretion and tact can play a prominent part in enabling you to stay out of trouble and remain safe.

Returning to the case in hand, our suspect was initially held in custody so he could be interviewed about the offences he'd been accused of committing and give his side of the story – and also to enable further enquiries to be conducted. When he gave his account, he refuted the allegations made against him, and insisted his visit to the property had been prompted by an invitation from the lady of the house. He disputed the claim made by the husband that he'd broken in, and we finally felt we were starting to get to the crux of the matter when he hesitantly explained that he'd formed a 'special bond' with the wife – which we thought was a delicate way of stating they'd been having a fling. According to him, his motive for going to the house was purely to see her and check she was ok. This of course needed to be checked out and verified but, as he had no history of being engaged in any form of criminal activity, we realised he might well be telling the truth and, quite possibly, was innocent of any wrongdoing.

Tommy therefore reached the conclusion we could justify releasing him on bail whilst he was under investigation, and we continued our enquiries into the conflicting accounts about what had occurred. There was a proviso, and his release was on condition that he didn't contact the other parties involved or visit their house. Letting him go on bail at this early juncture wasn't the norm for someone who had been arrested on suspicion of committing such serious crimes, but Tommy had significant doubts about the couple's version of events. With the evidence against our suspect looking increasingly dubious, he felt it was right to do so in this instance.

The following evening Tommy and I came on duty earlier than originally scheduled, so we could continue our enquiries into this case and speak with the couple who'd made the allegations. Initially we wanted to check out their stories now they'd had time to reflect on the previous night's events, and then, if appropriate, obtain written statements. When we arrived at the house the husband wasn't home, so this gave us the opportunity to talk to the wife without him being present. This was something Tommy was planning to do anyway, but now he could do so without making it too pointed. It also soon became blatantly obvious that the wife, a petite brunette who was probably in her early forties, was keen to talk to us whilst her husband was out of the way.

In his absence, she was eager to reveal the truth and be candid about what had really occurred the night before. She came clean about her 'involvement' with the chap we'd arrested, and embarrassedly informed us that they'd become close in recent weeks. It sounded like she had a tempestuous relationship with her husband, and she had befriended this other guy whilst in a vulnerable state of mind. He'd recently moved to the village and, in recent weeks, she'd started to see him as her confidant. We learned he'd come to visit her the previous night, solely because he was concerned about her welfare after she'd sounded upset during a telephone conversation they'd had earlier that evening. The lady apologised profusely for prevaricating the previous night, and effectively getting her 'friend' falsely arrested by being so secretive about what had really happened. She then told us she'd panicked at the time and been reluctant to tell the truth in front of her husband.

From the details she revealed, it became apparent her husband had returned home unannounced late the previous night, when she believed he would be staying away. She'd therefore been caught on the hop when her 'friend' had suddenly arrived shortly after her hubby's return. When the husband had answered the door to this 'stranger', who demanded to see his wife, he had seen red and an argument had ensued. The wife then explained that her 'friend' had forced his way in to check she was ok, probably because he thought she could be at risk.

Things had become increasingly heated between the man of the house and this 'stranger', especially as the husband supposedly had no idea who he was, or that his wife had developed a 'close association' with him. The wife admitted she'd also made matters worse by denying she knew this man, even when he'd shown his caring side by putting his arm around her in an attempt to lead her away from the house and out of harms way. Perhaps this was why the husband had mistakenly thought she was being molested, and then made the allegation of sexual assault against him – which now seemed somewhat extreme, based on the true picture that was emerging. She advised us she felt terrible about not contradicting this accusation at the time, by admitting she hadn't been violated, but said she was feeling so scared and confused she wasn't thinking rationally.

Everything made sense to us now and, although Tommy showed the wife sympathy, he did point out that her role in this situation could be seen as attempting to pervert the course of justice – because she had initially corroborated her husband's allegations of her own volition, whilst knowing them to be untrue. Tommy also stressed how damaging a false accusation can be for an innocent party, especially when someone bandies about a fake claim of this nature. However, in view of the mitigating factors that applied, and the underlying domestic issues she faced, he stated he would be recommending no further action be taken in regard to this matter.

In terms of the husband's complaint about the intruder molesting his wife, we had to presume he'd made the allegation in good faith, based on his knowledge of the prevailing circumstances when the incident occurred. Besides, we knew it would be impossible for us to prove otherwise, in spite of the lingering doubts we had about whether he'd been entirely straight with us. Our main concern now was deciding how to best present our findings to him without creating further friction between himself and his wife. With his suspicions having been aroused by the events of the previous night, he'd already be well aware something was amiss and be probing his wife for answers when he got home. Indeed, she admitted he'd already asked some searching questions immediately after the incident, and was therefore anticipating further interrogation. The last thing we wished to do was cause her additional problems, but Tommy made it plain we had to tell him why the police wouldn't be pursuing a case against the so-called 'intruder'. He also stated we'd have to inform her husband that the guy we'd arrested was known to her and had a legitimate reason for visiting their abode. Doing so was unavoidable, even though we knew it might antagonise him further – and meant there was a strong possibility we'd be returning to this household later that evening to deal with a domestic involving a blazing row – or worse!

When we eventually spoke to the husband he showed no emotion. He appeared nonchalant when informed that no charges would be brought against the alleged intruder – and we didn't need to be psychics to read his mind and realise he'd worked out what had been going on. The fact the police weren't asked to respond to a domestic at his address later that evening, nor anytime over the next few days, hopefully meant the couple had been able to resolve their differences amicably – although, once more, that could have been wishful thinking on my part.

The chap who'd been unfairly implicated in committing the alleged offences was rightly exonerated once the truth had been exposed and, on receiving this news, was very philosophical about what had happened. Considering he'd ended up being arrested after he'd 'mistakenly' been accused of committing such an abominable crime as sexual assault, which proved to be baseless, he showed a remarkable amount of humility and grace, particularly for someone who'd turned out to be a completely innocent party. He had every right to feel aggrieved and be a little indignant in his manner, but he didn't overtly show either emotion. Clearly, he wasn't a person who held grudges and, even though he'd been unwittingly sucked into this nightmare situation, I felt he came over as being very benevolent towards the complainant, the wife and, indeed, ourselves. That was the end of this matter, except to say he definitely won my admiration for his charitable attitude.

Within a few days of putting this case to bed, Tommy and I once again became immersed in dealing with another confusing incident where some form of sexual assault had allegedly occurred. This time it involved a group of teenage lads and lasses, who were pupils at the local grammar school. During a Saturday afternoon, a group of them, mustering six in total, had gathered at the school playing fields for a session of binge drinking. Although aged 15, they'd somehow acquired cans of cider, and by the evening they were all worse for wear. At around 2100hrs, we got a call to attend the school because one of the young ladies had been discovered by the caretaker wandering around the school grounds in a dishevelled and drunken state. When we arrived on the scene and tried speaking with her she was incoherent, so our initial plan was to take her home to her parents. However, as she became more lucid, and it dawned on her we were about to take her home, she had a bout of hysteria. She demanded we let her rejoin her group of friends, who were still hanging out on the adjoining playing fields. And, when she was denied this option, she started to sob and suddenly complained she'd been sexually assaulted.

It's fair to say that back then not all complaints of this nature were taken as seriously as they should have been, but Tommy and I did everything by the book and firstly enquired if she knew the person responsible for carrying out the assault. Her response was vague and she couldn't be that specific about exactly what had happened, or give a precise description of her attacker. This in itself isn't unusual when someone has endured such a dreadful trauma and is likely to still be in shock. The lack of clarity therefore didn't surprise us at this stage, especially as she was also suffering from the effects of excessive alcohol consumption. However, the lack of conviction she'd portrayed when revealing she'd been assaulted did give us slight cause for concern, and raise niggling questions in our minds about the authenticity of her claim. Even so, we knew it would be necessary to undertake a thorough investigation, and preserve the scene if she could pinpoint roughly where the assault had happened. Equally, it was essential we rounded up the rest of her group, not least because they were of similar age, likely vulnerable if drunk, and all potential witnesses. As she'd been unable to give us much detail about the age or appearance of the alleged assailant, other than he was male, we also needed to treat the three lads from the group as possible suspects. Once we'd traced her friends, we took them into our custody for their own safety and wellbeing. We then called up for the police mini-bus and had the five worried looking juveniles transported back to the station, whilst we escorted the victim in our patrol car.

By the time we got back to HQ the young lady in our care had started to sober up, and she was handed over to one of the Division's WPCs to be interviewed in more detail about the alleged assault. In those days this wasn't always the norm in this category of case, as it was usual practice for CID to conduct such interviews, but Tommy wisely chose to ignore force protocol and instead requested that a female officer perform this task. Things were very different back in the 1970's and female officers had their own separate Policewomen's Unit, and generally didn't work routine shifts with their male counterparts. Fortunately though, the differentiation between male and female officers gradually diminished, and before long they were rightly treated as equals and undertook exactly the same role. Eventually, even the 'W' prefix was discarded, with all officers of constable rank being referred to as a PC – however, to keep my memoirs factually accurate,

I will continue referring to female colleagues as WPCs.

The WPC leading the investigation into the alleged sexual assault required a responsible adult to be present when she interviewed the victim. She anticipated one of the girl's parents would perform this role – but this plan was scuppered because the young woman was resistant to having either of them involved. Not only was she adamant about that, but she also stated she didn't want them notified she was at the police station or to be told the reason she was there. The victim's strong feelings on the matter, and refusal to explain why she didn't want their involvement, aroused the suspicions of the WPC and made her wary of the girl's motives. Faced with a delicate situation though, she reluctantly agreed to instead get a social worker to act as the responsible adult, despite the delay this would cause. In view of the girl's age however, she insisted on notifying the parents of her whereabouts.

Our eminent colleague's attempts to gather any meaningful physical evidence were also hampered by the victim declining to undergo any sort of medical examination. She bluntly refused to see a doctor, even when the WPC explained it would be vital to determine the extent of any injuries she might have suffered during the assault, and to preserve any forensic materials linked to the alleged attacker – to help identify the culprit and bring about a successful prosecution.

When the young lady was finally interviewed by the WPC, in the presence of the social worker, she maintained she had been sexually assaulted. The female officer therefore sensitively probed further to establish what the attacker had done to her. However, she had great difficulty forming a picture of exactly what had happened as the victim reportedly stated everything was a bit of a blur, and she couldn't really be sure. Again, this can frequently happen when someone has been the victim of such an awful trauma, so this alone didn't seem surprising. In the circumstances the process was painfully slow but, to our fellow officer's credit, she persevered in an attempt to get all the facts – knowing it would be impossible to carry out a proper investigation into the allegation with so little to go on. In spite of this, no useful information had been forthcoming after a prolonged interview, and it appeared the young lady had suffered total memory loss. When, without warning, the girl suddenly blurted out she had made up the assault and hadn't been violated, I suspect the WPC was therefore relieved, and not that surprised.

Once the truth surfaced, we found out the reason the girl had fabricated the whole story. Despite her intoxicated state, she'd had enough gumption to realise her parents were going to be furious with her for getting drunk, and also for being out when she was already 'grounded' and on a strict curfew. Consequently, after we'd mentioned we had a duty of care and would be taking her home, she'd gone into panic mode and made up the tale about being attacked as a distraction. Once she'd embarked on this course of action, which had probably been influenced by her drunken state, things had rapidly progressed, and she didn't know how to stop the situation spiralling out of control – even though she'd known deep down she'd gone too far right from the outset. Hopefully, she learned a harsh lesson from this whole experience, and realised how quickly things can get out of hand when you cry wolf, especially if it is about something so serious, which will not only have major repercussions for the individual being untruthful, but also implications for other innocent parties – like her five friends in this instance.

Due to her age, no further action was taken against the girl for making up a misleading story that wasted a lot of police time, but she did get a severe reprimand from her parents once they finally found out what had gone on, which probably helped her see the error of her ways.

Bearing in mind how sexual assault allegations were sometimes handled in this era, I now realise that not all such cases were dealt with as empathetically as this one happened to be by our WPC colleague. She could easily have become dismissive early on, which was apparently what often occurred back then – but the fact she still sensitively and sympathetically persisted with the process when it became apparent the young lady's claim may not have substance, and continued doing so even after she'd retracted the allegation, showed this officer was probably ahead of her time in her outlook.

Working chiefly with uniformed frontline responders during the formative stages of my police career, meant this was a time when I only ever got involved on the peripheral of any enquiries into sexual offences. However, over the years I did come across several other similar cases to these ones, where false or frivolous claims were made about sexually motivated crimes – sometimes as a cover up to prevent a loved one from finding out what the claimant had really been up to. I even came across one vexatious claim where vengeance appeared to be the motive. Nonetheless, whilst false accusations aren't as uncommon as some people might think, they are very much the exception to the rule. It is, consequently, imperative to realise and accept that the vast majority of allegations relating to this heinous type of offence do have foundation, are truthful and will be genuine – and need to be thoroughly investigated by specialist officers. Nowadays, police officers are generally much more aware of the vagaries that can affect a victim's thinking after they've been subjected to a sexual assault – which, for all sorts of reasons, can even result in them withdrawing an allegation despite it being true. Therefore, I'd like to think that in modern times all investigations into allegations of this nature are undertaken diligently, showing the same degree of empathy and tenacity displayed by our wise female colleague.

Whilst on my next series of night shifts, I had my first encounter with a police dog. Tommy and I were on foot patrol, covering a beat that was on the outer fringes of the town centre, when a public-spirited member of the local community, who was out walking his mutt, summoned our assistance. He informed us that he'd recently seen two men climbing over the fence of a nearby scrap-yard and, believing them to be up to no good, he'd just phoned the police to alert them. To him it must have therefore looked like our seemingly rapid response to his call was impressive; in reality though, it was pure coincidence and good fortune that we happened to be in the vicinity. After thanking him, we quickly made our way towards the scrap-yard where he'd spotted the possible intruders. We only had one radio between us and Tommy tried calling in to tell control we were heading to the suspected break-in, but it didn't seem to be transmitting. It was, however, receiving transmissions and we heard that two mobile units had been despatched to the location.

Tommy and I were first on the scene, so we entered the premises in the same fashion as the suspects – by climbing over the surrounding exterior fence – and started looking for any signs of unwelcome visitors. Being a scrap-yard, it was an extensive area to search and there were plenty of places for someone to hide. We were some distance from where we'd gained entry when we heard over the radio that the other police units had arrived at the scrap-yard, along with the key-holder. Then, to our horror, we also learned that one of the police units was the dog-handler, and he was about to let his hound into the yard to sniff out any intruders.

Rapidly, Tommy informed me we may be in trouble because police dogs don't discriminate and are unable to differentiate between friend or foe. I could tell from the tone of his voice our predicament was serious and, with our radio not transmitting, we had but one choice – run for our lives! We charged back to the outer fence as fast as our legs would carry us, knowing that if the dog could smell fear it would definitely pick up our trail in no time. At one point when I glanced back while sprinting, I was certain the dog had us in its sights but, as luck would have it, the hound suddenly deviated from its course. It must have locked onto the scent of the two intruders before picking up our smell, and instead devoted its attention to seeking them out. As a result, we just about made it to the fence in the nick of time and managed to scramble over without coming to any harm. This near miss with 'deputy dawg' was something Tommy and I were able to laugh about with our bemused colleagues when we relayed what had happened – but it was pretty hairy at the time and an ordeal neither of us wanted to repeat in a hurry.

The fact the two intruders were apprehended did at least make us feel better about inadvertently placing ourselves in danger, especially when we discovered that our actions hadn't been totally in vain. It had likely been our presence in the scrap-yard that had caused them to hide, rather than attempt an escape before our backup arrived. This was one of those occasions that you encountered regularly whilst performing your duties where you therefore felt mixed emotions – a combination of excitement and fear in equal measure as you experienced that adrenaline rush.

6 Crossroads Reached

I DIDN'T KNOW AT THE TIME this bout of night shifts would turn out to be the last time I performed duties out on the streets as a police cadet. As soon as I'd completed my latest round of nights, I took some overdue leave, and this break became a time for reflection – a chance to take stock and properly absorb and assess all that I'd been through since joining the police force. I wasn't intending it to be an opportunity to consider my future or plan my next career move but, for several reasons, this was something I ended up doing.

In part, this development came about because I was still feeling a little guilty about deserting my dad's family business the previous year, following my spur of the moment decision to apply to join the 'fuzz'. It hadn't been a rash decision, but it had hastily come about on a bit of a whim, which had resulted in me abandoning my dad in the midst of turbulent times; the era of multiple strikes, power cuts, petrol rationing and the three-day working week. My abiding memory of those difficult days was one of strife, with many families struggling to make ends meet. Therefore, it wasn't a shock when I found out my father's company had been going through a tricky phase, and he needed to downsize. I knew he was too proud to ever ask for help, and he would never expect me to jeopardise my career to assist him during these challenging times. But, I was also aware my parents had made huge sacrifices for my siblings and me to ensure we had every chance of succeeding in life, and I wanted to repay the loyalty and commitment they'd shown me during my childhood and early adult life. So, I spent much of my leave wrestling with my conscience, deciding what to do for the best.

On the one hand my brief time as a police cadet had been career defining – because I'd caught the 'bug' and knew this was the life for me. However, family was also very important to me, and I wanted to support my dad as he worked hard to save his business and restore its fortunes. I faced an agonising dilemma, which caused me to look inwardly at myself so I could make the right decision – one that factored in what was best for my future career and wasn't purely altruistic.

The last 10 months or so had principally been full-on and all new territory for me; especially the seven consecutive months I'd spent out on Division, when I'd been learning the ropes and crammed a lot into the early stages of my police career. As already highlighted, during this brief period I'd attended my first murder scene, a fatal accident, several sudden deaths and a post-mortem – all this while still a novice. Such encounters had understandably been a rude awakening to the harsh realities of life. This was particularly so for a lad who'd led a life of blissful innocence and ignorance up to that point and, fortuitously, not suffered any serious trauma first-hand, other than a couple of nasty accidents whilst growing up, which I will elaborate on at a later stage. Therefore, these were overriding factors when I started to question whether I was ready for the next step in my policing career at such a tender age. It wasn't a case of self-doubt creeping in because I was sure I had what it takes to ultimately become an effective and rounded police constable, but my experiences had made me aware that first I needed to toughen up and be more assertive. In other words, to develop into the finished article I'd have to become more streetwise.

What I'd witnessed and been through since starting out in the police had definitely stopped me from being so wide-eyed; a trait I'd likely developed due to my somewhat middle-class upbringing. However, I was conscious I'd displayed a degree of naivety during my early days on the beat, and still lacked some of the key credentials required to be effective in a policing role; not least the level of wisdom every officer needs in order to be viewed as credible by members of the public. I intuitively sensed this would best be gained by broadening my horizons and undergoing a variety of different experiences outside of the police force, even though I had revelled in the excitement of carrying out police duties, and a large part of me wanted to continue on this path.

The brief time I'd spent as a cadet had done more to shape my life than the previous 18 years combined and, although I'd been thrust into confronting traumatic situations and gruesome sights that were alien to me, I'd still derived a considerable amount of satisfaction serving the community in this role. Therefore, I was very reluctant to leave; however, I knew I had to be honest with myself and let my head rule my heart. Accordingly, I made a decision based on common sense and pragmatism, as opposed to my passion for the police service. I chose to set about getting other experiences under my belt, which I felt would serve me well and allow me to hone my life skills, widen my sociological knowledge and further develop my emotional intelligence. I set myself a five-year target to achieve these objectives, which I felt would ultimately enable me to become a better police officer – providing they'd have me back at a later stage!

So that was the end of my first venture into police work. I just needed to return to Division to sort out all the formalities for my imminent departure and, most importantly, to bid a fond farewell to all my colleagues – many of whom had made a big impression on me, even though this initial episode with the Constabulary had been relatively brief. It was tough saying goodbye because several of them had become good friends, not least Tommy and CJ. Metaphorically speaking, they'd taken me under their wings and looked after me during my transient period on the beat. They both had big personalities and I was going to miss sharing their company. CJ was only 22 and, although he often displayed a youthful exuberance, he also exuded a lot of confidence that belied his tender years. As a result, it was sometimes hard to accept he was only four years older than me, and yet possessed so much street cred. He had already been married for over a year, and he made me laugh when he talked about his home life as though he was an old-timer who'd been wed since the year dot. Outside of work, trains were his passion, and he often described himself as a trainspotting geek. His favourite pastime was building his own model railway and, whenever he did anything to annoy his wife, he would apparently get banished to the shed to play with his train set. I therefore had this sneaking suspicion that he used to regularly upset her so he'd get dismissed to his man cave!

Tommy was a different kettle of fish. A 'tough cop' on the outside, but one with a soft centre. Now in his late twenties, he'd previously spent nine years in the army before switching to the police service, having originally signed up to the armed forces as a boy soldier aged 16. By age 22 he'd made sergeant, and I loved listening to him talk with real enthusiasm about his army adventures, especially when he incorporated some of the humorous colloquialisms he'd acquired from his northern roots in order to express himself. I recall him telling me about some of the missions he was involved in whilst on manoeuvres overseas, and vividly remember him recounting one particular story about his platoon getting lost in the jungle. With rations running low, he explained how they'd had to improvise and find some of nature's food to survive. I'm not sure if this tale was completely fictitious or simply embellished in part, but he told me that he'd led a group of his comrades to hunt for something suitable to roast on an open fire. According to Tommy, they'd come across a river where they'd been able to take pot shots at snakes swimming in the water, which they'd then managed to retrieve and cook for supper. This could well have been another of his tall stories, like the ones he would frequently tell my landladies in such a sincere and convincing manner. With Tommy it was hard to differentiate between fact and fiction, not only because he was somewhat wax lyrical in the way he relayed his tales, but also because he was so adept at modifying and turning even the most serious of matters or events into some form of spoof or parody. However, when he mentioned about the other half of his troop failing in their mission to track down a group of pigmies, so snake & pigmy pie was off the menu, it became clear he'd stretched the truth somewhat on this occasion.

When I visited CJ and Tommy, I also dropped in on my wise and wonderful sergeant to say goodbye and thank him for all his help and support. Incidentally, it was during this final meeting with him that I discovered he'd actually gained his stripes shortly after using his initiative to catch some serial burglars by hiding up a tree – although you could argue that a transfer to Special Branch would perhaps have been more apt!

In addition to saying au revoir to all my colleagues, I also had to say farewell to Mrs King and Betty back at my lodgings. Staying with them at their Victorian style house had been like travelling back in time but, as landladies, they had been kind to me and, in an odd way, I was going to miss all their fussing and nuanced idiosyncrasies. However, one thing I wasn't going to miss was stale sandwiches in my lunchbox. For some reason, they had this old-fashioned view that fresh bread wasn't good for you, and it needed to be at least a week old before it could be served up – even if that meant cutting off the mouldy bits! Something else I wouldn't miss was acting as their personal taxi service. Neither of them drove and, as I was the only cadet in residence with a car, they weren't slow in realising they could save a fortune on taxi fares by utilising my driving services. Generally, I didn't mind them taking advantage of my good nature and was happy to help out, but there were occasions when I felt they were taking liberties, especially when they started to rely totally on me to run any errands. One such errand that sticks in my mind – probably because it's a painful memory – was a trip to the bank with Mrs King.

It was only a short journey to the bank, but by the time we'd arrived at our destination it was raining hard, so Mrs King wanted me to drop her off right outside and then wait for her nearby, whilst she popped in to withdraw her weekly housekeeping money. I duly obliged, letting her out of the car close to the bank entrance. I then needed to move my vehicle to a parking space just up the road; however, before I could do so, I needed to reach over and close the front passenger door as Mrs King had failed to shut it properly. In fairness, it wasn't her fault as the catch on the door was dodgy, and it needed to be slammed extra hard before it would engage. Anyway, when I leaned across at full stretch from the driver's seat to shut it, the only part of the door I could reach and grab hold of was the handle to the quarter window – something that a 1963 Hillman Imp still possessed, unlike more modern cars of the 1970's era. I recall holding onto the small quarter window handle with just two fingers and a thumb, and then pulling the door using all my might – yet failing miserably in my effort to slam it shut. Instead of closing the door, all I succeeded in doing was wrecking my car as the quarter window flew out of its frame. Not only that, but as the window gave way all the power I'd used transferred to my right thumb and promptly dislocated it. The pain I felt caused me to yelp and, I'm ashamed to say, I cursed Mrs King for indirectly creating this situation. I then did something really stupid because I grabbed hold of my droopy thumb with my left hand and gave it a quick yank. This was something I'd seen done on a rugby field whenever a player dislocated a thumb or finger that then needed to be put back into its socket – and I think it was an action I performed instinctively without knowing the consequences, or having a clue whether it would work. The extreme pain this caused nearly sent me through the roof but, much to my amazement, the thumb did indeed slip back into its socket.

Looking back, I can only assume it was a combination of the anger and writhing agony I was feeling that made me resort to this drastic measure. Clearly, it would have been more sensible if I'd visited the local A&E department to have the procedure carried out by someone with appropriate medical knowledge – and probably a lot less painful if it had been numbed beforehand! Anyhow, as soon as the thumb was back in its rightful place following this jerking manoeuvre, the extreme pain started to ease a little and my annoyance rapidly subsided. So, by the time Mrs King came out of the bank clutching her money, I was more or less my normal self again – apart from a sore thumb. I wasn't, of course, overly pleased about now having a vehicle with natural air conditioning on a wet day but, hey-ho, it could have been worse – and a made to measure piece of perspex soon solved the problem on a temporary basis.

For the most part I enjoyed the time I spent living in the 'previous century' with my eccentric landladies, so saying goodbye to the delightful old biddies proved to be an emotional event for all parties, even though my short-lived stay had lasted barely nine months in total, including times away on exercise. It's odd how quickly you can grow attached to people who become a part of your daily life, and I missed them and their quirky ways more than I expected after my departure. I'd like to think they missed me too once I'd moved on, but I suspect they probably missed my car more!

7 Gap Years

Having left the force, it was on to pastures new as I now embarked on the next chapter in my life. True to my convictions, I spent the next five years getting new experiences under my belt, which I felt would serve me well when I hopefully returned to my police career. Although I went back to working in my father's business, I combined my job with a variety of other activities and escapades that took me out of my comfort zone. These included further studies, doing some travelling in the UK, France and Scandinavia, and undertaking a range of charity work. The latter of these challenges entailed briefly joining the 'Samaritans', setting-up and leading a community initiative for young people aged 18-21, and assisting at a club for people with learning disabilities. I also carried out some research projects into an array of different topics, took on some business ventures of my own and got heavily involved in several different sporting activities.

Throughout the time I was busy developing my life skills, extending my knowledge and trying out new experiences, I still longed to one day get back to fighting crime and retained the overwhelming urge to rejoin the girls and boys in blue. This yearning grew stronger and gathered momentum as the years rolled by. At the start of the summer in 1979, I therefore made myself redundant from my father's family business with the intention of applying to rejoin the Constabulary. I intended taking a few months off initially to do some travelling further afield, before hopefully returning to the police force in the autumn – however, my plans were interrupted. I registered at the local Job Centre to ensure I got NI credits whilst I was technically unemployed, and this unexpectedly led to me getting an offer to actually work for the Employment Service temporarily until the end of February 1980. I decided this would be another valuable experience and, therefore, made some adjustments to my original schedule. Unbeknown to me, just a few months up the road, there would then be a further delay to me implementing my intended career plan.

In the period leading up to Xmas 1979 I'd been experiencing chronic and debilitating stomach problems, which resulted in me suffering acute pain. I knew this needed to be sorted before I applied to get back to policing; so, after seeing my doctor, I underwent an endoscopy shortly before Xmas. For anyone unfamiliar with this procedure, it entails having a tube with a camera on the end inserted down one's throat to do some exploration of the gullet and colon. I don't know whether an endoscopy is carried out differently in the modern era but, back then, it required you to have an anaesthetic, which was described to me as a strong form of sedative that was being trialled – and it was this aspect of the medical procedure that went terribly wrong in my case and had a profound affect on shaping my future.

Whilst administering the anaesthetic, the consultant somehow managed to insert the needle into an artery in my left arm – rather than a vein – and inject the entire contents of the syringe before realising her error; the upshot being that I was ultimately left fighting for my life. Initially, I didn't twig that something was going drastically wrong when she began injecting the powerful sedative – possibly because I'd had inoculations in the past that hurt. Therefore, I thought the excruciating pain I had in my left arm must be normal and would quickly pass as I drifted off to sleep. But I soon found out this was far from usual. I made her aware I was in agony, and stressed my left hand was starting to blow up like a balloon and felt like it was on fire. And, when she glanced down and saw it for herself, she almost went into panic mode. I think she immediately recognised what had caused the problem as she instantly injected me with a strong painkiller to douse the pain. Presumably, this was some form of morphine-based analgesic because it soon had the desired effect and, much to my relief, caused the intense throbbing and burning sensation to rapidly subside.

I assumed that would be the end of this particular ordeal but, to my surprise, they then went ahead and did the endoscopy with me wide awake – and thus, all too well aware of what was going on. I recall that the tube with the camera on the end was much bigger than I'd anticipated. As they pushed it down my throat I had to swallow hard, and experienced this horrible choking feeling. It made me gag and gasp for air at the same time and, as I discovered later during my police service, this procedure is not dissimilar to what someone will endure when they undergo a stomach pump after overdosing.

As far as I'm aware, the only advantage of having an endoscopy whilst you are conscious and compos mentis is that you don't have a severe sore throat afterwards. I presume this is because you are able to swallow the tube, rather than having it forced down. Anyway, I still wouldn't recommend it – and not only because it's an unpleasant experience. There's also something really bizarre about looking up at the screen and seeing the inside of your own gut as the camera makes its journey along one's various internal canals.

Another strange phenomenon about this whole episode was being able to get off the surgical trolley and walk out of the operating theatre once the internal examination was complete. Whereas, everyone else undergoing the procedure had to be wheeled out still unconscious, and put to bed until the anaesthetic had worn off.

Once the endoscopy was over, I again made the mistake of thinking that would be the end of my nightmare. In spite of the anaesthetic having been administered intra-arterially, the consultant was confident there would be no lasting ill-effects. Therefore, after monitoring my condition for a couple of hours, they duly allowed me to go home. This was on the proviso I went to see my GP later that day to check that my left arm – which I assumed was still numb due to the painkiller injection – had come back to life. So, by lunchtime on that fateful day I was back home, still incapacitated due to my left arm effectively being paralysed, but otherwise feeling quite cheerful now that the internal examination was over.

Despite my bad experience, I was just pleased to have survived the trauma and come through it relatively unscathed – or so I thought.

As instructed, I'd made an appointment to visit my doctor later that same day, but I never got to see him. Around mid-afternoon he phoned me at home. He explained that he had some bad news, and I urgently needed to return to the hospital for some vital treatment. This sounded ominous, and I immediately sensed things were serious. Understandably, I was worried by this development and asked him to clarify why they were so concerned. He told me the hospital had contacted the manufacturer of the anaesthetic, and the prognosis for my recovery wasn't good unless there was further rapid intervention.

Apparently, the drug company's experts believed serious damage would have been caused to the blood vessels supplying my left arm and hand, and I would need urgent treatment to flush out the anaesthetic still circulating in this part of my body. My GP also advised that without this treatment there was an imminent risk I could develop a thrombosis. Furthermore, he stressed it was likely the misdirected anaesthetic substance causing the numbness, rather than the subsequently administered painkiller. It had most probably blocked off proper circulation to my left hand, which needed to be restored within a critical time period – otherwise gangrene may set in and amputation could become necessary! When I pressed him on this point, he informed me that once circulation has been compromised, it needs to be restored within six to eight hours before any damage becomes irreversible. This news sent a shiver down my spine as I knew we were already approaching six hours since the incident, and that the window for getting treatment to hopefully prevent any permanent damage was nearly up. Bearing in mind this time limit was fast approaching, I thought an ambulance would be on its way to collect me with sirens blazing, but I was wrong again. Instead, my father had to rush me back to hospital – because my doctor thought this would be quicker than waiting for an ambulance to arrive.

In the circumstances, I didn't think it unreasonable to expect priority treatment upon my arrival at hospital, but that proved to be overly optimistic. I wasn't greeted by a reception party of medical experts and taken immediately to a treatment room. Instead, with the clock ticking down fast to the point of no return, I just had to sit in a corridor and await my turn to be seen. Although I tried to put on a brave face, on the inside I was certainly panicking more and more as each critical minute went by because I knew the chances of them saving my hand were fading fast. Eventually, after what seemed like an eternity, there was a mad rush to get me sorted and it was all hands on deck once they began my treatment. It emerged that there was a justifiable reason for the interminable delay. Both the surgeon and the anaesthetist, who would jointly need to treat me, had been in theatre carrying out an operation at the point I arrived, and that was why I'd not been seen sooner.

One of these specialists rapidly informed me what they would need to do to try to save my hand. He emphasised they would be working against the clock to restore full circulation to my hand, fingers and lower arm – which had already turned a deep shade of purple. To my horror, he also explained the procedure would entail making an incision in my left armpit to locate the artery supplying blood to my arm, so they could then inject a medicated saline solution into it. They were hopeful this compound would flush out the anaesthetic and nullify the adverse affect it was having on the blood vessels. However, the specialist admitted this was very much a case of trial and error, primarily because they'd never had to respond to this type of medical emergency before involving this new form of anaesthetic drug. Finding this out didn't exactly fill me with confidence.

Performing the intricate procedure outlined was easier said than done. I discovered that getting a needle into an artery is incredibly difficult to achieve; making it all the more amazing that the consultant who'd administered my anaesthetic had managed to do so with consummate ease completely by mistake! Trying to repeat this feat as part of the urgent remedial procedure proved to be anything but simple. No sooner did they get the syringe into the artery, than it was forced out time and again. The pressure of the blood flow made it almost impossible to insert the hypodermic needle for long enough to inject any meaningful amount of the 'cleansing fluid' into the artery. It therefore proved to be a long and arduous process. Each time the needle was thrown out there was a gush of blood. Within minutes I was therefore soaked in my own blood and the sheet I was lying on had turned red. I was expecting a bed bath at some point whilst I was in hospital, but what I was getting was a bloodbath.

As a result of this massive blood loss I grew steadily weaker, and found it hard to focus on the mass of medical staff that surrounded my treatment table, eager to catch a glimpse of a procedure that had seemingly never before been conducted at this hospital. For the first time in my life I felt very much like a guinea pig – one that was being used as an effigy by someone that had it in for me!

After a surfeit of abortive attempts to inject the needle into my artery, the surgeon finally made a successful insertion, which had lasted long enough to infuse the amount of fluid required to hopefully have the desired effect. Once more, I was confident this would be the end of my woes and it would be downhill from hereon, but again my hopes were soon dashed.

Following the conclusion of this procedure, I was admitted to hospital to be kept under observation and receive further treatment, which included being placed on several drips. One of these was Heparin to thin my blood and minimise the thrombosis risk. My left arm was still paralysed at this stage, due to a combination of the analgesic and the partially restricted blood flow. A pulley was therefore used to raise it above my body to allow the 'toxins' to drain. Meanwhile, my right arm became a pin cushion for the variety of different drips. This rendered me useless, in terms of me being able to carry out basic functions using my hands, and reliant on nursing staff to meet all my personal needs. I found this a little amusing, especially when a young nurse came to give me the bed bath I'd anticipated. After she'd given most of my body the once over with a sponge, she then placed it on my stomach, and embarrassedly suggested I give my own nether regions a wash. I implied that achieving this expectation with neither hand at my disposal was going to be tricky, and I remember she made me laugh out loud when she acknowledged it would be nigh on impossible – and then, without fully realising the connotation, suggested I would certainly need to be a 'clever dick' to meet the challenge she'd set me!

The endoscopy had taken place on the Monday morning and, by the latter part of the following day, I was just beginning to think the worst was over. However, by around 9pm that evening I was facing another medical emergency. I'd become aware that my left arm was starting to swell up at a rapid rate and, within an hour of first noticing, it was alarmingly big. It had grown so much that in normal circumstances I'd have been proud to have an arm muscle that size – and I think even Mohammed Ali would have been impressed. I didn't want to make a fuss, but I was sure something definitely wasn't right, so I brought it to the attention of my nurse. Upon doing so, I could tell from her reaction that she was equally shocked at its size, and she immediately called for the consultant. When he arrived

I sensed he wasn't best pleased that he'd been summoned but, after seeing the size of my arm, his demeanour changed – doubtless he instantaneously realised he hadn't been dragged back to the ward on a fool's errand.

The speed at which he took further advice from the senior registrar instantly gave me an indication he had serious concerns regarding my wellbeing, and I soon found out there was a major problem. I'd been over-dosed with Heparin, due to it somehow being delivered too quickly into my body. This, in turn, was causing me to bleed internally. Although I didn't fully appreciate the severity of this situation, the irony of my predicament wasn't lost on me. It seemed like sod's law that a drug intended to combat the adverse health effects of being injected intra-arterially had actually compounded my problem, and ended up doing me more harm than good.

In view of the reaction I was having to the Heparin, reversing the process and rapidly getting the drug out of my system to prevent it from causing further damage became imperative. The senior registrar recommended I would urgently need a fast-acting antidote to make my body reject the Heparin and discharge it accordingly. To activate such a response, the antidote (another trial drug) had to be given via an injection; so, as you can imagine, I was insistent the consultant did his best to deliver it intravenously, and preferably not in my artery! Once this wonder drug had been pumped into my body to negate the affects of the Heparin, it was a case of wait and see – and hope that it did the trick.

The night that followed was a blur because my condition quickly deteriorated, and I received intensive care for the next 12 hours or so. However, I do remember being violently sick on several occasions, and a nurse sitting with me throughout the night checking my vital signs as I drifted in and out of consciousness. During this crucial period I felt like I was floating, and was pretty much oblivious to the seriousness of the situation I faced. That was probably just as well whilst this emergency was ongoing because it would have been very unsettling and extremely frightening. The fact I'm now able to give an account of my ordeal, confirms that I survived to tell the tale but, from what I learned subsequently about my plight, I think it was very much touch and go as to whether I would get through that night.

By the middle of Wednesday, the swelling in my left arm had started to dissipate and I was back in the land of the living, and feeling a little better. It wasn't all plain sailing from that point on because I was far from cured, but things were gradually moving in the right direction and my condition was starting to improve. The next few days were crucial, as they would determine whether there would be any lasting damage from either of the medical mishaps I'd endured. At that stage, the medical professionals and drug experts still didn't know if I'd have full use of my left arm and hand or, indeed, whether amputation would become necessary. Equally, they weren't sure if there would be any long-term repercussions resulting from the Heparin overdose, or the internal bleeding this had triggered. I can remember that as I lay in bed feeling a little sorry for myself, and pondering on what I'd been through over the previous 72 hours, I contemplated how this trauma may affect my future. As I did so, I also found my mind drifting back to my childhood and thinking about another nasty incident I'd been involved in when I was just nine-years-old, which could have led to the 'Grim Reaper' paying me an early visit!

This close encounter with death occurred whilst I was attending a friend's birthday party. For my pal's birthday treat, we'd gone to visit King Alfred's Tower for a picnic and, after we'd finished tucking into our party food, we played a typically boyish war game where I ended up as a real-life casualty.

There were around 10 of us young lads at the party and we split into two groups, and began charging around pretending we were soldiers. One side was trying to defend the castle, which was surrounded by fields, trees and plenty of fauna, and the remainder of us, who formed the invasion force, were trying to capture it from them. Being inventive, we armed ourselves with sticks and stones to act as our rifles and grenades. We launched our attack using the trees and bushes as cover and charged towards our playmates who represented the enemy. Whilst running full pelt at our foe, I never spotted the single-stranded barbed wire fence that surrounded the castle, which had been fixed around one metre up from the ground – or, in other words, at about neck height for someone of my age and size. As I went headlong into it at tremendous speed I was catapulted into the air and, as a result of the whiplash, effectively did a backward flip before crashing down on my backside. Amazingly, I wasn't instantly decapitated and didn't break my neck on impact. However, I was completely stunned after accidentally trying to garrotte myself, and initially had no idea what I'd collided with or why I'd come to such an abrupt halt.

Whilst I was lying on the ground trying to regain my senses and work out what had just happened, I became aware something warm and sticky was trickling down my neck and turning my tee-shirt red. Upon putting my hand up to my throat, I soon realised this was in fact blood, which was gushing from a deep puncture wound under my chin. There was a lot of it, but it didn't cross my mind the collision might have inflicted a serious injury, and wasn't really conscious of the implications. I even recall laughing with my chums about the incident that had caused the injury, especially when they described what they'd witnessed, and how I'd performed a high-speed backward somersault that any Olympic gymnast would be proud of.

At that point I honestly thought I'd just need a sticking plaster, and then we could get on with playing our game. However, when we went back to see the birthday boy's mum, so she could administer some basic first aid, the look she gave me was one of sheer horror. She immediately got everybody back in the vehicle and rushed me off to the nearest Casualty department, which was around 10 miles away. I genuinely didn't know what all the fuss was about, and just felt disappointed that our party had come to a premature end. It wasn't until a doctor in Casualty was treating me that it started to sink in I was lucky to still be alive. The puncture wound had come within a whisker of penetrating my windpipe, and much too close for comfort to catching and severing my jugular – in which case it would almost certainly have been curtains for me! The doctor said it was miraculous the impact hadn't ripped my throat open, and that I'd only been pierced by a single barb. There was no doubt I got incredibly lucky, since the accident could have proved fatal. However, I still didn't grasp the gravity of the situation, and it was only when I got home to my parents that I finally felt some emotion and burst into tears – although, even then, I'm not sure I knew why I was crying.

Puncturing my throat wasn't the only serious accident I experienced due to my own misadventures while growing up. From 11-years-old I was a day boy at a private school where the majority of pupils were boarders, and this establishment was very different to typical state-funded senior schools. Not only was it a very strict environment, where there was as much emphasis on etiquette as there was on education, but it also had some uncommon sports that featured in its curriculum, including fives and soft-ball. Whilst once playing the latter of these games, I again came perilously close to receiving a life-changing injury. I was aged 13 at the time and, for some stupid reason for which I was entirely to blame, I got far too close to the striker as he hit the ball with considerable force, and it caught me square in my right eye. You could say that I followed my PE teacher's instruction about 'always keeping your eye on the ball' to the letter – although, I don't think he meant it quite so literally. My eye socket and nose took the brunt of the impact, and I can testify that the ball is definitely not in the least bit soft, so the name of the game is not at all befitting. Once more I was lucky not to experience a serious outcome, such as losing my eye or having my skull fractured, although my nose was badly broken and I did suffer a hairline fracture of my cheekbone, along with mild concussion. According to the school nurse, the larger size of the ball used for this particular game, in comparison to a cricket or hockey ball, probably spared me from suffering irreversible damage to my eye.

By the time of my near-fatal hospital-related incident I was, of course, older and wiser, and appreciated more deeply how dicing with death at a young age brings your own mortality sharply into focus. It puts into context just how precious life is, and indeed good health, especially when you realise it can be snatched away in the blink of an eye. Such an experience also makes you acutely aware you should treasure every future day and treat it like a bonus. I'm sure that was a big factor in me becoming very philosophical in my view of life, and developing a more laid-back and tolerant manner as I matured.

Returning to my hospitalisation for treatment to my left arm, by the Thursday I'd recovered enough to cope with visitors. One of them was the consultant who'd injected the anaesthetic intra-arterially. She was very apologetic and looked mortified when she discovered the extent of my consequential injuries, and also the amount of trauma I'd suffered both directly and indirectly as a result of this mishap. I was grateful for her visit and appreciated her apology, but told her it was unnecessary as I fully understood that it had been a freak accident and I was just unlucky. Injecting me into an artery had simply been a fluke, and the chances of it happening were probably millions to one; after all, we are only human and anyone can make a mistake.

While I've never been someone who has adopted a blame culture, I can't deny it had a devastating impact on my physical and mental wellbeing – it would be foolish to pretend otherwise, especially as I suffered the physiological after-effects for several months. From a psychological perspective, I also found it hard to have faith in our medical services following my traumatic experiences at the hands of specialist staff. Ultimately though, I knew it could have been so much worse, and I was just relieved to still be alive and fully intact with two arms and hands!

In this respect, my good fortune was poignantly brought home to me just a couple of years after my drama, when I learned the terrible news that a young girl from East Anglia had suffered the same fate. My heart went out to her, and I was deeply saddened when I first spotted this shocking story on the front page of a tabloid. She'd also been accidentally injected into an artery before undergoing minor surgery and, from recollection, I think she was just five-years-old at the time and the outcome had been catastrophic. Sadly, she had ended up losing a hand as they'd had to perform a life-saving amputation once gangrene had taken its toll. Considering my own case had evidently made medical history, and actually been reported on in a well-known medical journal – and I'd been reliably informed that lessons would be learned following my experience – this awful news was particularly hard to stomach. It certainly put my own misfortune into perspective, and I experienced pangs of guilt because it seemed so unfair that I'd more or less made a full recovery, whilst the end result for this young girl had been far more devastating and life-changing.

Regarding the early stages of my recovery, towards the end of my first week in hospital there were promising signs because I was beginning to get some feeling and movement back in my left arm and hand. As the weekend approached I was desperate to get home, although I had an ulterior motive for wanting to do so. Xmas was less than a week away and, on the Saturday preceding the festive season, I was due to go out with my brothers and friends for a meal at our annual big bash; a customary celebration I didn't want to miss. Somehow, I managed to convince my consultant I was well enough to be released from hospital. This was far from the truth and, by misleading the consultant, I was effectively discharging myself. I had to promise him I wouldn't do anything strenuous, and would remain bed bound for several more days to aid my recovery and ensure I didn't suffer a relapse. Therefore, I made no mention of our habitual festive social and my intention to go out on the town on the Saturday night.

To be frank, I don't think I fully appreciated just how unwell I still was at this point in my recovery. I could barely walk, my left arm remained partially paralysed, and I was in a lot of discomfort. Perhaps worst of all, I was still suffering the ill effects of all the Heparin-related haemorrhaging. This meant I was incredibly weak and should undoubtedly continue to be confined to bed. I was definitely in no fit state to be out and about but, regardless, I was determined not to miss out on our social gathering and duly went along. With hindsight, I know it was a pointless and stupid thing to do because I couldn't really focus, was unsteady on my feet and felt faint. I only have a vague recollection of the evening, mainly because I was as high as a kite from all the drugs I was still on, including some exceptionally strong painkillers.

Not surprisingly, I didn't last the duration, and just about got through the meal before I had to be taken home. On reflection, I wonder what anyone who saw me out that night must have thought because I would have been a weird sight to behold. My left arm and torso were wrapped in thick wads of cotton wool, and I probably looked like a replica of the 'Michelin Man'. This cotton wool served a dual purpose; it was meant to preserve my body heat and also afford me some protection, as the slightest knock could possibly cause further internal bleeding and significant bruising, at least until any remnants of Heparin had completely dispersed.

In terms of the side effects I suffered as a result of my hospital traumas, the bruising was the most disconcerting aspect. Over the course of the next few days, following my release from hospital, the extent of my internal bleeding became increasingly noticeable. The left side of my body, from the top of my shoulder to the tips of my toes, gradually turned completely black, including my naughty bits! As the earlier blood loss spread a little further each day, and appeared as bruising on the surface of my skin, I began to wonder how on earth I'd survived, and whether there'd been any of this vital fluid left circulating in my veins at the point my internal bleeding had reached its peak. I regret not taking any pictures for posterity because I genuinely looked like someone who was half black and half white, and I'm sure that in the olden days I'd have been signed up for some sort of freak show.

What happened to me in hospital was horrendous but, in spite of everything I went through, I was still able to retain the same sanguine view of life that I'd had for as long as I could remember. Since a young age I'd been happy go lucky and an eternal optimist, so I was determined that wasn't going to change. Therefore, despite this medical episode affecting my plan to imminently resume my police career, I nonetheless just saw it as a temporary setback and maintained my insouciant outlook – and my fervent enthusiasm to get back into police work didn't diminish one iota.

The next three months, or thereabouts, were essentially a period of convalescence, and included a few weeks off work whilst I recovered my strength. During this time, I slowly but surely started to get further feeling and life back in my left arm and hand and, thankfully, it became increasingly apparent it wasn't going to remain paralysed. Routine medical check-ups lasted for several months, and finally my consultant was able to give me the good news that neither the mal-administered injection, nor the Heparin overdose, appeared to have done any lasting damage. On hearing this diagnosis, I was naturally over the moon. I considered myself to be very fortuitous, especially when I reflected on just how serious the consequences could have been for me.

For some weeks, the complications I'd had to overcome as a consequence of the misdirected injection, and the subsequent internal bleeding, had enveloped my life completely – so much so that I'd forgotten about the reason I'd had to undergo the endoscopy in the first place. The stomach problems and chronic pain I'd been suffering, prior to having this investigative procedure, had paled into insignificance in contrast to everything else I'd been through; so, when the consultant enlightened me about the result of the endoscopy, it came a bit like a bolt out of the blue. He explained this examination had revealed I'd developed a hiatus hernia, which he described as nothing untoward, providing I managed my diet carefully. I found out this condition is quite common, and the treatment can range from dietary management to invasive surgery, depending on the severity of the symptoms. In my case, he was confident the former would apply unless the problem worsened, and resulted in the pain becoming more acute or the acid reflux symptoms posing a greater risk to my wider health. I'm glad to report that his outlook on my condition proved to be right, and I managed to keep my hiatus hernia in check by sticking to a sensible diet, and minimising my alcohol intake!

In terms of any ongoing problems, which could adversely affect my left arm or hand and limit their use, the prognosis was equally positive. As the weeks went by and I started to get the strength back in this limb, the feeling returned to normal most of the time and my sinistral mobility steadily improved. Long-term, the only issue that remained was poor circulation whenever it was cold; meaning I occasionally experienced some numbness in my fingers. As another side effect, my arm and hand would also turn a purplish blue when there was a substantial drop in the temperature. This colourful pigmentation therefore only manifested itself on really cold days. It arose as a result of damage caused by either the anaesthetic or the Heparin because I'd never had this occur previously when it was chilly – but it didn't actually cause me any problems and just looked weird. I was more than happy to settle for both these outcomes and, until this day, have always viewed them as minor inconveniences compared to the possible alternatives.

By spring in 1980, my recovery was going well. Physically I was in reasonable shape and, even though my resilience had been tested to the limit by the medical drama I'd endured, I was dealing effectively with the resultant psychological scars. I was therefore determined to be resolute and not dwell on what had happened; so I once more began to mull over the options regarding my future career. At this point I just wanted to get on with my life and fulfil my aspiration to return to police work.

Despite this positive outlook, I knew I still had to be realistic about my prospects of returning to full-on police work any time soon. My strength was slowly getting back to normal, and I'd more or less recovered power in my left arm and hand, but I still wasn't sure if I was yet fit enough to cope with the rigours of police duties day in day out. I suffered with fatigue, even though I was working in a sedentary job, and it bothered me that I was getting really tired when not exerting that much energy. This would likely impinge on my ability to function as a fully operational officer. At the very least, I sensed this lack of durability would mean I'd therefore need to postpone re-applying to join the police for several months. My head told me that remaining in my role at the Employment Service was the sensible and rational thing to do at that stage, especially as my contract had been extended. In my heart, however, I desperately wanted to overlook my shortcomings and just get back in the fold, so I still agonised over my decision for several weeks before accepting the inevitable.

Since my brief time as a cadet, a big part of my psyche had become indelibly linked to the police force, and during the intervening years I'd been well and truly smitten with the idea of rejoining. Having to further delay my return wasn't something I found very palatable, but common sense had to prevail. However, just as I'd resigned myself to that being the case, an alternative plan started to hatch.

Shortly after my hospital mishap, and while I was still convalescing, I'd been out for a drink at our local with one of my brothers, and we'd met a young chap called Nev who'd just been posted to my home town as a police constable. Nev was at the bar and overheard my sibling and I chatting passionately about rugby – and, being an avid fan of the game himself, he'd joined in our conversation. Our chance meeting turned out to be the start of a lifelong friendship. Not only was rugby a mutual interest but, naturally, so was police work. As we got chatting during that first encounter, we also discovered we'd shared a common path. It uncannily transpired that Nev and I had both served as cadets in the same seaside town, albeit five years apart. We'd also stayed in the same lodgings with Mrs King and Betty – what a weird coincidence! Bumping into him at that stage in my life made me feel like we were fated to meet.

As Nev and I became close friends we talked at length about his role and my plans to hopefully get back to policing and, indeed, how any resumption had been delayed due to me being incapacitated. It was during one of these conversations that the idea of joining the Special Constabulary came up. This wasn't something I'd previously considered but, once the seed had been sewn, I did some research to find out exactly what joining up as a special would mean, and also to check out the requirements. I was amazed to discover that a special police constable effectively has the same powers as a fully fledged police officer, and after minimal training can perform active duties working alongside regulars. Once I'd found out what the role involved, deciding to join was a no brainer because it would mean I could get back to undertaking police work – but on a part-time voluntary basis in the first instance, which would suit my current circumstances. Through my research into voluntary policing, I also discovered that I definitely met the generic profile of most special constables. This role generally attracted recruits who were either very community focused or hoping to become full-time officers at some stage – and, in my case, I fitted both categories.

I was confident I'd be able cope with the more limited duties of a volunteer bobby – in terms of the hours I would need to work – and that signing-up as a special would enable me to ease my way back into policing. I was also satisfied

I'd meet the requirements for joining the Special Constabulary, and could get through the requisite physical tests and medical checks. Consequently, I felt this option presented me with an ideal solution to my current situation and was delighted to enlist.

Joining in this manner allowed me to have the best of both worlds, as it meant I was able to pursue my dream of being a copper once more, but without giving up my job with the Employment Service. At the time, this position was a safety net for me in case I suffered any relapses in my health. Having to continue being gainfully employed at the Job Centre, for longer than originally intended, was no big sacrifice as I enjoyed the work and got on well with my colleagues – and, besides, at this juncture, I still anticipated my stay would be temporary.

8 Back in the Fold

So, six years on from my first venture into police work, and after minimal training, I was back in uniform and out on patrol for a 2nd stint. This time I was policing the area where I grew up – a quaint market town with a rich tapestry dating back to medieval times, and featuring a variety of unique buildings, architectural structures and cultural landmarks that are characteristically linked to such historical origins. Located in a valley and surrounded by undulating terrain and scenic views, it's the type of landscape and picturesque rural setting one might associate with picture postcards. However, its idyllic outlook could easily belie the problems it faced. With a population that had rapidly doubled in recent years to around 25,000, and pockets of deprivation being interspersed with more affluent areas, it could sometimes be a challenging place to police. That was especially so during the 1980's, when it was in decline and experiencing high levels of unemployment. Crime rates were at a peak, particularly in regard to anti-social behaviour and criminal damage, with many shops being boarded up as a result of vandalism. Still, by the late 90's, my home town had recovered its vibrancy and once again regained its appeal – being voted one of the top 10 places to live in the UK.

As a special police constable entering a professional occupation as a volunteer, you rightly have to prove yourself to regular officers and gain their trust. In some ways, this was easier for me because of my previous experience as a cadet, but I was still careful not to appear too presumptuous or over-confident. Anyone can put on the uniform, but that in itself doesn't make you a competent police officer. To be accepted, and gain the respect of your colleagues and the public, you have to demonstrate you are worthy of wearing it. Proving yourself out on the streets is what resonates with your full-time buddies, and gives them confidence in your ability to work alongside them. The vast majority of police officers put body and soul into doing a first-rate job in order to protect their communities and keep the public safe; the last thing they need is a bunch of amateurs out there ruining their hard-earned reputations. Most regulars really welcome the support of anyone who is prepared to give up their own time to help with policing their local community – providing they are up to the task.

My first duty following my return to the police family was a morning shift on a market day in the middle of summer in 1980. I was partnered with my mate Nev on this first occasion – an outcome we'd done our best to contrive. This initial shift proved uneventful, although my appearance in uniform caused a few quizzical glances from people who knew me, but didn't know I'd rejoined the 'fuzz' in the role of special constable. Whilst on patrol Nev and I responded to a few minor incidents, but nothing of any real significance, and I was relieved to have the chance to be broken in gently during my inaugural shift as a special. Despite it being quiet, I enjoyed every minute of being back out on patrol. As expected, the session also confirmed that the bug I'd caught for police work was very much still in my system, and I excitedly looked forward to joining my regular colleagues on the beat again sometime soon.

After working a few more relatively quiet day shifts and providing police cover at a couple of local events, I performed my first twilight tour of duty (1800hrs - 0200rs) as a special constable. It was a mid-week evening and I was paired with another SPC – an old-timer and distinguished looking volunteer called Frankie – to undertake foot patrol in the town centre. It was the first time I'd been let loose without being under the direct supervision of a regular colleague. Initially we encountered no major problems, but later that situation changed dramatically.

Unlike me, my partner Frankie had to be up early for work the following morning, so around 2330hrs he'd returned to the police station to sign-off, leaving me to continue my foot patrol solo. I thought I'd therefore be on my own for the remainder of my shift, but around mid-night my mate Nev, who was single-crewed in the response car, picked me up so we could spend the last couple of hours of my duty working in tandem. No sooner had he done so than all hell broke loose. We received an urgent call over the radio to attend a break-in at a nearby house, where it was suspected there were intruders on the premises. Simultaneously, it was reported that a group of hooligans were driving around the gardens of a nursing home, in close proximity of where the burglary was taking place, and vandalising the lawns. Nev and I responded to the suspected break-in, whilst Billy and Demi, who were also on mobile patrol, went immediately to the nursing home.

We reached the scene of the reported burglary in less than a minute of receiving the call, but the intruders had already scarpered. They'd been disturbed by a neighbour from the adjoining house, who knew his next-door neighbours were away on holiday, and had gone outside to investigate a noise. The intruders had spotted him coming and done a runner after leaping out of a downstairs window. This witness informed us there had been three male intruders, probably aged in their late twenties; beyond that, his description was sketchy. However, he was able to tell us they'd run off towards the town centre. Nev asked me to stay at the house to preserve the scene and continue interviewing the witness, while he went in search of the culprits.

Whilst doing so, I spotted several pairs of footprints in a flower-bed just below the window from which the intruders had made their escape. The prints looked fresh, and I presumed they must have been left by one or more of the intruders. I immediately radioed control to give a description of the footprints, which appeared to be from a pair of 'Doc Marten' boots – or possibly several pairs. As luck would have it, my timing was impeccable because Jezza, the only other officer on duty that night (apart from those already mentioned) had just intercepted three well-known villains who were running away from the vicinity of the crime scene. Jezza had been out on foot making enquiries when he'd heard the call over the radio about the suspects, and it had been pure coincidence they'd come running towards him in the direction of the town centre, just as he'd resumed patrol after taking a statement.

Not surprisingly, all the suspects denied any involvement in the break-in; however, it was the information about the type of footwear likely worn by the offenders that provided sufficient evidence for him and Nev, who had now joined him, to arrest them on suspicion of burglary – as they were all wearing 'Doc Martens'! This certainly put me in Jezza's good books; even though he had a distrust of volunteer bobbies. He'd had a bad experience whilst working for a different Constabulary, when a special constable had let him down, and he usually gave them short shrift. However, on this occasion, Jezza (who became known as 'Officer Huckleberry' after the 'Police Academy' character!) was happy to sing my praises, and admit it was my timely information about the footprints that had armed him with the evidence he'd needed to take the suspects into custody. He even commented positively about my attention to detail and announced he was impressed with my conduct, so it was a fillip for me to learn I'd gained his respect. Ultimately, I was also chuffed that my powers of observation contributed towards three prolific burglars being convicted. Not bad for a rookie!

Whilst Nev, Jezza and I had been focusing on the break-in, our colleagues Billy and Demi had been doing a brilliant job sorting out the issue at the nursing home. With some backup from the sergeant, they'd managed to apprehend the four occupants of the Mini involved in vandalising this establishment's grounds. All of them were high on drugs and had been taken into custody on suspicion of causing criminal damage. The driver had also been arrested on suspicion of committing a number of driving offences, and he was the one causing the greatest amount of aggro following his arrest.

With our resources stretched to the limit, Demi had been singularly tasked with placing him in his cell. Shortly after doing so, he'd become intent on causing himself harm by constantly banging his head against the wall and she'd been struggling to keep him under control. Consequently, she'd called out for assistance and I'd gone to her aid. This was the first time I'd encountered someone in such a psychotic state due to drugs, and I was shocked by how much extra strength he'd seemingly gained from being in this condition. Trying to calm him down and prevent him from self-harming took all our combined efforts, and I was relieved that the violence he was exuding was directed at himself and not us. It was a good 20 minutes before he finally started to come down from his high, and by then Demi and I were completely knackered. By the time I finally finished my duty around 0300hrs, I was very much in need of my bed, but at least I was feeling like I'd done a reasonable job and actually made a difference – and it had certainly been an excellent night's work by the team, with seven suspected criminals being arrested in one fell swoop.

The next time I worked with Nev, just a couple of nights later, we had another successful shift in terms of tracking down a criminal who'd committed an offence. We'd been despatched to a local Italian bistro, where a young lady wanted to report that her jacket might have been stolen. After the diner had enjoyed a romantic dinner date, and was about to head home, she'd discovered that her denim jacket was missing. It had been left in the cloakroom, so she was sure it had either been taken by mistake or, more likely, stolen. She favoured the latter because she was certain she would have noticed if someone had inadvertently taken it, as the only other customers had been a group of lads. Without much to go on, Nev and I weren't confident we'd be able to track down the thief, but that night luck was on our side.

Shortly after we'd left the restaurant and started patrolling the surrounding area, we spotted a young guy who aroused our suspicions. He was known to police as a petty criminal and happened to be wearing a denim jacket, which not only matched the description of the one that had disappeared from the bistro, but also looked far too small for him. We therefore approached him and explained our reason for wanting a word. Instantly he protested his innocence, and then became indignant when we suggested he might have stolen the jacket. He insisted it was a man's jacket, and told us it was tight fitting because he'd shrunk it in the wash. At first I thought this explanation, likely concocted, could be enough to get him the benefit of doubt, but he was outwitted by Nev, who had one more trick up his sleeve. Nev requested he remove the jacket, so he could search it and check for any evidence of ownership. Our suspect was happy to comply, probably because he'd been through the pockets and didn't think there would be any incriminating evidence. However, when Nev discovered a tampon discreetly tucked away in the lining of the jacket's inside pocket he was stumped, and unable able to provide us with a rational explanation for it being there. He was therefore detained on suspicion of theft and transported back to the police station.

At interview our prisoner admitted stealing the jacket; he was gutted that he'd been caught out and realised he'd made a fundamental mistake when we'd first confronted him. Had he told us he'd acquired the jacket in a charity shop, it would have been hard for us to prove otherwise and he could have got away with his crime, despite the tampon – simply by claiming a previous owner must have left it there. Nev and I were delighted his calculated attempt to avoid culpability had failed, and pleased we were able to return the jacket to its rightful owner.

This incident wasn't my most vivid memory of that particular tour of duty, as earlier during this shift we'd also had the dubious pleasure of having to arrest a man for being drunk and incapable. He was so paralytic he couldn't even stand up, let alone walk home. Reluctantly we'd therefore had to place him in custody for his own safety, even though we'd been loath to do so because we knew there was a strong chance he'd be vomiting in the police car. Nev had previously dealt with this none-too-bright nefarious character. He was anti-police and, according to a tattoo on his forehead, a member of a banned paramilitary organisation. However, I somehow suspect that if this had actually been the case, they would have considered him an embarrassment and disowned him because he spent most of his time either blind drunk, or flat on his back sleeping off the affects of the booze he'd consumed. We had no choice but to arrest him, and our worst fears soon came to pass. On the way back to the police station he'd been as sick as a dog, and I recall it was like having 'Special Brew' on tap when it spewed out of him. My last task that night was therefore reluctantly helping Nev thoroughly clean the inside of the police car – although, despite our best efforts and using a vast quantity of disinfectant, it still smelt like a brewery!

Over the next few months I crammed in as many duties as possible, largely working Friday or Saturday evenings, which were usually the busiest shifts. Whenever I got the opportunity I would pair up with Nev, but I also worked frequently with Ivan, whose appointment to my local nick had coincided with Nev's posting. They'd embarked on their police careers at the same time and become really good buddies. I'd already met Ivan on several occasions prior to joining the Special Constabulary, having been introduced to him by Nev, and we'd immediately hit it off and developed a good rapport. Like me, Nev and Ivan were fun-loving and had happy-go-lucky approaches to life; so, the bond the three of us formed in those early days soon blossomed into long-term friendships, and the pair of them became two of my best mates. For several years we were inseparable. I often ensured that my availability for shifts matched occasions when either Nev or Ivan would also be on duty, as I enjoyed working with them and learnt a great from doing so. However, I by no means worked exclusively with them. I wanted to ingratiate myself with all my new colleagues and develop effective working relationships across the board, so I also did regular tours of duty with each of the four operational groups. At that time, each group consisted of half-a-dozen or so constables, an inspector and two sergeants; one of whom assumed the operational role of section supervisor, whilst the other was station based and performed the function of custody sergeant.

Briefly during their respective probationary periods, Nev and Ivan had been allocated to the same section and, as they shared a similarly warped sense of humour, soon established themselves as team jesters. It could be a laugh a minute whenever they were working together and you never knew what they might get up to if the opportunity to let their hair down arose; although they could instantly revert back to the requisite police personae as soon as duty called. In the eyes of the public, they always appeared to be enthusiastic, dedicated and discerning police officers – and, in my view, based on witnessing them perform their duties, that is exactly what they were. They did a brilliant job. There was one exception though, when their tomfoolery could easily have backfired and they were literally caught with their pants down.

The local motel had been cultivated as a coffee stop by Nev and Ivan, and the resident night porter had become something of a pal. Quite frequently, when they were paired up on night duty, they would drop in for a beverage and a catch up in the wee early hours. Their mate, who encouraged them to call in regularly, was pro-police and had an infectious sense of humour, not unlike their own. On one occasion, when they popped in around 0200hrs, there was no sign of the night porter. Assuming he must be doing his rounds, they therefore obtained cups of coffee at the self-service dispenser and made their way to the motel reception area to await the return of their mate.

Prior to arriving at the motel, both of them had been attending an RTC in the pouring rain and they'd been absolutely drenched. In particular, their police issue trousers were soaked right through; so, before sitting down to enjoy their hot beverages, Ivan suggested it would make sense to slip them off and place them on the radiator to dry. They hadn't deliberately planned to play a practical joke on the night porter, but both agreed that finding the pair of them with their trousers removed would give him a good laugh, so duly stripped off – believing that nobody else would be about in the early hours except their mate, and he would be highly amused.

When the night porter finally returned to the front of house, he was therefore greeted by the sight of two burly coppers in full uniform from the waist up, sitting on the reception sofa in their boxer shorts and hob nail boots, sipping coffee. Normally, he would have found this sight hilarious but, in this instance, he was aghast because he'd just been showing two new guests around the motel, and they were still with him as he walked back into the reception area.

The married couple had arrived late due to a hold up and, having been shown to their room, had now returned to reception to complete the checking-in process. Quite what they made of the situation when they came across two of her Majesty's finest constables in such an undignified state of dress is anybody's guess, but doubtless they were flabbergasted. And being members of the gentry, I expect their bizarre encounter with this zany pair of exhibitionists featured regularly as a conversation piece during future dinner parties!

Nev and Ivan somehow got away with this escapade as there was no forthcoming complaint from the shocked couple. I can only assume they came up with a plausible excuse for being partially dressed when they explained the reason for their unprofessional appearance to them. This was by no means the only time my partners in crime caused considerable amusement acting like buffoons, so you can imagine how much fun it could be to work with them, and appreciate why we developed such a close bond in the early days of our association. It was a connection that grew stronger over the years, due in part to all three of us uncannily enduring near-death experiences at some stage in our respective lives as a result of freak accidents, and having to overcome medical emergencies (as already alluded to in regard to myself).

9 A New Dawn

THE LATE 1970'S HAD HERALDED a number of changes to the way the police service operated – and most of these had led to a vast improvement, not least that policewomen were now treated as equals, and had rightly become fully operational in all aspects of police work. They now worked the same shift patterns as their male counterparts, and were allocated to sections as fully integrated police officers. In contrast to 1973, another noticeable change was that uniforms were now much more practical, and we were no longer issued with whistles or capes!

It also struck me that the relationship between senior officers and their subordinates might have altered. High-ranking officers were still treated like demigods by rank and file bobbies, but most big bosses no longer appeared so omnipotent or fastidious in the way they behaved. I don't think they'd mellowed, as those with scrambled egg on their cap and two or more two pips on their epaulettes remained imposing figures – and senior officers continued to be feared, or even revered by some in the lower ranks. However, I felt they were no longer so brazenly aloof or unapproachable, and seemed inclined to exhibit more empathy towards their junior colleagues. Importantly, they came across as being more in touch with the impact of work-related stress, including the frailties this can cause. Equally, despite their superiority, I sensed they now rarely exuded the level of arrogance I'd witnessed during my first stint in the force. My initial view of very senior officers had undoubtedly been influenced by my first experience out on Division as a cadet. In those days, I'd constantly seen officers at the helm take advantage of their seniority by routinely ordering those in the lower ranks to run errands they deigned beneath them. This included our chief superintendent expecting his Sunday paper to be collected from the newsagent and delivered to him at home. Nobody dared to challenge such behaviour back then, when those at the top often gave the impression they were untouchable. It was heartening to think that maybe bosses were now more accountable, and no longer prone to taking such liberties.

As you'd expect, special constables were often called upon to supplement their full-time colleagues at a range of events that attracted members of the public in large numbers. One of these was an annual agricultural show, which required extra officers to manage the crowds of people that flocked to the event, and direct the increased volume of traffic in the area. On one such occasion, I was actively engaged in traffic control at the entrance to the event, trying to direct vehicles in and out of the showground whilst maintaining a steady flow of vehicles along the main road. Standing in the middle of a busy road amongst fast-moving traffic puts you in a precarious position, so you need to have your wits about you at all times – especially when it's teeming with rain and visibility is poor, which was the case on that particular day. However, despite being focused on the job in hand, I became aware there was a young lad, aged about five-years-old, stood on the verge watching me. Like me, he was getting soaked. He didn't appear to be accompanied by an adult responsible for his guardianship, so I was concerned for his welfare, and knew that taking care of him would need to take precedence over my traffic control duties.

I'd vaguely picked up over the radio a missing child report and, as he matched the description, I was confident he could be the lad in question – though goodness knows what he was doing about a mile away from the main arena. He didn't appear perturbed about being lost, or getting drenched, and just seemed fascinated by my gesticulations as he watched me perform my duty. Equally, once I'd abandoned my post and taken him into my care he didn't seem overly bothered, and simply came across as being disappointed that my one-man traffic control show had come to an abrupt end. Having alerted control to my find, I soon got some assistance and was able to hand over the young lad to one of my colleagues so he could be returned to his relieved parents. With my rescue act complete, I was then able to resume controlling the traffic. Shortly afterwards, I got a radio message advising me the boy's parents wished to express their gratitude.

Traffic control was something I got plenty of practice in during my early days of service in the Special Constabulary, and I remember another occasion when I was assigned a task involving this activity, and asked to tutor a newly appointed special constable. The new recruit, who became affectionately known as Spud, was a complete novice and out on his first ever duty – and, despite having a stern look, he was actually a jolly fellow. He accompanied me to a street market where we would need to put in place a road closure, and then re-direct vehicles. It was my responsibility to show him the ropes so, for the first 20 minutes, Spud therefore took a back seat and observed me directing traffic.

Once I felt he should have grasped the fundamentals of traffic control, I said to him:

'Ok Spud, hopefully you should have got the hang of it by now, so would you like to have a go?'

His response was not what I expected because he replied in his dulcet tone:

'No thanks mate, I think I'll I just stand here and watch you!'

It was from that day forth that I realised he had leadership qualities – obviously a born leader who was destined to go far. And I was right because less than three years later he was promoted.

The pair of us became close buddies and I developed the greatest of respect for him, as did all his colleagues. He worked on the land for his day job and was a real down to earth and likeable character, whose family came from a military background; therefore, it was no surprise when he was readily accepted into the police family from day one, even though he could occasionally be an irascible and cantankerous old bugger. Despite this, he also had a good sense of humour, which was just as well because I did play a joke on him some years later when he asked to borrow my long service medal. This medal was issued after 10 years of service and, as I'd joined a year prior to Spud, I already had mine by the time his was due. He'd become entitled to his, but it hadn't yet come through, so he enquired if I would lend him mine in order that he could wear it at a forthcoming Remembrance Day parade. In view of his proud military heritage, he was very much into regalia and I was more than happy to oblige. However, I thought it would be amusing if I replaced the long service medal with my coveted 'Blue Peter' badge, so when he opened the box he would be pleasantly surprised – and no doubt honoured to have such a sought after accolade that he could display with pride at the parade. Well, apparently he wasn't too keen on that idea. It was, therefore, just as well I'd handed the medal to another colleague, who was also going to the parade, so he could pass the genuine article onto Spud just before the event began.

It wasn't long after I'd inducted Spud that I was once more required to help out with traffic management duties at another large weekend event, which was known as 'Wings & Wheels'. This time my traffic directing duties were also interspersed with crowd control. As the title of the event suggests, the main attraction was a combination of motor vehicles and aeroplanes, and the occasion attracted a lot of spectators – in fact about 10,000 in total – many of whom were 'petrol heads'. The crowd also included several hundred bikers. Amongst these bikers was a contingent of 'Hells Angels', whose numbers far exceeded the volume of we 'wooden tops' on duty at this venue. In the event of any trouble, the maximum resources we could immediately muster was a group of just six of us – comprised of four regular officers and two special constables. We also had at our disposal a couple of traffic units that were in the area to assist when the crowds were due to leave, but we knew any other backup was some distance away.

Up until mid-afternoon on the second day all had been going reasonably smoothly, and it had been peaceful. In fact, up till then, the most memorable thing that had happened from my perspective was meeting Keith Chegwin (AKA 'Cheggers'). This had occurred during the first day when I'd briefly joined him on stage with a lost child, so he could make an announcement to alert the young boy's parents that their son had been found, and hopefully get them to reclaim him – which they'd duly done. Anyhow, as we approached the latter stages of the event this situation changed because a disturbance arose near the main arena – a fight involving bikers. As I was in close proximity when things kicked off, a call went out over the PA system requesting I please make my way to the area in front of the stage to deal with the matter.

I recognised it was unlikely I'd be able to singularly sort out the problem and, as I didn't have a radio, I first visited the PA announcer, who was based in a nearby caravan, so I could get him to summon further assistance over the loudspeakers. I then went to investigate the cause of the trouble, keeping my fingers crossed that my colleagues would have heard the announcement and also be making their way towards the reported disturbance.

Luckily, by the time I arrived on scene, things had started to calm down, although I sensed there was still a lot of underlying tension. A chief inspector, an inspector and the acting-sergeant – three of the four regulars on duty at the event, and all from outside of my borough – subsequently joined me. Jointly we took stock of the situation, and tried to establish the facts. It appeared there'd been a minor skirmish between several of the 'Hells Angels', who'd been drinking heavily, and another group of bikers. I would describe it as a bit of argy-bargy based on what we were told. However, a few of the bystanders did also advise that the 'Hells Angels' were the main instigators as they'd been trying to stir up trouble by deliberately antagonising the other bikers. In his wisdom, the chief inspector therefore concluded there was every likelihood of further trouble brewing – or, as he somewhat melodramatically put it:

'Under the surface we could have a simmering volcano, which we will need to keep a lid on and extinguish if necessary!'

That description sounded rather poetic and fanciful to me, but I got the gist of what he meant. In order to achieve his objective, he then determined I should keep an eye on the 'Hells Angels', discreetly if possible – which, paradoxically, can be virtually impossible when dressed in uniform – and try to identify the key protagonists in the group. With there being four possible parking zones, he also requested I follow them until I'd discovered where they'd parked their motorbikes and then report back, so he could arrange for the traffic cops to pull them over as soon as they departed and got on the highway. As there was a strong possibility they'd be over the drink-drive limit, there was some logic to this part of his thinking. However, his cunning plan did have one major flaw because, as mentioned, we didn't have personal radios available to use at the event. Communicating their whereabouts was, therefore, going to be tricky. He wasn't deterred though, and simply decided that I could hoof it back to the site's police office after I'd ascertained their location, so he could then relay the information by phone to the central control room. Since it was going to take me at least five minutes to get from any of the car parks back to our office, even if I sprinted all the way, I still wasn't sure how his plan was going to work but, as a junior rank, it wasn't for me to question his dubious thinking. Both the inspector and the acting-sergeant expressed their reservations, but our glorious leader wouldn't be swayed. I therefore did as I was told. Wherever the 'Hell's Angels' went, I dutifully pursued them like a shadow for the next couple of hours. Not only did I find out where they were parked, but I also managed to get the number plates of the bikes belonging to the ringleaders.

Having completed my mission, I ran all the way back to the little police office on site, whereupon I discovered to my astonishment it was locked up and deserted. I was utterly flabbergasted. It took me a few seconds to work out that all my colleagues must have forgotten about me and gone home for the day. In effect, I'd been abandoned by the very personnel I thought had my back and, was it not for the fact their actions could have put me in jeopardy, it would have been calamitous in the comical sense. I probably should have complained about the chief inspector, since he had overall responsibility for the welfare of those officers under his command at the event but, instead, I magnanimously accepted it was just one of those things. I realised leaving me all alone must have been down to human error – at least I hoped it was an oversight, and they didn't just view me as expendable! Anyway, for me, this was the only occasion I felt let down or left in the lurch by my colleagues throughout my service, so I'm confident blips of this nature are something of a rarity.

10 In at the Deep End

FAIRLY EARLY DURING MY TENURE as a special constable, I became involved in another murder case; my first having arisen whilst I was a cadet – as already outlined. On this occasion, I was away at an evening training session when our chief inspector came into the classroom to announce he had just heard that a serious incident had occurred in the borough where I was based. Details about the ongoing incident were just starting to unravel, so he placed us all on standby in case our assistance was needed. Shortly afterwards, he returned to inform us that the services of myself and one other special constable (Robbie) would be required.

On speaking to me, he explained that it appeared a woman had been viciously attacked and killed back in my home-town, and requested that I return immediately to my station to support the Murder Squad. It came as a real shock that my services could be required by such a specialised team, considering my limited experience, but he pointed out that my local knowledge (much of which had been acquired from working at the job centre) may prove to be invaluable – and that the detective sergeant from this squad would meet me back at the station and explain how I could contribute. I should have felt elated at being asked to assist in such a high-profile case but, on the contrary, I was filled with apprehension and sadness knowing that someone has lost their life in such appalling circumstances. Before I set off, our chief inspector also revealed one other shocking piece of news. He enlightened me that my fellow SC (Robbie) wouldn't be participating in the investigation, as he was required for an alternative task connected with the identification of the body. My boss told me the victim was likely Robbie's mother-in-law; so his involvement in the case was linked to his role in the family, and would undoubtedly be far more heart-wrenching and upsetting.

The DS duly met me upon my arrival back at my local nick and gave me a brief account of the situation they were dealing with, based on the information gleaned so far. He explained the body of a woman aged in her forties had been discovered, and the incident was being treated as a probable murder case because she had a stab wound to her neck. The suspected murder had likely occurred earlier that evening, and had almost certainly taken place where the body had been found, which was in the grounds of a former school located close to the town centre.

Due to the time and location of the incident, the first officers on scene had come across numerous people in close proximity – some walking home from town after work or shopping, and others queuing at the nearby cinema. This meant there were plenty of potential witnesses who might have seen something untoward or noticed someone acting suspiciously. My colleague informed me the details of all these possible witnesses had been acquired by the officers who'd responded to the incident – and, although unlikely, it was also feasible that amongst this list were the details of the killer. Over 250 names and addresses had been obtained and, in the first instance, the DS wanted me to sift through them and identify anyone that I recognised and might have concerns about. He acknowledged this was a subjective approach, being undertaken more in hope than expectation. Nonetheless, he felt it was worth doing in view of my extensive knowledge of local people – just in case it enabled me to spot someone on the list who set alarm bells ringing. Indeed, this did prove to be so, and there were several individuals that jumped out at me, where their past behaviour had given me cause for concern. They were followed up on, but in all cases it proved to be a dead end because each of them had a solid alibi for the approximate time the fatal attack had occurred. Ironically, however, one of these individuals did go on to commit a murder some years later.

At this preliminary stage in proceedings, some of the Constabulary's big wigs were considering whether the fatal stabbing could possibly be linked to another serious attack on a young lady, which had occurred the previous year within close proximity of the murder scene. Much to my amazement, the head of the force's CID, a detective chief superintendent, asked for my opinion on such conjecture. My knowledge of this former incident was limited, but I told him I'd heard that the officers involved in that investigation thought the assault was linked to some form of 'domestic' altercation – and the victim, who'd spent several days in a coma after sustaining a head injury, likely knew her assailant but had declined to identify him. I also advised him the victim had claimed she had no memory of the assault, and that was why she couldn't give any details about her attacker. I wasn't sure if I was speaking out of turn by commenting on this matter, but any thoughts of a connection between the two events were soon dismissed; so, hopefully, that decision wasn't based entirely on my limited knowledge!

My minor role assisting the Murder Squad that night, entailed spending a couple of hours working closely with the DS, after which he decided it was unlikely I'd be able to have any further meaningful input during those early stages of the investigation, and I may as well clock off. I thought that would be the end of my involvement, and that any useful contributions I could make had been exhausted, so it came as a surprise when he then asked if I could return the next day to provide further assistance. Willingly I obliged, and presented myself for duty at 0800hrs the next morning as requested, expecting to once again be engaged in sifting through witness testimony and other intelligence as it came into the temporary incident room. However, by the time I arrived, there'd already been a major development and a significant breakthrough in the case, so my services were no longer required by the Murder Squad after all. Instead I was diverted to help out in the Operational Support Unit, and asked to relieve a Task Force officer who'd had been guarding the scene of the murder since the start of his early shift. When I got to this location it was a hive of activity, with members of the Forensic Team actively involved in searching the area. This included the local scenes of crime officer (SOCO) and he updated me on developments, and explained why my period assisting the Murder Squad had been short-lived.

Evidently, at first light, a police dog had picked up a faint trail of blood leading away from the site of the murder. Luckily, the overnight weather had been kind to the police, with no precipitation falling to wash away the evidence. Consequently, the dog had been able to follow this trail all the way to a house on an estate not far away and, after officers had gained entry, they'd discovered blood-stained clothes at the premises. The householder had insisted the clothes didn't belong to anyone living there, and stressed she had no idea how they'd come to be in her home. However, she had been able to state the distinctive items looked familiar, and were certainly very similar to an outfit regularly worn by a young man who was known to her son and lived just a few doors away. This information had given detectives another lead to pursue and a justifiable reason to visit the address she'd provided for the youth.

According to my colleague, upon doing so they'd discovered a male teenager at home who resided at this abode. Apparently, this young man was just 18 years of age and had admitted being an acquaintance of the nearby householder's son, but initially denied possessing any attire matching the clothes found in his neighbour's house. However, I'm told he changed his tune once he'd been confronted with evidence that suggested otherwise. That admission, combined with him being unable to account for his whereabouts the previous evening or give a reasonable explanation about how he'd acquired a recent deep cut to one of his thumbs, had resulted in him being arrested on suspicion of murder. Therefore, he was now in custody waiting to be formally interviewed under caution.

Clearly things about the case were starting to unfold at a rapid pace and, in my position, I wasn't privy to all the facts that were emerging. However, I did know the background to the events leading up to the attack, and was aware that during the preceding weeks several worrying incidents had occurred in the vicinity where the murder actually took place. There had been reports of a young guy acting strangely while sitting on a wall that ran adjacent to the pathway connecting the town centre and a large housing estate. This wall also happened to surround the former school grounds where the body was ultimately discovered, and effectively formed the boundary edge to this complex. It had been reported that the young man – who turned out to match the description of our murder suspect – had been lobbing stones at pedestrians who happened to walk by and, on one occasion, had actually hit a young woman on the back of the head. Miraculously, it hadn't done any major damage and she'd been able to run away, even though she'd been left stunned and in shock. Naturally, this serious incident had caused considerable consternation within police circles, and local beat officers had been instructed to give the area frequent passing attention. Regrettably, this action, combined with an ongoing and extensive investigation by C.I.D, hadn't led to the perpetrator being identified, tracked down and apprehended before he'd almost certainly committed this next very serious assault, which had tragically resulted in the death of his victim.

Once the suspect had been interviewed and charged with murder, I subsequently learned a little more about what had happened, and how the events of that evening had materialised. During his interrogation, the accused had been presented with damning forensic evidence that implicated him in the attack, along with an abundance of circumstantial evidence that demonstrated he'd likely been the person seen sitting on the wall lobbing stones at passers-by. Faced with indisputable evidence, he'd chosen to admit his guilt and made a statement confessing to the heinous crime. Quite what the initial motive for his behaviour had been was unclear, and even during his interrogation I believe it remained uncertain as to whether he'd set out to commit a specific crime, such as murder, robbery or sexual assault. However, from comments he'd made to his interviewers, it was now plain that his contemptible actions had, at some point, become sexually motivated.

He told them that on the evening of the attack he'd been sitting on the wall when a lady had walked by carrying two bags of shopping, and from close range he'd forcefully thrown a brick at her as soon as she'd passed by. The missile had been aimed at the back of her head and caught her full-on at the base of her skull. As a result, she'd been knocked out cold and had instantly collapsed to the ground. While the poor woman was unconscious, he'd then dragged her some 50 feet or more from the pathway to the other side of the wall, and into the undergrowth in the grounds of the former school site. There he'd carried out a gratuitous sexual assault on his victim, before fatally stabbing her.

This truly despicable and callous crime was compounded by the fact this unfortunate lady had been a victim of circumstance. Normally she never walked home along that pathway, as she nearly always drove to work but, on the day she met her untimely death, her car had been booked into the local garage, and her husband was intending to pick her up. However, something delayed him getting there at the agreed time; so, presuming he must have forgotten, she'd made the catastrophic decision to walk home alone via the pathway where she sadly met her demise. It was also most unusual for her to take that shortcut in the dark but, being on foot with two bags of shopping to carry, she was probably keen to take the quickest route home. Destiny therefore played a cruel twist, as the encounter with her killer would surely not have come about but for this ominous series of events causing her to be in the wrong place at precisely the wrong time.

She was also incredibly unlucky to come face-to-face with her assailant when there was nobody else about, especially as this walkway is usually a busy thoroughfare at the time of day she was attacked, with many people using it on a daily basis. Equally, it's incredulous her attacker wasn't spotted by any members of the public whilst he was dragging her out of sight, bearing in mind this must have taken him at least a minute or more. Indeed, if the passer-by who came across her shopping strewn across the pathway only moments after the attack had come along a little sooner, perhaps the outcome could have been so very different. Sadly, that wasn't the case, although this man's discovery of the shopping did lead to him alerting police to a potential problem – which then led to a search of the area and the discovery of the victim's body.

Life is full of 'what ifs' and 'maybes' but, as with many tragedies, it can be a fine dividing line that determines someone's fate. In this instance, that was most certainly the case because, if the victim had walked by just a few seconds earlier or later, there is every chance she may have survived or not been attacked at all. Dealing with their loss in such awful circumstances must have been unbearable for the victim's loved ones – and I doubt the murderer's eventual guilty plea and mandatory life sentence, with a lengthy minimum tariff, would have eased their pain in the slightest.

In terms of guarding the scene of the atrocious crime, I was at the site until the evening. At this point it still wasn't public knowledge that an arrest had been made in connection with the murder, so I was amazed at how many people were still using the pathway once it had turned dark – particularly the number of women who were walking home alone. A murderer could still have been on the loose for all they knew. There were also a surprising number of sightseers hoping to get a glimpse of the scene, presumably because they had some sort of morbid fascination. Some of them did get a bit of a shock though once the light had faded. I was stood out of view in the shadow of the street light where nobody could see me. Therefore, when I emerged from my sentry point, it was obvious that certain individuals thought they'd seen a ghost. I wasn't deliberately trying to scare them but I couldn't help thinking it served them right.

Once I'd been relieved from my post around 1900hrs, I was then asked by the station sergeant to accompany another SPC on foot patrol around some of the nearby housing estates. Although I was exhausted by this time, having been on duty for 11 hours, I still stayed on for a little longer in order to help out. On this occasion, performing foot patrol around the housing estates was chiefly about having a visible presence to help restore confidence in these neighbourhoods. It was important to ease the fears and concerns of elderly folk and other vulnerable people following the dreadful event of the previous day, especially as an announcement regarding the arrest of a suspect wouldn't be made until the following morning. And, based on the positive comments we got from members of the public, it certainly seemed our appearance in uniform gave them the reassurance we hoped.

Shortly after my very brief attachment to the Murder Squad, I then had an opportunity to take part in my first drugs raid. This came about by chance whilst I was on duty working with Nathan, a PC who'd been in the job for three years. The sergeant supervising our shift requested we accompany him on a drugs search at a house located just outside of town. This sergeant had recently transferred from the Drug Squad, and had been appointed as the local point of liaison for any drug-related investigations, so he was assuming direct responsibility for serving this particular warrant. The large property we were due to visit was currently occupied by a known drug dealer, and intelligence gathered by the Drug Squad had indicated that a large stash of illegal drugs were being stored on the premises for a brief period; meaning there would only be a short window of opportunity to seize them. With prompt action therefore being needed, the enquiry had been handed over to the sergeant to co-ordinate locally – and that was how Nathan and I had ended up being involved.

Before we set off on our mission, our sergeant told us the guy suspected of dealing was well-known to him. He explained the chap had been a user for many years, and like many hardened drug addicts, had become fixated on how he was going to fund his habit, and acquire enough money by any means to purchase his next fix – and how this obsession had typically led him down the path of criminality, and ultimately triggered his involvement in dealing.

When we arrived at the property the suspected drug dealer was at home and, since we had a search warrant, reluctantly let us into his abode. He wasn't happy about our presence, and as an act of defiance muttered a few expletives under his breath, but he wasn't obstructive, so we were able to immediately get on with the search. I have to admit I was completely out of my depth. My training in drug-related matters up to that point had been minimal – in total, it amounted to attending a single workshop! While conducting a search of the kitchen, I came across a pantry that housed dozens of jars containing herbs and spices and, to be honest, I think I would have been easily fooled if he'd hidden his stash in amongst them. For that matter, I'm not sure I'd have been able to tell the difference between the various types of illicit street drugs, let alone spot them if they were concealed amongst an abundant cache of dried herbs. Being serious, in all probability I'd likely have realised if cannabis had been present, due to the distinctive aroma emitted by this drug – although the pungent smell being given off by the wide variety of herbs and spices would have made it tricky. In that respect, it would probably be the ideal place to hide illegal substances if you wanted to put a sniffer dog off the scent.

Ultimately, we didn't find anything that matched the substances we were seeking, and our thorough search only uncovered a small amount of a Class A drug and couple of cannabis wraps, which could at best be described as sufficient for personal use. We did, however, come across a number of items associated with supplying drugs including scales, small plastic bags and paraphernalia, along with some incriminating correspondence, which provided further intelligence about the criminal network involved in the conspiracy to supply. Therefore, even though the search didn't uncover a large haul of drugs, it still proved to be a worthwhile exercise.

After all my recent insights into the more specialist aspects of police work, I was actually pleased to resume routine patrols – not that anything about frontline policing is ever routine as you never know what awaits. Anyhow, much to my delight, when I returned for my next tour of duty, I found myself once more in the company of my mate Ivan covering response. Around 2100hrs we got an urgent call to attend an address on the north side of town, where a brick had been thrown through a downstairs window of a house belonging to a retired couple. Luckily, we were in close proximity of the property when we got the message, and therefore arrived on scene shortly after being alerted. The offence had occurred only minutes before our arrival but, even so, we'd not spotted any likely perpetrators of the crime in the vicinity as we'd approached the address.

As soon as we got to the property, a detached house located on a main road on the outskirts of town, we could see the extent of the damage. There was a large hole in the lobby window situated just to the right of the front door, and the distressed occupants of the house were outside waiting to greet us. They were an elderly couple and you could see they were visibly shaken, which was entirely understandable. At the point the brick had been hurled through the window they'd been sat quietly watching TV, and must have suffered the shock of their lives. The brick was about the size of a loaf of bread, so you could just imagine the shattering noise it would have made as it came crashing through the large plate glass window.

The victims were a gentle unassuming couple, aged in their 70's, and it seemed unlikely they would have any enemies. It was therefore hard to see why they would have been targeted. Nothing appeared to have happened recently or in their past lives that might have led to them being involved in some sort of vendetta, which had then resulted in a revenge attack. Neither had they been engaged in any form of dispute with a neighbour. Consequently, it looked like it was either a case of mistaken identity or, more likely, a motiveless act of wanton vandalism. Our house-to-house enquiries led nowhere and, with little to go on, it regrettably ended up as an unsolved crime. Perversely however, I did discover some years later why the vandalism had arisen, although I still wasn't able to identify the perpetrator.

Many moons after the incident had taken place, I had a brief relationship with a young lady who lived quite near to where it occurred, and during our time together I found out by chance what had happened on that frightful night, and how the window had come to be smashed. While dating, we went out with some of her friends one night and they began talking about a party they'd all attended as teenagers. My girlfriend mentioned an odd gatecrasher at this event who'd tried to incite the other guests into performing a series of outrageous dares. My ears had pricked up when she recalled a particular dare that resulted in a window being smashed in a neighbouring house. Naturally, I enquired where and when this party had been held. I discovered it had taken place around the time we'd attended the incident of criminal damage, and in the same street; so I rapidly reached the conclusion they'd been talking about the unsolved crime that Ivan and I had investigated a few years earlier. Following further searching questions, it became clear that neither my girlfriend, nor her friends, had a clue about the identity of this uninvited stranger. However, they did inform me he'd been responsible for smashing the window and give me a detailed account of how it arose.

They were convinced he was already drunk and high on dope when he arrived at the party, and this accounted for his puerile behaviour. I was told he instigated a drinking game that involved party members having to perform a variety of forfeits or dares and, as the game progressed, things got completely out of hand. As a dare, he'd proposed that someone should run across the road and lob a brick through a window of the house opposite – and, when other partygoers had sensibly declined, he called them chicken, and then performed the sick deed himself. Everyone else present at the party had been shocked by his drink and drug-fuelled action, but too scared to intervene or report him to the police; so, when Ivan and I had turned up at the scene they'd turned off the lights and hidden. On hearing this I could have kicked myself. As part of our house-to-house enquiries following this incident, I recall I actually knocked on the door of the address where the party was being held – but, with it being in darkness and there being no answer, I'd assumed nobody was in.

It was a shame that finding out how this futile act of vandalism had arisen didn't lead to the culprit being identified and brought to book. He deserved to be punished for his totally unacceptable and irresponsible behaviour. In an ideal world, it would also have been much fairer if he'd had to face up to the impact his actions had on his innocent victims, and how his senseless act adversely affected them long-term. Sadly though, it wasn't possible to apply restorative justice in this instance, although maybe he got his comeuppance through other unknown means.

Within days of the window-smashing incident, I was helping out on another night shift and back on patrol with Ivan again. This time we were on foot and covering the town centre as the pubs and clubs were chucking out. Invariably this could be a busy part of such a shift and, whilst we were keeping tabs on the situation, we were joined by Beth, a WPC on Ivan's section who'd completed two years of service. It was a cold winter's night with snow in the air, and by 0100hrs the three of us had reached the point where we were confident the vast majority of late-night revellers had made their way home.

Up to that stage, the latter part of the evening had been unusually calm and passed by peacefully, without us encountering any major incidents of anti-social behaviour. We were therefore in the throes thinking we might be in for a quiet night – but such sentiments proved to be premature. Suddenly we heard a raucous crowd heading towards us and, based on the direction they were coming from and the nature of their chanting, we immediately presumed they'd been attending a social event at the local football club.

As they neared the town centre we approached them and simply requested they keep the noise down as they made their way home. At first, it appeared as though they would respond positively to our polite request and heed our advice but, for some reason, one of them took umbrage at being asked to lower the volume. He started swearing at Ivan and, without warning, everything kicked off. There were eight of them so we were totally outnumbered, even though a couple of them thought better of getting involved and did a runner. As things got quickly out of hand, the three of us soon became separated.

I ended up confronting one member of the group, who took up a boxing stance and started goading me to throw the first punch. Although his behaviour was threatening, I initially focused on trying to calm him down by advising him I wasn't looking to fight him, but would need to arrest him for breach of the peace unless he immediately went on his way without further ado. With that, he threw a punch, which caught me on the shoulder – and then, much to my surprise, just ran away. In all honesty there didn't seem to be much conviction in the way he landed the punch, and I felt it was a bit half-hearted; so, when he legged it, I decided not to pursue him at that stage, especially as I knew who he was and where he lived. At the time I was more concerned about what had happened to Ivan and Beth, and I thought finding them to check on their welfare and see how they were coping was more important. I'd heard Ivan call for urgent assistance over the radio, so I headed off up the side street where I'd last seen him running after the yob who'd triggered the mayhem by his aggressive reaction to our polite request.

When I reached Ivan, he was on the floor wrestling with his adversary trying to get him under control, but his exceptionally violent opponent was doing everything he could to resist being arrested. As the aggressor lashed out during their struggle, Ivan had no choice but to use his truncheon to stop him inflicting serious injury. His attempt to detain the violent lout and place him in handcuffs was also being hampered by another member of the rabble, who was attempting to pull him away from his prisoner. This particular thug – the leader of the gang – was massive and, through size alone, came across as intimidating. I appreciated he was going to be a handful, but knew I had to intervene and somehow get him away from Ivan. I therefore shouted at him to back off and used all my strength to push him away. Much to my amazement, he was initially compliant, and I briefly managed to get him far enough away from Ivan to stop him assisting his mate. Despite this, I anticipated I wouldn't have the upper hand for long and was much relieved when two traffic officers arrived to help me out just in the nick of time, before he had a change of heart. Between us we were then able to get the situation under control and complete the arrest of both offenders.

On reaching the police van that had arrived on scene to transport the prisoners, it was a relief to see that Beth was already in the vehicle and still in one piece. She was actually accompanied by her own detainee – who just happened to be the guy who'd thrown a 'soft' punch at me! My assailant had apparently handed himself into Beth for committing an assault on police, and had duly been arrested. Much to my surprise, he apologised for striking me and, in response, I thanked him for not launching a 'haymaker' towards my face or head, which could have done some serious damage if it had connected. Consequently, when the charge of assault on police was ultimately dropped, and he was only charged with breach of the peace, I was actually pleased with the decision. Although he'd been confrontational, it seemed to me that his posturing had been more like someone trying to engage in a play-fight, and I felt the punch he threw in my direction wasn't intended to do me any real harm. His actions didn't warrant a conviction for 'assault on police', and I wouldn't have been comfortable trying to justify such a charge or giving evidence in court to that effect. However, the outcome of my skirmish with this young man did come back to haunt me at the ensuing trial.

This arose because when I testified against the other defendants during court proceedings, the barrister for the defence team tried to use my evidence to undermine the prosecution case. He suggested that Ivan had used excessive force to gain control of his prisoner by bludgeoning him with his truncheon; whereas, I hadn't resorted to such measures in what he described as similar circumstances. I totally refuted this claim, and categorically stated that the threat I'd had to deal with had been significantly lower, and was nothing like the extreme level of violence Ivan had faced when his defendant resisted arrest. Equally, I stressed that based on what I'd witnessed, my colleague had solely used reasonable force to protect himself, and hadn't used his truncheon excessively as I'd only seen him strike the offender once – and this had been in the region of his lower limbs to stop him from kicking out. Hopefully, the responses I gave during cross-examination helped to thwart the barrister's slightly devious tactics as he failed to convince the court that Ivan's level of force had been unreasonable. A guilty verdict, which resulted in a tough sentence being dished out, exonerated Ivan and ratified the prosecution's view that his action had been justifiable in the circumstances.

At the start of my next duty, a Saturday evening stint, I'd not even had time to grab a radio or all my equipment before I was accompanying the section sergeant to investigate a possible burglary in progress. As I'd arrived in the enquiry office that evening the phone had been ringing and I'd answered the call. The call was from a concerned member of the public, who wished to report that he'd just seen someone break into his next-door neighbour's house. He told me that his neighbours were out, and he could now hear what sounded like someone ransacking their home. Having obtained details of the address of the potential break-in, I advised the caller that officers would be despatched immediately to the location. I then rushed to find the section sergeant, who was just about to head out in his patrol car, and informed him about the alleged crime that was taking place, so he could determine who should attend. In view of the urgency, Sarge said he would go himself. He also told me to jump in the car to join him on the shout – hence how I ended up heading off to this incident not even partially equipped.

The location of the reported burglary was close-by so we raced to the scene on a blue light run in under a minute – but, annoyingly, just missed the intruder by a matter of seconds. In the brief time the thief had been in the house he'd wreaked havoc searching for valuables. This disgusting member of the low life had also found time to leave his 'calling card' before departing from the property, inexplicably by relieving himself in the corner of the living room. Breaking into someone's abode is despicable in itself, but to then defile another person's property in that way is incomprehensible. I've never understood why some criminals occasionally stoop so low, and anyone who gets the urge to desecrate somebody's home like that must surely be a complete sicko. Unfortunately, this incident happened before the era of DNA, so the gross evidence he left behind couldn't be used forensically to help identify him. We also didn't have any luck tracking him down that evening because any leads soon went cold, even though we summoned the assistance of the dog handler. The case was therefore handed over to CID – although I never found out whether they succeeded in tracing the person responsible.

The next time I was on duty, it was this same sergeant who came to my assistance, and likely saved my bacon when he responded robustly to an imminent threat that I faced from an aggressive prisoner. In this instance, a fellow officer and I had been sent to arrest a violent suspect, who was wanted in connection with a serious case of GBH, where he'd left a young lad unconscious in the road after kicking him in the head. Once we'd returned to our local police station with the alleged assailant in custody, I'd been left alone guarding him in a makeshift interview room. It had been a busy night and we'd had to await our turn to book in our prisoner with the custody sergeant and, for some unaccountable reason, my colleague had removed the suspect's cuffs prior to going off to check how long a delay we faced. Whilst I was on my own with the prisoner his mood changed dramatically. Initially he had appeared to be reasonable, but in a flash he reverted back to being the thug we suspected of carrying out the violent and unprovoked assault earlier that evening. He refused to sit down and kept making threatening gestures, which were designed to intimidate. His behaviour was disconcerting and, when he started to jostle with me, I decided it was time to call out for assistance before the situation deteriorated further, and progressed to the point where we became embroiled in a full-on scuffle.

Before help arrived, the prisoner also put his fists up and started making frequent and sudden lunging movements towards me – so I attempted to get him back under control by trying to apply an arm lock. However, due to his fierce resistance, I was unable to get a firm grip and, literally as the duty sergeant entered the interview room to assist me, my adversary completely escaped my grasp and threw a punch, which I just about managed to dodge in the nick of time. Upon seeing this, my colleague immediately recognised I was at serious risk of being harmed and came charging across the room to my aid. As he did so, he slipped into a table that was between himself and the prisoner, which resulted in the table being accidentally shoved into the detainee's midriff and pinning him up against the wall; thus ensuring that the next wild punch he threw in my direction didn't reach me. With him now being constrained by the table, it also enabled my sergeant to reach across it to grab him, so between us we could then get him restrained once more. Although the suspect didn't seem to be injured by the table being unintentionally rammed into him due to the sergeant's clumsy intervention, I think the resultant impact had a chastening affect, and the shock of the collision took a while to wear off. Once it did, his bravado appeared to have deserted him and he no longer posed such a physical threat; however, he still possessed the effrontery to be verbally abusive as he was booked into custody.

11 Variety – The Spice of Life

FOR A CHANGE I FOUND MYSELF WORKING with Beth when I next offered my services for a weekend duty – a Friday late shift. We were mobile covering some of the more rural areas of our patch, when we got a call to look into an incident of gunfire on some farmland. The report, from a concerned farmer, suggested there were some poachers at work in the area, so we set off to investigate. By the time we'd tracked down the precise field from where the gunfire was emanating, the light had faded and dusk had turned into night. We could see torchlight flickering in the distance and were confident this would be our poachers at work. Beth therefore determined one of us would need to enter the field to fetch our would-be poachers. Since she was wearing her police issue skirt, which was totally impractical when it came to climbing over farm gates, she kindly volunteered me for that privilege! I duly obliged and, after clambering over the gate, I strode off towards the torchlight hoping to round up our night-time thieves.

It was while I was making my way across the field, with guns blazing intermittently, that I suddenly appreciated the sheer folly of my actions. Neither Beth nor I had thought to assess the risk before I'd set off. So, there I was in the pitch dark, putting myself in a precarious position, with poachers potentially about to aim their shotguns indiscriminately in my direction. I had no desire to become their prey for the night, and soon realised I needed to rapidly extricate myself from this predicament to minimise the chances of them mistaking me for a moving target. For the sake of self-preservation, I was eager to make a hasty retreat, but I knew that I could still be in the firing line if I took that course of action. Instead, I immediately fell flat on the ground and frantically waived my torch, whilst also hollering 'police' at the top of my voice. I shouted out we had the field surrounded and ordered them to lower their weapons and make their way towards me – not really expecting them to do as they were told. At best, I thought they would probably run off but, much to my amazement, they did as I instructed and within a couple of minutes I had three poachers handing themselves into me.

I'd never handled a shotgun before but, before I carried the weapons across the field to where Beth was waiting for me, I had enough gumption to know the barrels needed to be broken open and any cartridges removed to make them safe. I did just that, and then escorted the prisoners back towards Beth and our police car.

Our poachers weren't best pleased when they realised they'd been hoodwinked, and there wasn't a whole possê of constables waiting to run them into jail for the night – just good old Beth and me to do the honours! However, I was told that by next morning they found it bemusing, especially when they were released on bail. And as for me, I was just grateful that I'd not been used for target practice, and vowed to learn from this experience and make more reasoned judgements in future to avoid unnecessarily putting myself in peril. However, as I reveal more about my police experiences, it will become obvious that I failed miserably to live up to that vow.

The following Friday I again found myself supporting Beth on mobile patrol – this time covering the town rather than outlying rural areas. Just after 2300hrs we checked out the Market Place, which was busy with night-time revellers. As you might expect, many of them were drunk by this time, but generally the mood was pleasant, with the majority merrily going about their business. Even so, you still anticipate you'll come across the odd troublemaker looking to disturb the peace, and this night was no exception.

Whilst driving slowly up a narrow street we passed a throng of people queuing outside a fish & chip shop, and one young man decided to take a pop at us by kicking the side of our police car. Once the culprit had done so, he quickly tried to blend back into the crowd before we had an opportunity to identify him. As luck would have it though, I'd spotted his drunken action in the wing mirror and was able to recognise him amongst the queue of people. I was also able to identify him by name. This stunned him because he'd only just moved to the area that week, and clearly thought he would be anonymous to the police. He didn't recognise me in uniform, but I'd recently dealt with this young man in my day job, so knew all about him – even where he was residing.

Fortunately for this lad, his karate kick to the side of our police vehicle hadn't caused any visible marks or dents, so there was no point in arresting him for criminal damage. Apprehending him for an alternative offence was an option, but we decided suitable words of advice would suffice. We gave him the benefit of the doubt because he seemed repentant and immediately apologised for his stupid behaviour. Importantly, he also appeared to accept that his impulsively foolish action could have proven costly if it had resulted in him getting his first criminal conviction – and appreciate how easily youthful exuberance can adversely affect someone's whole future. With our work done at this incident we resumed our patrol, and then shortly afterwards attended a break-in at a flat located on the town's largest council estate.

An emergency call had come in from a neighbour reporting that someone had just kicked in the door to the flat opposite, and that the intruder was still on site. We instantly responded to this emergency and arrived on scene within minutes of getting the call.

As we approached the flat in question, we could see the door had been well and truly kicked in as reported, and we could hear there was definitely someone inside. To say we were a little apprehensive about entering the flat would be an under-statement, and we both drew our truncheons before cautiously stepping over the threshold to the doorway. However, it transpired we needn't have been so worried. Inside we found a very drunken man stretched out on the floor of the lounge, who just happened to be the occupant of the flat. Once we'd identified ourselves, and checked he was indeed the tenant, we got him to explain why he'd broken into his home using such brute force against his own front door. He told us he'd been out on a bender, and couldn't get in on arriving home because he'd lost his keys to the flat. In his drunken state, anger had then taken over and he'd simply kicked down the front door to gain entry – setting off panic amongst his petrified neighbours, who believed a burglary must be in progress. For Beth and I, dealing with this peculiar incidence of 'housebreaking' was all in a night's work, although we were relieved to discover that a dicey situation turned out to be more amusing than threatening.

The next time I worked, I was part of a team of specials out in the crew bus operating as a rapid response unit. It was all happening on this particular late night shift, and we were soon in business. Our colleague Damian had requested backup to deal with an incident outside the local kebab house, so we rushed to join him at the scene. Damian had issued a parking ticket to a driver who'd left his car on double yellow lines, and a drunken customer at the kebab house had become annoyed at him doing so, even though he wasn't the owner and the matter didn't concern him. The burly drunk had been told to stop interfering but had declined and become disorderly, leaving Damian no choice but to arrest him. Being an expert in several martial arts, Damian was more than a match for his detained prisoner, but needed help to quell a raucous crowd that had started to gather around him, and also to physically remove the offender from the scene. With seven of us rapidly on hand to assist, calm was soon restored and the matter resolved; however, we were back in action again within a matter of minutes when a fight began not far from the kebab house.

As we were on hand to instantly deal with the incident, order was again quickly restored, but not before one young man had received a nasty punch to the face, which had split his lip and likely broken his nose. The victim was able to point out his assailant – who I recognised as the captain of our local rugby team – but insisted he didn't wish to press charges. Despite him not wanting the matter taken further, I still went to speak to the lad who'd punched him. We knew each other through our connection with the rugby club and, without hesitation, he embarrassedly admitted he'd caused the injury to the afflicted party; although he was adamant he'd only thrown a punch in retaliation after the other guy had taken a swing at him. Nevertheless, I advised him I'd need to take his details in case charges were subsequently made against him, and it became necessary to arrest him on suspicion of committing ABH – so he could be interviewed under caution and give his side of the story. He duly obliged and I hoped that would be the end of the matter.

Later that night, however, when I was back at the nick and helping out in the enquiry office, I happened to deal with the mother and girlfriend of the injured party when they called into the station. The mother told me she wanted action taken against her son's attacker and wished to press charges. I explained that I'd been present at the scene of the incident, and at the time had spoken to her son about making a complaint but he'd declined to do so. Therefore, I also pointed out that as her son was the injured party he would need to make the complaint himself if he'd changed his mind and wanted the matter taken further.

Before they left to ponder on the information I'd imparted, I also mentioned to them that I'd spoken to the person who'd punched their loved one, and he had claimed he'd only done so in self-defence, and may even choose to make a counter complaint. From the reaction of the girlfriend, who'd been present at the incident, this didn't appear to come as a surprise, and she certainly didn't deny her boyfriend had instigated the confrontation. Her reluctance to do so left me wondering whether this had indeed been the case, and accounted for the victim's initial reticence about pressing charges. And, since a complaint never did materialise, I can only assume the victim accepted he was equally culpable for causing the fight to erupt, and didn't feel it was appropriate to proceed with a case.

Anyway, there was no let up in demand after we'd finished dealing with the latest fracas and had resumed our patrol. As we cruised the town's backstreets we happened upon a disconcerting sight – a young woman, dressed in a skimpy outfit, spread-eagled on the pavement. She was out for the count lying prostrate on her back with her legs akimbo and, since she was in a compromising position as she laid there displaying more of her feminine charms than she no doubt intended, it was fortunate we'd stumbled across her before she'd come to any harm. From the smell of alcohol, it soon became clear she'd probably had a heavy night of drinking out on the town, and had then failed to make it home before succumbing to the urge to take a nap.

As she was drunk and incapable we could have taken her into custody but, since our primary concern was her safety and welfare, we instead chose to get her out of harm's way by taking her home. With this in mind, several of us lifted her up and bundled her into the back of the crew bus, but not before I'd covered her up with my police anorak to belatedly preserve her modesty. On getting close to the young woman, I realised I knew her – again from my day job. I had a vague idea she lived somewhere nearby, but we still needed her exact address before we could act as her taxi service. With her being in no fit state to tell us, it was therefore fortuitous I was able to recall her name, so we could obtain details of her current residence through control and then deliver her home to her grateful parents. The next time our paths crossed, I'm glad to say this young lady had no recollection of this event or my involvement in her rescue, which was just as well – otherwise I'm sure she would have been mortified knowing I'd seen her in such an ungracious and humiliating state!

The following weekend I was paired up with Doug to undertake foot patrol of the town centre. He was a regular PC who'd been in the job for more than a decade and, just before midnight, I knew exactly where we would be heading – the local Chinese takeaway for one of their curries. I could have put money on it as I'd been warned Doug was a creature of habit; a man with a voracious appetite and an insatiable penchant for curries – or, more to the point, an absolute glutton for any type of food, especially when it was being offered buckshee. At well over six feet tall, with a build to match his height, he could eat for England, and food was always on his mind. Perhaps it wasn't therefore surprising that certain undesirables were known to occasionally refer to him as a greedy pig – a description that in some respects was undeniably apt and deserved!

Doug had recently returned to routine duties after spending the previous three years attached to the Division's Task Force, and it hadn't taken him long to set up a network of refreshment stops on his beat. In that time he'd also gained a reputation for being something of a gannet amongst local restaurateurs and takeaway owners, all of whom welcomed him with open arms whenever he called on them during a night shift. I think they were pleased to have his attention when the pubs and clubs were chucking out, and felt his presence would prevent any trouble occurring in their respective establishments; so they made a point of regularly inviting him in to partake in a free feast when he happened to be on duty in the vicinity. Besides, as it was generally late at night when he paid a visit, I suspect most of the food they dished out to him gratis was destined for the waste bin – so you could argue he was doing them a favour.

Anyhow, on this particular night shift my premonition that a food stop would be on the agenda proved to be right, and we did indeed end up calling in at Doug's favourite takeaway. This Chinese takeaway, the only one based in the town centre, had an eating area at the back, and there we indulged in a flavoursome curry - supplied on the house of course. Once we'd finished our splendid meal we continued our foot patrol feeling replete. However, this didn't stop Doug also accepting the offer of a coffee at a bistro located just up the road from the Chinese takeaway.

The bistro, which was attached to a bakery, was one of his regular coffee stops, and the proprietor (Marge) was working late getting a variety of pies and pastries ready for baking the next day. She was always pleased to have some company when working alone late at night, particularly from members of the Constabulary. During this visit though, I think Doug almost cooked his own goose with his cheek. He mentioned to Marge that he'd forgotten to bring his truncheon with him on duty, and then asked if he could have one of her French sticks - as he was confident it would have the same affect if he needed to bop anyone with it!

Before we left this haunt, Doug decided we might as well make good use of the facilities and write up our pocketbooks, which made sense; so, whilst we were out of the cold and sitting comfortably, we did just that. Naturally, your pocketbook is like your gospel for recording everywhere you've been and everything you've dealt with during your shift and, while I was in the midst of writing mine up, I couldn't resist winding him up by saying:

'So, what time was it Doug that we had that curry?' (Thus implying I was going to include this event in my contemporaneous notes!)

Clearly this wasn't something you would normally record, and definitely wasn't a matter he would want me to note down, but I could tell from his reaction that he briefly thought I was genuinely going to include this in my pocketbook entry - at least until the smirk on my face gave it away that I was only joking.

Once we'd finished writing up our pocketbooks, Doug and I resumed our patrol and, at 0130hrs, we took over the response vehicle. It was while we were covering response that we got a rather strange request to attend a mystery job at an address located on a new housing estate. The message we got from the control room was a bit cagey, and we were advised that the emergency caller would meet us at her home and explain the nature of her problem. Wondering what was in store for us, we made our way to the address in question, where a glamorous woman met us outside.

We soon gathered the lady of the house and her beloved husband had returned late at night from a party but, once home, she'd been unable to get her other half out of the car because he'd fallen into a deep, drink-induced sleep. No matter how hard she'd tried to wake him from his slumber, she hadn't been able to get him to come around. In the circumstances, the petite wife had immediately concluded that in his inebriated state he would be a dead weight, and there was no way she'd be able to get him out of the car and into the house without help. Worried it wouldn't be safe to leave him sleeping in the car all night – in case he was sick and then choked on his own vomit – she'd therefore tentatively phoned the police in a panic; knowing full well it wasn't really a police matter, and that putting people to bed wasn't normally part of the service!

Upon discovering the reason this lady needed our assistance, Doug and I appreciated why the control room operator had been somewhat coy with us over the radio about the exact purpose of the job he'd asked us to attend. We could only assume that when she'd rung up in a panic he'd taken pity on her, and decided to summon our help with this matter; despite knowing perfectly well that the difficulty she faced wasn't an emergency requiring the attention of the police. Doubtless that's why he hadn't wanted to broadcast the exact details of the job when contacting us – in case doing so aroused the suspicions of his control room supervisor, who was a stickler for following protocol. The boss would certainly have questioned why two of his officers were effectively being used as 'errand boys', and never have authorised our attendance if he'd known the reason. Anyway, we were there now, so Doug and I thought we may as well see what we could do to help.

From one look at the drunken hubby it was obvious to us he was out for the count; in fact, virtually comatose! All attempts to rouse him failed, so we advised the wife the only option would be to manhandle him out of the car and carry him into the house. She was in agreement and happy for us to do so. We not only achieved our objective, but even managed to carry him upstairs and deposit him on the matrimonial bed; however, this was the limit of our service, and we made it clear that getting 'Sleeping Beauty' ready for bed wasn't part of the deal – so we declined her request to help remove his clothes. Nonetheless, she still saw us as her saviours and, as a sign of her gratitude, she served up coffee and biscuits, which went down well – and, of course, once again complemented the midnight snack we'd consumed earlier. Having fulfilled the odd challenge we'd been set, which gave us a good laugh along the way, we left her house in a buoyant mood and once more resumed our patrol.

As this particular event illustrates, police work isn't solely about responding to full-scale emergencies with blue lights flashing and sirens blazing. Much of the time it's about community policing – such as undertaking patrols aimed at preventing crime by your very presence. This formed a major part of my role as a special and I derived as much satisfaction from this proactive side of policing as I did from the reactive aspects, which naturally could be exciting at times and get the adrenaline pumping. Responding to incidents was great, but I got a real buzz from being out on the streets pounding the beat and having face-to-face contact with members of the public. The part I enjoyed most about high-profile policing, especially foot patrols, was having the chance to interact and build a rapport with local people, whilst also being a visible deterrent to anyone with criminal intent. Not only were you out there getting noticed and giving reassurance or crime prevention advice, but you were also on hand to support citizens whenever they needed your assistance or intervention. Being able to serve in this way is both critical and rewarding, and wanting to contribute to this element of policing was a major factor in me joining up and being a voluntary bobby for over 20 years.

Shortly after I'd worked with Doug for the first time he was out of commission for a while. Following a routine traffic stop, he'd attempted to arrest the driver after he'd provided a positive breath test, but his prospective prisoner had resisted and kicked Doug as he'd tried to detain him. The severe blow had struck Doug in his 'undercarriage', which had resulted in him suffering bruised 'plums' and being signed off work. Ultimately the driver had been tracked down and charged with assault on police but not drink-driving because, due to him fleeing the scene, it regrettably hadn't been possible to obtain a blood test in time. Anyway, when Doug finally returned to duty it coincided with another of my shifts.

On this occasion I was on foot patrol, accompanied by Spud, whilst Doug was in the response car. Around 2100hrs a call went out over the radio for Doug to attend a disturbance at a location near to where Spud and I were patrolling, so we also made our way towards the incident. The report indicated there was a large gathering of youths in the road, who'd been trying to gatecrash a party being held in the area. Doug arrived on scene before us, and we heard him give an update stating he'd checked the area, but there was no sign of a disturbance or large crowd. We therefore assumed the call had either been a hoax or the youths had already dispersed by the time he'd arrived; so, when we got to the vicinity just a few minutes later, we were expecting it to be all quiet on the Western Front. However, much to our consternation, there were about 30 youths, aged in their mid-teens, lingering in the road or hanging around on the pavement. Another dozen or so were gathered in the garden of a terraced property where the party was presumably being held. As we approached, I therefore alerted control to the revised situation and, in view of the numbers present, requested assistance. Consequently, Doug was asked to make his way back to the scene that he'd only recently vacated.

One could only assume that when he'd visited the location the youths had spotted him coming, and somehow managed to scatter and hide from his view as he patrolled the area – and then emerged again as soon as he'd left. The fact Doug had failed to spot such a large contingent of youths in the area left him a little red-faced, but it was perfectly understandable as there were plenty of potential hidey-holes in close proximity, even for a crowd of that size.

Due to the volume of young people present, which in itself was intimidating, we realised this was one of those situations where things could easily flare up and get out of hand if they suddenly transformed into an unruly crowd of louts. That didn't prove to be the case this time. The vast majority went on their way as soon as we suggested they leave the area. Likewise, even those that displayed a little more bravado and chose to hang around for a while being vociferous, also backed down and went quietly once warned they'd be arrested for affray if they didn't depart.

With our duty done at this location, Spud and I resumed foot patrol for another hour, after which we were paired up with regular officers for the rest of our shift. I found myself with Doug again, once more covering response, and we had another eventful session together. Around 2300hrs we were doing spot-checks close to the market place, when a lad came down the road on his motorbike without a helmet on and, much to his dismay, bumped into us. After we'd stopped him, he attempted to argue that he hadn't ridden on a public highway, and had actually been in a nearby supermarket car park when we'd spotted him – and therefore, in his opinion, didn't need to be wearing a helmet. Despite his protestations, we knew this definitely wasn't the case, and he'd certainly come down the road in full view of us before entering the supermarket car park; a favourite gathering place for boy racers at night-time.

I mention this because, when the ensuing court case arose, he tried to use this as the basis for his defence, and claimed he hadn't been riding his bike on a public road without his helmet. Consequently, when Doug and I gave evidence during these proceedings, the defence solicitor challenged our assertions that we'd seen his client riding on the road. To this end, he requested that we mark on a map exactly where we'd first seen him riding his motorbike. Doug was first up to give his evidence and, during his cross-examination, he had to mark the map with a cross to show where he'd first observed the defendant. When I took the stand, I then had to do the same to corroborate Doug's evidence – which really wasn't a problem, as we'd both spotted the defendant as he'd come down the hill towards the car park. However, much to the embarrassment of the defendant's solicitor, this attempt to catch us out using such means spectacularly backfired. It resulted in something of an own goal because I had to point out that the map, which Doug had marked his cross on, had inadvertently been left in the witness box for me to view! This blunder earned both the defence solicitor and the court clerk a stern rebuke from the magistrates; although it didn't adversely impact on the outcome of the proceedings, as the defendant was rightly found guilty and fined for his misdemeanour.

On the same night as the helmet incident, Doug and I were also treated to an explicit and erotically charged demonstration of unbridled passion, just a short while after we'd finished dealing with the motorcycle rider. We'd swapped the response vehicle for an unmarked police car and were parked up keeping a close eye on the local nightclub, which was sited in the precinct. The club's night-time revellers were generally behaving in an acceptable manner as they were coming or going, even though many of them were clearly drunk. We were parked under some trees towards the rear of the precinct's car park and, in the dark, nobody was noticing us as we were camouflaged by the surrounding foliage. Keeping a low profile was intentional because we were on the lookout for a known drug dealer, who we were hoping to catch plying his trade. He regularly frequented the area in the expectation he would encounter plenty of the club's patrons as they arrived or left – and that some of them would be seeking to 'score'. The fact we were well hidden was presumably why a woman didn't spot us when she exited the night-club, and then sat on the loading bay at the rear of some shops smoking – probably dope, based on the wafting aroma. There she was subsequently joined by a man, who seemed similarly unaware of our presence nearby. At least, bearing in mind what happened next, I'd like to think they were completely oblivious to our presence.

As it was a warm evening, and we had our car windows down, we could easily hear their conversation. It soon became apparent they had most likely been complete strangers to each other up to that point, which made what took place next even more bizarre. Little time was wasted on chat up lines, and there was nothing implied when the chap enquired if she was up for sex there and then – except the language he used was a lot blunter when he asked her whether she'd like to join him in the act of fornication, as his precise question was:

'Do you fancy a shag?'

We expected the woman to reject his impolite suggestion in no uncertain terms but, much to our amazement, she did the exact opposite. After nonchalantly accepting his proposal, they both stripped off and engaged in full-on sex like a pair of prostrate doggers.

Doug and I were flabbergasted, and normally we would have intervened well before it got to that amatory stage; however, we were initially reluctant to do so whilst nobody else was about as we didn't want to blow our cover. Also, just after concluding things had gone too far and it would be necessary to take action, we'd received a radio call putting us on standby to attend another more pressing matter, where a colleague would likely require backup. Knowing we may have to imminently dash off had then made us even more hesitant about getting involved – and that was why the horny couple got away with their daring act. It wasn't a case of turning a blind eye – it was about prioritisation.

Luckily, there were no other witnesses to this primal activity who might have been offended; otherwise we would have been forced to take action and report the over-sexed couple for indulging in an indecent act in a public place. Anyway, their uninhibited cavorting was all over in a flash because something spooked them and brought their carnal antics to a premature end. At this point we were even more taken aback by their behaviour. They simply got dressed and casually walked off in different directions – without as much as a parting word or a peck on the cheek. It had all been so matter of fact, and there wasn't even an exchange of names and phone numbers to our knowledge, despite the fact they didn't appear to know each other, except in the intimate sense!

Weirdly, a few years later something similar to this happened to my mate Ivan. It was at a time when he'd been on escort duties, and he was returning to the police station along with some other colleagues after they'd transported several prisoners to the custody suite. Upon approaching a busy mini-roundabout not far from their destination, they encountered a long queue of traffic, so Ivan volunteered to get out of the crew bus to investigate the cause of the hold-up. When he got to the mini-roundabout he was gob-smacked. There he encountered a naked couple copulating in the middle of the road, wearing nothing but a smile! Clearly, they were even more brazen than the amorous couple Doug and I had observed because this pair of lovers seemed unfazed about performing in broad daylight in front of an audience, whilst lying starkers in the centre of the roundabout with their legs entwined. Naturally Ivan took appropriate steps to deal with the situation. He used his police jacket to belatedly preserve the modesty of the young lady, and his helmet to cover up the guy's ample manhood – which had been pointing traffic in the direction of Land's End as soon as he stood up!

Once the offending exhibitionists had been duly arrested and placed in the crew bus, it had soon become obvious to Ivan they were both as high as kites on dope. He thought this probably accounted for them being so blasé about revealing their bodily charms, completely losing any inhibitions and failing to control their carnal desires. In their trance-like state they apparently had no idea just how much bother they'd been causing – or, for that matter, how much trouble they were going to be in as a result of their outrageous, drug-influenced behaviour.

Sex alfresco might not be that uncommon, but putting on a live show in the middle of a mini-roundabout, in front of stunned drivers, has to be a one off that was bound to hit the news. It was therefore not surprising when such impropriety attracted a lot of interest from the media, and numerous reporters from the national press and TV stations descended upon our town. Once the story broke, it crossed my mind it would be amusing if they managed to interview the over-amorous male fornicator for a comment because, when asked during his police interview what he could recall about the incident, he replied:

'Not a lot really, but I'm told I was wearing nothing but an earring and a hard-on when I was caught by the fuzz!'

The performance of this lustful couple wasn't quite a case of 'dèjá vu', but there were a number similarities between this incident and the one Doug and I had witnessed; so, after I heard about this second event, I wondered whether there must be something in the local water, which was causing such unbridled displays of animal passion to be openly committed by members of our community. And, if that was the case, then maybe the local Water Board ought to strongly consider changing the additive from an aphrodisiac to bromide, in order to curb such libidinal instincts.

As many people know, the South West is renowned for its carnivals, pageants and parades, and the services of special constables were routinely utilised during these events. For me, policing such community celebrations stand out because doing so was always one of my favourite duties. However, I think my abiding happy memories of patrolling at carnivals might have been slightly skewed by a couple of pleasant experiences that occurred whilst doing so. The first of these arose at the end of a parade, when a fellow special and I received an invite to attend a party being held in honour of the carnival queen and her attendants. Fortuitously, the end of our stint coincided with the start of their party, so we were able to join the celebratory event – and wow, were we treated like VIP's! Not only were we given ample helpings of food and plied with plentiful amounts of punch, but we also got to spend lots of time with the queen and her maids of honour – and neither of us raised any objection when we got more than our fair share of attention from them. This was probably not surprising since we were relatively youthful at the time, while most of the blokes present were old enough to be their fathers – if not their grandfathers! Anyhow, it was a lovely way to finish off the evening after overseeing the procession, and certainly left me with some endearing memories.

The second carnival-related incident that sticks in my mind as a treasured memory took place the following year, and was actually over in a flash. On this occasion, I was stood minding my own business doing crowd control close to the town centre as the carnival floats passed by, when this beautiful young woman suddenly made a beeline towards me. Based on the fact she was wearing sports gear and carrying a hockey stick, I presumed she was part of the procession and was in a fancy dress outfit – perhaps trying to depict a character out of the St Trinian's film. As she approached, my assumption was confirmed because I spotted a whole bunch of young ladies on a float adorning similar attire. Anyway, she came bounding up to me and planted a big 'smacker' on my lips, before running back to rejoin her gang. Her amorous display left me pleasantly stunned, but I imagine the impromptu kiss I received was most likely as the result of a dare set by her chums, rather than her finding me irresistible and having a momentary loss of self-control – more's the pity!

As previously indicated, I do wonder if these couple of enjoyable episodes have in some way distorted my overall view of policing carnivals, and whether they possibly masked what such duties were really like in the main. There was certainly a fun side to overseeing these types of family events and, generally, a good atmosphere existed, with the vast majority of people behaving responsibly throughout. However, there was always the potential for that to change, so you constantly had to be on your toes. As the night wore on, carnival fever could sometimes transform into unruly behaviour amongst certain elements within the crowd. Unsurprisingly, excessive drinking was normally the underlying cause that turned a small minority of high-spirited people into objectionable troublemakers. Fights could then break out, which required police intervention. Such instances were rare during actual processions, and tended to arise later in the evening. We still needed to be alert at all times though, just in case trouble started brewing sooner.

In addition, we also had to be on our guard in case we were targeted by yobs using coins as missiles. This particular problem was an issue we faced back in my early policing days, when there were normally several carnival floats in each procession being used for collecting money for charity, with members of the crowd being urged to donate their loose change by lobbing coins onto the back of the designated vehicles. It was a fun but dangerous practice and, for those thugs who disliked the police, it was an ideal opportunity for them to take pop shots at us. They would deliberately aim their coins at officers with the intention of causing injury; knowing full well they could do so under the pretence they were targeting the collection vehicle. Naturally, such a projectile thrown with considerable force could do some serious damage, especially if it struck someone in the face. Not only was this reckless behaviour a concern to police officers who were in the firing line, but also innocent bystanders, including children, as they could easily be hit if the coin missed its intended target. In view of the large number of people at such events, it was virtually impossible to ever identify anyone who had thrown a coin that had caused injury – meaning yobs that engaged in this activity realised they could do so with almost complete impunity. They knew that in the unlikely event they were identified, they could simply claim it had been unintentional, in the sure knowledge it would be difficult to prove otherwise. I was therefore delighted when this method of charity collection at carnivals was banned under health & safety rules; on the grounds it was an unsafe practice, which put members of the public at risk.

From what I've highlighted so far, it should be apparent that carnivals could be typically lively events from a policing perspective – and that was definitely the case one year when I had to deal with a car going up in flames whilst a procession was in full swing. I was on point duty when a member of the public alerted me that a car was on fire in a side road, adjacent to where I was located, so I straightaway rushed to investigate. The vehicle was well alight by the time I got to it and, once I'd checked there was nobody in the car, I urgently requested the fire service attend. I discovered the driver had pulled over and exited the car upon realising the engine was on fire and, apart from being a bit stunned, he was otherwise fine. My immediate priority was therefore keeping members of the public back because a crowd was already starting to gather to observe the spectacle. I was staggered by just how many of them were getting really close to the blazing inferno, despite it being a dangerous situation, considering the petrol tank could explode at any moment. It was a very narrow street, with shops on one side and domestic dwellings on the other, and it amazed me that passing pedestrians also thought it was perfectly reasonable to walk by the burning car, without fully appreciating the risk they were taking. Some of them even had children with them they could be putting in jeopardy.

Whilst I was doing my utmost to keep people back from the danger zone, I had a brainwave. I remembered there was a petrol station nearby and they would definitely have a fire extinguisher on site, so I rapidly persuaded a willing member of the public to go to fetch it. For obvious reasons I didn't want to leave the scene, but maybe I should have gone myself because this helpful member of the community soon returned empty-handed. Unbelievably, the forecourt attendant had refused to hand over the extinguisher without a £50 deposit!

By now things had deteriorated further as I'd just heard on the radio that the fire tender that was en route in response to my transmission had headed to the wrong location. The driver had unwittingly gone to a street with a similar name to the one I'd given as the site of the fire. And, since the fire engine had already had to weave its way through the carnival procession whilst heading to the wrong end of town, I knew it would likely be another 10 minutes before the appliance manoeuvred its way back to the correct spot. However, all was not lost and more help was at hand.

A resident from the street, who'd come out to see what all the commotion was about, offered to run a hose from his house, so we could aim a jet of water at the fuel tank to keep it cool, and hopefully prevent it from exploding. That's exactly what we did until the fire brigade finally arrived and soon extinguished the flames – by which time the car was a burnt out, smouldering wreck and, without a shadow of doubt, a complete write-off. Still, the main thing was that nobody was hurt; although that was more through luck than any degree of sensible behaviour on the part of those people who treated it like some sort of display, which had been laid on for their amusement.

12   Twists of Fate

Around five years into my service as a special constable, I was really disappointed to learn that my mate Nev would be transferring to our Divisional HQ. He had recently become engaged to a local young lady (which was my fault because I'd originally introduced them!), and she was keen to settle down in a new location away from her home town. Nev had ultimately agreed, and they'd purchased a lovely little cottage in a village located in the south of the county, quite near to his new workplace, in readiness for when they tied the knot. This made perfect sense, and I was delighted for them, even though it meant I would rarely get the opportunity to work with Nev in the future.

As their nuptial date was fast approaching, Nev and his fiancée were busy sorting out all the arrangements for their forthcoming matrimonial ceremony. This included returning to the bride's home town to have the bands read on several consecutive Sundays in the run-up to the wedding. It was during one of these trips that tragedy struck, which resulted in Nev suffering a life-changing injury.

Shortly after setting off one Sunday morning, Nev stopped at his local garage to get petrol and, whilst there, also decided to top up the oil – a decision that he would live to regret because it led to a catastrophic series of events. Just after leaving the garage he realised he'd forgotten to put the oil cap back on and pulled over to the side of the road to remedy the situation. It was a wide road, where cars routinely parked on the side of the street, so technically it should have been safe to do so, especially as there was little traffic about. However, whilst he was at the front of the car with the bonnet up, the unthinkable happened. A car suddenly veered into the rear of Nev's vehicle at about 40mph, and the impact threw him backwards into a stone wall. The fact that Nev demolished the wall gives you some idea of the force at which he struck this solid mass and, inevitably, he was critically injured. I imagine anyone's initial chances of survival after undergoing such a forceful collision must be slim, so whether Nev being tall and muscular with a massive frame was a factor I don't know – because, survive he did. The back of his head and rear of his upper torso took the brunt of the impact, which resulted in him suffering a life-threatening brain injury.

He was rushed to hospital and, subsequently, transferred to a major trauma unit that deals with serious head injuries, where he underwent emergency brain surgery. Other injuries Nev incurred included significant damage to one of his knees, caused by the impact of his own car being forcefully thrust into him, but this was deemed secondary compared to the extensive wound to his head. Everyone feared the worst, even his surgeon who was concerned that the brain damage would leave him in a vegetative state, or at least severely impaired in the event he survived. However, to everyone's relief and delight, he not only came through the surgery and regained consciousness after being in a coma for two days but, at an early stage, also showed signs that a good recovery in the longer-term was a distinct possibility. He was still able to talk, even though his speech was a bit garbled – and his first few words sounded like gibberish. In fact, the reply he gave to a question I asked him shortly after he'd come around, probably gives an indication of just what a confused state his mind was in at that point. During my visit, I'd noticed that he kept taking hold of one of the many tubes connected to various parts of his anatomy and giving it a squeeze, so I enquired why? His response was:

'It's not a tube I'm holding; it's the US President's finger!'

Nevertheless, discovering he could speak at all was amazing – and completely surprised the surgeon.

This initial outcome was far better than anyone could have anticipated or hoped for based on the original prognosis and, once Nev had come out of his coma, we found out why the surgeon had at first thought his prospects of recovering were so poor. Most of the damage to his brain had affected the left-hand side, which would normally have serious ramifications for a right-handed person – but, unbeknown to the surgeon, Nev is fortunately left-handed. Having assumed Nev was right-handed, the brain surgeon's diagnosis had understandably been very pessimistic. In the circumstances, he had therefore suggested that the best-case scenario would likely be that Nev could retain some basic mental faculties – but, overall, the brain damage would probably inhibit his capacity to ever function normally again. Once he became aware that Nev was actually left-handed, he was able to revise this forecast and, without being overly optimistic, predict there was every chance he could make a reasonable recovery and, ultimately, continue to lead a relatively normal life. Considering the original prognosis was so bleak, this represented a substantial stride forward, and restored everyone's hope and belief that his condition would steadily improve. However, Nev's loved ones still recognised his injuries were going to be life-changing, and the road to recovery a long haul.

I'm glad to say the anticipated improvement did come about, and gradually Nev recovered to a point where he was able to leave hospital and continue his convalescence at home. Slowly but surely he was nursed back to good health. Sadly though, the extent of his injuries meant he could not resume his police career and had to be medically discharged from the force. Due to the swelling on his brain, they'd had to remove part of his skull, which had been replaced with a metal plate. Therefore, it was deemed too risky to let him once more undertake frontline police duties in case he ever took another blow to the head. It also meant he had to give up contact sports, including rugby, which was such a shame because he was a brilliant player and this was one of his main passions in life. Another of his favourite sports, cricket, was also a no-go area. As a result of his accident, Nev was also left deaf in one ear and susceptible to epileptic fits – although these were kept under control through medication.

Naturally, all Nev's colleagues, especially Ivan and me, were bitterly disappointed to find out his police career was over and that we were never again going to have the opportunity to work alongside him out on the beat. In many respects, this sad news was tempered by the fact that he was still very much alive and kicking, with the prospect of living a long and meaningful life. For this we were extremely grateful as it was an outcome that looked unlikely during his darkest of hours.

In spite of all these repercussions from the accident, Nev always accepted things could have been so much worse and somehow remained positive. Bearing in mind the devastating impact it had on his life, he had every right to feel resentful and aggrieved; especially when he learned about the combination of unfortunate events that brought about his freak accident, and how easily it could have been avoided.

It emerged that the car, which had careered into him on that fateful day, was being driven by a young lady who was transporting her partner to a psychiatric hospital. Apparently, the boyfriend had suffered a breakdown and been sectioned by his doctor earlier that day. The doctor had visited his patient at home, and come to the conclusion he needed treatment at a secure unit due to his irrational and unpredictable behaviour. However, for some inexplicable reason he allowed the young man's girlfriend to drive his agitated patient to hospital, rather than arrange for him to be transported in an ambulance. This decision had terrible and far-reaching consequences because, as a result of the young man grabbing the steering wheel, he caused the vehicle to swerve into the back of Nev's car.

At the time the accident occurred, the doctor responsible for sectioning the young man was following his patient to hospital in his own car, so it did mean he was immediately on hand to begin treating Nev. Ironically, a doctor also lived in the very house that was surrounded by the wall Nev had been flung into by the impact of the crash, so there was also a second person with medical expertise to tend to him until the ambulance arrived. In combination, they were able to check Nev's vital signs and provide essential early treatment to prevent rapid deterioration. Having the two experts there to instantly intervene almost certainly made the difference between life and death, when you consider the severity of his injuries. However, it's debatable whether this was of much consolation to Nev. He would no doubt have been gutted once he found out the reason this accident arose in the first place, which was effectively due to the decision made by the doctor responsible for sectioning the mental health patient. Quite why the doctor unaccountably allowed someone in this condition to be driven to hospital by his girlfriend is a mystery but, despite this travesty, I've never known Nev to moan about his plight or the injuries he sustained as a result of this error of judgement – even though he had every right to think it was grossly unfair. He just accepted his lot and searched out other opportunities to enrich his life, including a variety of new career paths.

This accident, which nearly ended Nev's life, wasn't' the only occasion when he suffered a severe blow to the head. There'd been at least two previous occasions where he'd taken hard knocks to that part of his body. One of these came from a fearsome left hook that he was unable to avoid when he encountered a violent assailant whilst on duty. It was the type of punch that would have floored someone of smaller stature. However, I'm told Nev just shook off the blow, a bit like the 'Hulk' does when he gets struck, and then put his prisoner in a headlock until help arrived.

The second occasion when Nev endured another ferocious smack to his skull was down to him having to take evasive action by behaving like a 'Superhero'. Whilst he was on foot patrol during a night shift, his fellow constable Paolo was driving the response car and spotted him out on his beat, so decided to pull over to have a catch up. As Paolo slowly pulled up in front of him, Nev saw the police car coming his way and, assuming it was going to stop imminently, stepped out in front of the approaching vehicle with the intention of walking around to the driver's side. However, he got his timing wrong because the car didn't come to a halt as rapidly as he'd anticipated. This left Nev with no choice but to throw himself onto the bonnet of the police vehicle just before it struck him. Having ended up spread-eagled on the front of the car, it probably looked like he was attempting to emulate the type of daring stunt normally associated with 'James Bond' – but it transpired he wasn't as nimble or athletic as Ian Fleming's premier spy, nor as indestructible as the UK's super-human secret agent! He promptly slid off, fell backwards, and hit his head on the kerb. The kerb won the contest and

Nev was left with a large bump to the back of his bonce, along with a gash that required several stitches – so, the outcome of this stunt indicated he was less '007', more 'Frank Spencer'!

What made this situation worse was the knock-on effect of this initial calamity, because one man down soon became two. On that particular night, there were only three officers on duty at the outset but, before the shift was over, there was only one fit enough to continue working. Along with Paolo and Nev, the third member of the team for that tour of duty was a probationer called Tobias, who was still very green in terms of his service. He was accompanying Paolo for the shift and, therefore, was present during the fiasco, and when Nev was transported to the local A&E department in the response car. Likewise, he was also there watching when the duty nurse stitched up Nev's head wound.

It was whilst Nev was having his sutures inserted that Tobias suddenly turned very pale at the sight of this procedure and then fell flat on his face – knocking himself out cold! His injuries were actually worse than those experienced by Nev. He not only broke his nose when he fainted, but also suffered such a severe bout of concussion that he ended up being admitted to hospital for several days – whereas, Nev was allowed home and just had a splitting headache for a day or so. I later heard that when Tobias came around, he had no recollection of the incident, and told everyone he'd been hurt playing rugby – even though he'd never played a game of rugger in his life.

Luckily, neither of the injured parties did themselves any long-term serious harm, but it did mean all three of them had some explaining to do when the bosses became aware Paolo had ended up covering the rest of the night shift working solo. Knowing the guys involved, I'm certain they would have come up with a convincing story, without ever having to admit the injuries were effectively self-inflicted as a result of their own foolhardiness.

Having survived all these bangs to the head, plus others no doubt throughout his rugby career, it was no wonder that some people came to the conclusion that Nev must be a hard nut to crack!

As mentioned previously, Nev, Ivan and I all experienced near-death experiences whilst relatively young, whereby our respective lives were left hanging by a thread. Ivan's close encounter with the 'Grim Reaper' came about a few years later, after he'd transferred to the Regional Crime Squad. He was travelling back home on his motorbike to spend his rest days with his wife and children, following a period away on a tour of duty, when he was involved in a near-fatal incident with a van. As I understand it, the van driver pulled across his path and forced him into a stationary vehicle at speed. Due to the impact, Ivan suffered serious internal injuries, including a split liver, and had to be rushed to hospital to undergo emergency surgery.

For several days it was touch and go as to whether he would survive, and when I first visited a couple of days after the accident he was still in a bad way in ICU, but at least he was no longer connected to the assisted-breathing apparatus. Although it was difficult for him to talk, he tried hard to make light of his situation and was typically upbeat. I therefore acknowledged it was great he could look on the bright side as every cloud tends to have a silver lining. I told him that had even been the case with this unfortunate event – because it had enabled the surgeon to kill two birds with one stone, and take the opportunity to also give him the snip whilst performing his life-saving surgery. I could tell from his reaction that his sense of humour hadn't deserted him as a broad smile confirmed he saw the funny side of this comment. However, I think he might have misunderstood my remark, and interpreted the term snip as meaning the surgeon had given him a sex change during the operation because I did notice him discreetly check down below, presumably to make sure everything was still intact and that nothing was missing!

The next time I visited he was out of ICU and well on the road to recovery. His internal wounds were healing well, but the effects of the accident had taken their toll and he still had to overcome the psychological scars of his brush with death. However, Ivan is a tough cookie and, following several months off work, including a spell at the police's national convalescence centre, his recuperation was complete and he was able to return to active duty.

13 'Minding the Shop'

EVERY SO OFTEN SPECIAL CONSTABLES would take over the running of a borough within our Division for a 24-hour period. Doing so served a dual purpose. It aided the development of practical skills amongst the force's contingent of specials, and also gave the bosses a chance to test out the capabilities of such personnel, and gauge their capacity to cope with the pressures and demands of frontline duties. On the whole, policing was down to specials during these specified periods, although regular officers were always on standby in case things went pear-shaped, or they needed to assist with emergencies outside of our scope. As the years rolled by, and I became steadily more proficient in the many facets of police work, I especially looked forward to these occasions. They gave me the opportunity to really test myself in challenging circumstances, and hopefully demonstrate my prowess as a voluntary bobby, without having to rely on a full-time colleague to take the lead. However, the first time I took part in such an exercise, things could easily have gone seriously awry.

The occasion was a Saturday during the latter part of summer in the mid-1980's, and we were due to take over policing my home town from 1400hrs. Just before I headed to the police station, I pulled a muscle in my back whilst getting ready for duty. Initially, I thought it was a minor strain that wouldn't hamper me too much, although I was conscious my movement was a little restricted. Sensibly I should have withdrawn from carrying out any active duties, especially as my condition worsened during my drive to the nick, but I was keen to get out on patrol and thought the problem would gradually ease if I kept mobile. So out I went, covering a beat that took in the south of the town.

I'd barely been on patrol for more than a few minutes when I got a radio call asking me to make my way to the scene of a domestic, which was in progress on my patch. There was no marker on the address to suggest the occupants were known to the police and presented a cause for concern, so I was despatched to investigate on my own. Clearly, had any of the occupants residing at the address had a history of violence towards the police, or previous convictions for assault, additional resources would have immediately been requested to back me up. However, as things stood, there was no reason to think I would be confronted with anything other than a routine domestic to deal with, or that anyone living at this abode may pose a serious threat – but on both counts this proved not to be the case.

As I neared the address where the reported domestic incident had occurred, I could see there was a guy sat on the roof of a car in the adjoining road. He was casually sipping from a bottle of beer and, once I got close enough to observe his facial features, I instantly recognised him. This chap was known to police, and was one of the most violent adversaries that resided in our town – in fact, he was the same nutcase who'd only recently been released from prison after committing a series of unprovoked assaults on unsuspecting members of the public. He had a string of convictions for committing violent offences, including ABH and GBH, and had received this particular custodial sentence for indiscriminately punching seven people in the face (six men and one woman) for no apparent reason, other than they'd happened to walk by him in the street. I also knew he hated the police, and it was a loathing that frequently manifested itself in extreme violence towards any officer who happened to cross his path. Indeed, as indicated, he could be aggressive towards anyone with whom he came into contact if he took a dislike to them.

The minute I'd spotted this well-known convicted criminal in close proximity of the address I was about to visit, I instinctively knew his presence was likely to be more than pure coincidence – and there would almost certainly be a connection to the domestic incident I'd been directed to attend. An urgent radio call, telling me to wait for assistance before approaching the vicinity, ominously confirmed my suspicion was justified. Control had received an update about the nature of the domestic and, more importantly, the parties involved – which included the person I'd already spotted, who was known to have psychotic episodes and, as stressed, tended to be exceptionally violent.

I rapidly explained that I'd already got wind of the situation, and was aware of this person's presence at the scene because I'd observed him whilst walking towards the location of the domestic – and, more to the point, he'd already eyeballed me as I'd neared the address (as it's not really feasible to keep a low profile when you're in uniform!). This news caused considerable consternation in the control room, and I was further instructed not to approach him under any circumstances. However, I had to advise it was too late for me to back off because I was already at the scene and a retreat at this stage would not be feasible – so I'd appreciate some backup as a matter of urgency.

I knew something about the history of the chap I was about to confront, who could pose a serious threat to my wellbeing – not least that he would be agitated and exhibiting obvious signs of his mental disorder if he was off his meds. I was also aware that whenever he came into contact with anyone from police or prison circles, he would go through the ritual of offering to shake hands. This was definitely not because he wanted to be friendly, and adhere to one of the usual social graces you'd observe when meeting someone. It was actually because he was known for the disgusting habit of wiping his own faeces over cell walls, or even the rooms of his own dwelling place when he was completely out of it, and realised that police or prison officers would be disinclined to accept such an offer! In essence, it was a form of deliberate baiting to see how an officer would react. Knowing this was his party trick, I therefore managed to discreetly slip on my police issue gloves as I approached him, which I conveniently had in my pocket, even though it was the height of summer.

Just as I anticipated, my prospective adversary did indeed greet my arrival by gesturing to shake hands and, not wanting to rile him by rejecting his offer, I cautiously obliged. Luckily, he seemed to be unusually chilled and in a world of his own, most likely due to the affects of an illegal substance, or the alcohol he'd been consuming, and didn't notice I was somewhat oddly wearing gloves on a warm summer's day. He gave the distinct impression he was impervious to what was going on, and that any trouble I was there to investigate was nothing to do with him. This suited me fine as I knew I had to keep things calm and remain vigilant until I got some assistance. I was in no fit state for rough and tumble, and taking on such a formidable assailant with my bad back wasn't something I relished. Besides, I knew perfectly well that trying to restrain him on my own would be more or less impossible – and something I'd have been unlikely to achieve even if fully fit. In the circumstances, I soon worked out that this was definitely one of those occasions where discretion was the better part of valour. However, although the last thing I wanted to do was lock horns with him if it could be avoided, I also realised it wasn't within my gift to dictate the terms, and that I may have no choice but to get in a tussle if he chose to turn nasty.

Once I'd accepted his welcoming handshake gesture, I then explained that I just needed to briefly make an enquiry at a nearby address – but, at that stage, I deliberately didn't tell him why, and simply said I would return shortly to have a word with him. I made a mental note to wash my gloves at the earliest opportunity, and then made my way to the house where the domestic had reportedly taken place. Upon my arrival, I soon discovered I vaguely knew the couple living at this abode, and that the disturbance they'd reported to the police had no direct connection to them. Furthermore, they were able to confirm my fear that the incident involved the villainous thug I'd encountered loitering on the car roof. In fact, his mother was being harboured at this couple's home after she'd escaped from her own house and come to seek refuge. Their respective rear gardens backed onto each other, and the distressed mother had arrived at the couple's back door after scaling the fence to get away from her son following a row, which had culminated in him threatening her with violence. In spite of his threats and his violent track record, she declined to press charges against her son, and simply told me she wanted him to leave the house and go back to his hostel.

Back then it was difficult to justify an arrest without a complaint being made by the victim, so that tied my hands in regard to any action I could take. Next, I called up control to update them on the situation, and also to check the whereabouts of my backup. I was relieved to hear that the regular officer on standby to assist us with any serious incidents was en route and due to arrive any minute. Following this update, I advised the occupants of the house to lock themselves and the mother inside while we dealt with the lady's son, and tried to persuade him to return to his hostel. I then joined my full-time colleague upon his arrival, so I could update him on the background to the domestic and agree our collaborative approach before we jointly spoke to the alleged aggressor.

Much to my amazement, upon doing so he was compliant and agreed to his mother's request that he vacate the family home and return to his hostel; although I'm not sure if it was much to do with our powers of persuasion. I think it was more to do with him being on a drug or alcohol-induced high, as he didn't seem to know what planet he was on, let alone where he lived. Anyway, whatever the reason for his better nature on this occasion, we were simply pleased we'd been able to defuse and resolve a delicate and tricky situation without things turning ugly, especially as we knew his demeanour could change in a flash.

Once he'd departed from the scene, my full-time colleague was able to revert back to being on standby, whilst I was able to resume my patrol – and, shortly afterwards, I got a message from the control room operator. He apologised for sending me solo to a potentially volatile situation but, as I pointed out, there was no way he could have known this was the case at the time. When the initial call had come in, the person reporting the incident had understandably given their own home address, not that of the complainant under threat, who had taken refuge with them after fleeing via her back garden. Therefore, since the caller actually lived in a different street to the one where the offender's mother resided (whose address would have had a warning marker flagging it as high risk), it was easy to appreciate why it would not have initially raised suspicion, or given undue cause for concern. The risk posed by this individual had only become apparent following a further call from another concerned neighbour, who lived next door to the victim. In turn, this had caused alarm in the control room and resulted in backup being immediately despatched to assist me. Ultimately, I was just grateful I'd received support before things turned nasty, and come through the incident unscathed; although this event did act as a reminder that my regular colleagues have to face this type of situation day in day out.

My next port of call was to a house occupied by several vulnerable adults who experienced a variety of learning difficulties. The residents had encountered some trouble with a group of youths, so I'd been sent to investigate as the location was again on my plot. Those in residence at this abode had recently moved to their communal dwelling, following the launch of a new 'care in the community' strategy. This programme had been introduced to facilitate the integration of people with learning disabilities into their local communities and, as part of this new approach, they had acquired far more independence; however, it appeared that some local youths had decided they could perhaps exploit this situation to their advantage.

Upon my arrival at the complainants' home, I discovered that a small group of young lads had thrown a stink bomb into their house causing panic stations. At first, it appeared this could be a simple case of youngsters misbehaving and requiring a good ticking off, but there was actually more to it than one might have reasonably assumed. After speaking to the residents, it became clear the lads in question were known to them, and had effectively been demanding money in payment for 'essential supplies' they had allegedly delivered to this address. From what I was able to glean, it seemed that the stink bomb had been lobbed into the house in retaliation because the residents had refused to pay the bill. However, from the explanation I obtained from the residents, I couldn't really work out whether they had actually ordered and received these items and genuinely owed money for them. It was possible they had unwittingly done so, without realising the implications. Equally, it was also perfectly feasible these youths were just taking advantage of the residents, due to their lack of mental agility – and could well be claiming payment under false pretences, or even demanding money with menaces.

In the circumstances, I wasn't anticipating a quick fix, especially if this was indeed some form of demanding money through false representation. I didn't have much to go on to help me carry out an investigation, largely because the residents were unable to give me a detailed description of those responsible for the alleged intimidation – even though they were supposedly known to them. Nonetheless, I did try to track down the youths who'd been terrorising them, so I could get their side of the story and deal with them in respect of their threatening behaviour. This initially proved to be unsuccessful, despite me searching the surrounding the area. At that stage, I therefore thought the only thing I'd be able to usefully do was provide the victims with plenty of reassurance, by giving their address passing attention throughout the remainder of my shift. However, then I got lucky.

I decided to make a speculative enquiry at a local grocery store, on the off chance the residents might have ordered some goods from this shop – and voila! The owner was able to confirm this was the case, although he hadn't personally dealt with them and had no idea they experienced learning disabilities. On finding this out, and then hearing about the plight these unwitting customers had endured at the hands of the young lads – who turned out to be this store's weekend delivery boys – the shop boss agreed to waive the cost of any items they'd received. He was a decent man, and appreciated they'd ordered them without fully comprehending the financial consequence of doing so.

Next, the shopkeeper directed me to the lads responsible for trying to get payment using intimidatory means, including the despicable act involving the stink bomb. I reprimanded them for their unacceptable behaviour, and made it clear they'd been totally out of order, even though the residents technically owed money for the goods in question. As part of this process, I also pointed out that in due course an officer would be visiting each of their respective parents to bring this matter to their attention.

Thankfully, the rest of my shift passed by without me having to confront anything too threatening or problematic; although, in between dealing with a couple of minor matters relating to lost property, I did have to contend with a rather strange allegation of assault made by one of my traffic warden colleagues. In regard to this incident, the traffic warden was incensed because a florist had thrown a bucket of dirty water towards him, just as he'd passed the flower shop's doorway. His trousers had been soaked, and the victim of this dousing was sure it had been a deliberate act on the part of the proprietor. Therefore, when I arrived to investigate, he wanted him arrested for common assault.

As soon as I identified the florist, I had no doubt the complainant was probably right in his assertion that the water thrower's action had been intentional. The guy was not only a known drug user, who had a tendency to be anti-establishment, but also someone with a history of being hostile towards traffic wardens. However, despite this, I also knew it would be hard to prove he had deliberately thrown the water at my colleague, especially when he pleaded his innocence and declared it had been a complete accident. He explained that he'd been washing the shop floor and, once he'd finished, he'd as per usual thrown the water out of his shop doorway towards a drain that's sited in the gutter running parallel to the pavement. In his defence, he claimed he'd done so without realising someone was in his line of fire, and it had been an unfortunate coincidence that the traffic warden had walked by at the very second he'd deposited the water.

I knew this was a 'likely story', but realised a charge of common assault was never going to stick in these circumstances, so arresting him for committing such an offence would be futile. The best I could do was warn him about his behaviour and give him suitable words of advice about his irresponsible action, including that he needed to be more careful in future. I also persuaded him to begrudgingly apologise to my colleague, even though I knew there would be no genuine conviction in his apology – bearing in mind it was coming from someone who frequently verbalised his distaste for anyone in authority. Taking everything into account, my colleague acknowledged my hands were tied and, therefore, grudgingly accepted the meaningless apology that was full of hollow words, before trudging off to the station to change out of his wet garments.

The next couple of times we took over running boroughs in my Division they were both away from my home town, and nothing quite as hair-raising happened in comparison to the domestic that featured during my first such exercise. However, within my team, I did always seem to be the special constable that encountered the most challenging situations to deal with once I was out on the beat. The second occasion I took part in one of these operations, I immediately witnessed a collision involving three vehicles. It occurred right in front of me when I was no more than 50 yards from the police station, so naturally I was the first officer at the scene. Although it wasn't too serious, being a non-injury accident, it still required a lot of work to sort everything out and I had no choice but to get stuck in. By the time I'd organised for the damaged vehicles to be removed, arranged for all the drivers to be breathalysed, checked documents, taken all the statements and compiled an accident report, my eight-hour tour of duty was virtually up – and I'd spent most of it either in the police station or in close proximity, mainly on the road just outside its perimeter!

The third time I was involved in a takeover exercise, the start of my duty wasn't dissimilar to my previous experiences, in terms of me once more being required to attend an incident early on during my shift. On this occasion it was a night duty, and I was paired up with another special constable to undertake foot patrol of the town centre. Before we'd even made it that far, one of the Division's 'jam sandwich' cars came screeching to a halt beside us and the driver, who was an inspector in the Road Traffic department, requested we jump in and accompany him to a brawl, which had broken out at a night-club in a neighbouring town. We duly complied, and went with him to assist local officers, who were struggling to get the situation under control and needed all available hands on deck.

By the time we arrived on scene about five minutes later, the situation had started to calm down and we weren't desperately needed, so the inspector apologised for unnecessarily dragging us away from our beat; however, with it being a chilly winter's evening, neither of us had any objections about getting a ride in the traffic car instead of pounding the beat in the cold. Besides, it wasn't a complete waste of our time as we were asked to remain in the area for a while in case trouble flared up again.

In addition to these types of takeover exercises, members of the Special Constabulary were also used to carry out designated assignments aimed at meeting a specific objective; for example, crime prevention operations or targeting particular criminal activities and localised problems.

One such deployment involved policing an area in town that had been experiencing a significant amount of anti-social behaviour. It was a Saturday evening in the height of summer and I was part of a detail, consisting of four special constables, who'd been requested to patrol the streets between the town's main nightclub and the Market Place. We were there in response to complaints from residents about the unruly behaviour of some of the clubbers, especially when they were leaving the venue. Our specific mission involved undertaking foot patrols in the area to combat any acts of anti-social behaviour, including shouting, swearing and criminal damage. Along with me in the team were my volunteer colleagues Spud, Mike and Katie – a relative novice. We split into pairs – with me joining forces with Mike, and Spud accompanying Katie – and duly spent the initial part of our shift patrolling the area where the problems outlined were likely to occur. Nothing much happened early on but, around 2300hrs, which back then was chucking-out time for the pubs, we were alerted to a disturbance in close proximity, which warranted our attention – and, ultimately, this proved to be a situation that led to me making my first solo arrest.

Mike and I were just making our way back up the town's steepest hill, which ran from the Market Place towards the location of the nightclub, when we heard someone shouting and swearing somewhere near the top of the incline. As we made our way towards the noisy reveller, I radioed Spud and Katie to check their whereabouts. They'd also heard the shouting and were heading to the area it was coming from, but were approaching from the opposite end of the road to Mike and I. This effectively meant we could implement a pincer movement, and would have all four of us on hand to deal with the situation if it proved necessary.

Upon reaching the brow of the hill, Mike and I could see the person responsible for the rowdy behaviour; a tall, well-built young man that I'd dealt with before. He was very unsteady on his feet and, as he stumbled along he was bouncing off shop windows each time he lost his balance; meaning there was a high risk he could smash through a plate glass window and do himself some serious harm, as well as cause criminal damage. As he wandered towards us, he was also singing at the top of his voice – it was just about recognisable as a well-known Tina Turner number, but I was not familiar with the version he was singing because it was interspersed with a range of swear words!

Once we got close enough to speak with the budding pop star, I blocked his path to prevent him from bumping into any more windows, and then politely asked him to stop the singing and swearing. I explained that his behaviour was far too raucous for that time of night, especially in a residential area where people were trying to sleep, but I could tell immediately that my words of advice were falling on deaf ears. He became abusive and let rip with a barrage of choice words, so I again tried to calm things down by asking him to lower his voice and stop swearing. However, he had no intention of obeying my polite request and instead barged me out of his way and told me to 'f… off'! In view of his recalcitrant behaviour, I therefore had no alternative but to arrest him for being drunk and disorderly. There was no way he going to come quietly, and he immediately started to grapple with me as I attempted to get him under control and take him into custody; fortunately though, with immediate help on hand from my three colleagues, I was soon able to restrain him, put on handcuffs and call up for transport to ship him back to the station.

In spite of his drunken state, our prisoner seemed to settle down whilst we awaited the arrival of the police vehicle – and then, as soon as it arrived, he kicked off and again became an awkward, belligerent cuss. The PC and our sergeant, who had turned up with the police car, got out to assist when our drunken prisoner refused to get into the back seat and, during the ensuing struggle, the detainee somehow managed to trap my left elbow in the rear door, causing me considerable pain. Adrenalin got me through it at the time, and between us we were eventually able to manhandle him into the vehicle, whereupon he continued to wrestle with the sergeant and me during our trip back to the police station, despite being shackled in handcuffs. Then, once more his behaviour and mood changed when we arrived at the nick, and he became more malleable as I booked him in with the custody sergeant.

By this stage, he seemed resigned to the fact he would be spending a night in the cells to reflect on his unacceptable actions and, ultimately, a day in court to face a charge of being drunk and disorderly. My sergeant was also keen to add assault on police to the charge-sheet, but I was apprehensive about doing so because I wasn't convinced he'd deliberately caused me harm by catching my elbow in the car door. I appreciated he'd been aggressive towards us, and it was probably one of those borderline cases but, knowing I wasn't comfortable with making such an allegation, the sergeant agreed not to pursue the additional charge. However, as my left elbow was swollen and I was having some mobility issues, he did insist that I went to hospital for a check-up, so I reluctantly complied with his request. As hoped, the X-ray showed there was no break. I'd primarily suffered severe bruising as a result of the trauma, along with some temporary soft tissue and nerve damage that was affecting my movement. That aside, I was fine.

At his subsequent court appearance, our rowdy night-time reveller pleaded guilty to being drunk and disorderly and was duly fined for the offence. I didn't think anymore about the incident until it was reported on in the local press; whereupon it embarrassingly stated the offender had slammed the arresting officer's arm in the police car's door during the course of his duty. That simply wasn't correct and, in my view, the reporter had embellished what really happened. Presumably this was to sensationalise the story by making it sound somewhat worse than it was. Reading it made me even more relieved that my so-called assailant hadn't been unfairly charged with assault.

My embarrassment at being in the local news was further compounded when I was then 'mentioned in despatches', along with my fellow special constables who'd been present when the incident occurred. The citation, written by our superintendent and published in Divisional Orders, specifically commended me for my prompt and positive action in making the arrest.

Although the last thing I wanted was any sort of recognition for effectively performing my duty as a volunteer bobby, I could see why the bosses wanted to make a big thing of it from their perspective – and therefore ensured that details of the citation were also conveniently leaked to the press. I guess for them it gave out a strong message on two counts; firstly, to the small element of unruly clubbers who were causing grief to those living in the neighbourhood that such behaviour wouldn't be tolerated – and, secondly, to residents that the police were taking positive steps to address the problem. However, from my point of view, I just wanted to stay anonymous and get on with my duties in the background, as opposed to being in the limelight. This was also the case when an arrest I made whilst off-duty a few years later hit the headlines, and even attracted interest from the national press. It's a story I will elaborate upon further in the next chapter.

14 When Duty Calls

IF YOU ARE INVOLVED IN ANY TYPE of law enforcement role and sign up to keep the peace, then technically you are never off-duty – and there are inevitably times when you'll come across serious situations whilst you are not officially on duty, where you will feel compelled to do something. However, you have to be selective, and it's vitally important you learn to differentiate between situations when's it's necessary to step in and take action, and those that can be ignored. There have been several occasions when the former of these options applied, and I felt I had no choice but to act, even though I appreciated that intervention in such circumstances can sometimes mean risking your own personal safety. As a result, I was always a little uneasy about getting involved when faced with something of this nature – especially as you never knew how soon backup would arrive once you'd placed yourself in jeopardy. One such occasion when this type of scenario arose was back in the early 1990's, shortly after I'd become a married man.

I was just leaving home in my car around 8pm for an evening out with my recently betrothed, when I noticed a man in his early 20's striding purposefully across the parking lot located at the rear of my abode, and heading towards the back gate of a neighbour's house. He was someone I recognised immediately and seeing him gave me cause for concern, not only because he already had a string of convictions for various acts of criminality, but also because he was the same guy I'd had several confrontations with in the past. These included the incident when my arm got 'accidentally' shut in the police car door. Since that clash, I'd had a few more run-ins with him and his level of anti-social behaviour and violence had worsened considerably. In many respects, he'd become a constant thorn in my side; whilst I'd possibly become his nemesis.

My suspicions were instantly aroused when I spotted him, so I therefore suggested to my wife it would be wise if we briefly hung around to see what happened, just in case he was up to no good. I didn't explain the reasons for my concern, but I was conscious that the address this man had headed towards was the home of a young woman who'd recently been threatened by someone matching this guy's description. Neither did I mention it was a concern that the police deemed serious enough to warrant fitting an intruder alarm to her property. Clearly, if this was the chap who'd been harassing the young mother living in close proximity to myself, then he posed a serious threat and the woman was in danger – and I didn't have long to wait to have this confirmed.

Shortly after he'd disappeared through the back gate of the young woman's house, there was the sound of breaking glass – followed by a lot of commotion, including the noise of the intruder alarm ringing loudly. The minute I heard glass smashing I jumped into action, and ran to my next-door neighbour's house. I asked him to call 999 and report the disturbance taking place at the nearby house – and also to request urgent assistance! Next, I went to investigate what was going on at the house that was under attack.

As I neared the property, I first spotted the lady of the house leaning out of a bedroom window screaming for help. Once she saw me approaching, she shouted that an intruder had broken in via the back door and attacked her boyfriend, who happened to be visiting at the time. She looked petrified, and went on to tell me that as soon as the intruder had burst in she'd run upstairs and barricaded herself into her bedroom, along with her two terrified children – leaving her boyfriend to confront the uninvited visitor. Knowing there was no time to lose, I hastily made my way up the garden path towards the rear of the house belonging to the distressed lady, wondering exactly what challenges and sights would greet me on my arrival.

I'm neither fearless nor gung-ho, and this was one of those situations where you are torn between self-preservation and doing the right thing. Whenever you are going to be putting yourself in the firing line and encountering danger, you naturally feel some degree of trepidation and have to overcome the urge to just walk away or turn a blind eye, and that's when you learn which category you fit into – freeze, flight or fight! All your natural instincts tell you not to put yourself in harms way but, as you wrestle with the dilemma about whether you should intervene or not, the fear you feel can be overridden by the desire to protect your fellow beings. For me, I guess that was the driving force whenever I was faced with situations where I could be putting myself in peril, even though I dislike confrontation and try to avoid it. However, I would never judge or criticise anyone who chooses not to do so and, when one of my special constable colleagues decided he couldn't hack it, and chose to jack it in after being sent to a fight during his first duty, I totally understood and sympathised with his sentiment. Police work's not for everyone and clearly wasn't his forte.

Once I reached the open back door, which had been forcibly kicked in, and warily walked into the kitchen, I came across two men still grappling. One was the intruder, whilst the other was presumably the boyfriend – who had clearly fared worse in the fight so far, based on the wounds to his face. He was bleeding profusely from both a cut to his lip and a gash above his right eye, but was bravely and steadfastly blocking the path of his fearsome assailant to prevent him from getting beyond the kitchen. Immediately upon seeing me, the intruder came away from the boyfriend, and acknowledged my arrival on the scene by somewhat oddly saying to the victim of his unprovoked attack:

'It's ok mate, he's police'.

His strange comment sounded as though he was trying to make it appear that the boyfriend was at fault and the cause of the disorder, rather than himself. From my perspective, I was just pleased that the fighting had ceased and, now they were separated, I could focus on getting the intruder under control before he did anymore harm. I knew this guy could be a tricky customer, so my initial aim was to get him as far away from the house as possible to put some distance between him and the occupants. Therefore, rather than arrest him straightaway and perhaps antagonise him, I decided it would make sense if I could coax him outside into the back garden of the property so he could tell me 'his side of the story'. At first he was compliant but, after I'd talked him into accompanying me to the bottom of the garden, the situation suddenly deteriorated and he became increasingly threatening in his manner.

Even though being diplomatic is one of my strengths, and I can sometimes be an effective negotiator when trying to defuse volatile situations, I soon realised that attempting to keep him calm through words alone in his emotional state was likely to be a non-starter. Consequently, I made an early decision that I couldn't rely solely on my persuasive charm to win him over, and needed to get the upper hand by being assertive. Somehow, I managed to manoeuvre myself into a position where I was able to get him into a bear-hug and, once I'd done so, I held on for dear life as he struggled to get out of the restraint I'd placed on him. He was much bigger than me and it took all my strength to hold on, but I was determined not to let go – and, while I was doing so, I also kept trying to talk him around. This seemed to work to some extent because his anger and resistance came in waves. One minute he would be really stroppy, but that could change in a flash as his aggression subsided. At one point, he even apologised for his behaviour and became distraught at the prospect he'd be returning to prison due to his transgression. As he bemoaned the fact he would likely face being incarcerated once more, I couldn't help but think of that old adage, 'if you can't do the time, don't commit the crime'

Given his capricious behaviour, I had to be ultra-careful not to relax to my grip on him whenever he showed signs of contrition, and appeared resigned to his fate. In that regard, his fluctuating mood certainly tested my resolve to the limit, and he nearly caught me off guard on a couple of occasions when he reverted back to being recalcitrant and aggressive. This was definitely the case when my next-door neighbour turned up with his broom in hand to clear up the broken glass, and came over to check whether I needed any help keeping him restrained. He took real exception to this offer, and I had to be resolute to maintain control when he almost managed to force his way out of my grip.

It was about 10 minutes before two regulars (Ricky and Malcolm) arrived to assist me, but it felt like a lot longer. Apparently, at the time they got the call, they were heading out to a local village to do an enquiry, and had to quickly make their way back to attend the incident. As they were the only officers on duty in the vicinity that evening, I was fortunate to get help as rapidly as I did.

The longer I'd been alone with my prisoner in such an emotionally charged and volatile state, the more precarious my position had become, so I was relieved to finally have some support; although, in some respects, he became even more violent and obstructive once they arrived on scene. He resisted our attempts to walk him to the police car and, even though we were able to over-power him, it became necessary to actually drag him along as he kicked out and gave us a volley of abuse. During his tirade he made threats to kill, aimed mostly at me – and, by the time we'd reached the police vehicle, we knew there was no way he was going to get in without a struggle. Our prediction proved correct, and he did everything he could to stop us getting him in the car. At one stage, his resistance even caused us to all fall against a garden fence and bring it tumbling down. Finally, after much pushing and shoving, we achieved our objective and he was able to be transported to the local nick, where he continued to shout about how he was going to exact his revenge the next time he encountered any of us – and I think his precise words were:

'Next time I see you I'm going to punch your f...ing lights out!'

The main target of his verbal abuse was still my good self, but I didn't take it too personally as I knew it was chiefly aimed at the police in general due to his loathing of anyone connected with law enforcement.

After all the kafuffle, I then had to spend the rest of the evening writing up my statement and, by the time I got home, it was gone midnight and my bed was beckoning – so my wife never did get her night out on that occasion.

Whilst I'd been at the police station doing the paperwork, I'd learned more about the background to the situation I'd ended up dealing with earlier that evening, and the link between the two parties. I discovered the lad we had in custody, following his intrusion at my neighbour's house, had reputedly met the neighbour (a single mum) at a nightclub a couple of months earlier, and had been completely smitten by her – even though they'd never really embarked on a relationship. On the night they'd originally met she'd invited him in for coffee after he'd walked her home; a decision she had good reason to regret. Clearly, this lad had interpreted her invitation as a green light to make his move on her, but she'd apparently spurned his advances after deciding she didn't want to take her involvement with him any further. I was informed that although he'd only just met this young woman, he'd already become besotted with her and hadn't taken this rejection well. Initially, he'd pleaded with her to give him a chance, but when she'd again rebuffed him, he'd become threatening towards her. He'd then gone on to start a campaign of harassment – hence the intruder alarm – which had ultimately culminated in me coming to her rescue, and reluctantly being viewed as her knight in shining armour.

My intervention that fateful evening left me feeling a little apprehensive for a while because the offender had threatened to seek vengeance for the part I'd played in apprehending him. Receiving threats isn't that unusual when you're engaged in police work, and it's something that goes with the territory, which you learn to expect and accept – so, normally, I wouldn't have been too worried. In this instance though, it was slightly different because the intruder now knew roughly where I lived. I therefore half-expected a brick to come hurtling through a window any moment over the next few days. Thankfully, that didn't happen during the immediate aftermath, which was just as well because it would have been so unfair if my actions had somehow impacted on my wife and put her in danger.

Once the defendant had appeared in court several weeks later, and pleaded guilty to forced entry and assault causing actual bodily harm (ABH), for which he received a six-month prison sentence, I thought that was the end of the matter and didn't think much more about it. However, I suddenly got a call from the Chief Constable's office about three months after the incident, informing me my actions that evening were going to be formally recognised, and I would be receiving a 'letter of thanks' directly from the man at the top. It was humbling to learn that the hierarchy saw me as this distressed woman's saviour, and thought my intervention warranted some form of commendation. Despite this, I still wasn't convinced that what I did made me worthy of such adulation, or think I deserved the accolade they wanted to bestow on me – even more so when they told me they'd be making a press release to coincide with the letter being issued and presented. The thought of this placing me in the public eye filled me with dread. It was scarier than actually dealing with the incident – as I'm not the type of person who seeks notoriety or likes to be the centre of attention. Besides, I couldn't help feeling there are so many unsung heroes out there who regularly perform genuine acts of bravery and merit recognition far more than me.

Although I've always been protective towards my family, friends and anyone who is vulnerable and at risk of being exploited or abused, I don't consider myself to be brave, and the last thing I wanted was a lot of fuss. To make matters worse, the whole situation seemed to escalate as soon as I'd been presented with the letter. The media really went to town on the story and totally over the top when my actions made headline news in our local rag. Some of the regional newspapers described my intervention as some sort of heroic act, which it truly wasn't. All I did was the same as any police officer or upstanding citizen would do in such circumstances. There were even some national papers and radio stations that decided to get in on the act, so I had no chance of avoiding publicity and keeping a low profile once they'd jumped on the bandwagon. In fact, their exaggerated portrayal of my actions made it even more embarrassing for me – and a little disconcerting for my wife, considering the offender had threatened to avenge his arrest.

With the press now prominently displaying lots of personal information about me, and drawing even more attention to the part I'd played in taking away this intruder's freedom, I very much appreciated this could have repercussions, especially for my wife if he targeted my house once he was released from prison. Whilst I knew the offender's ranting about getting even had likely been an idle threat, I didn't see the sense of doing anything to possibly provoke him. Therefore, I resisted the attempts of some reporters to make it into an even bigger story by declining to be interviewed or have my picture taken. I felt this could make me appear to be some sort of glory seeker who enjoyed having his details splashed all over the newspaper, which was definitely not my intention or desire. Additionally, I refused to have a photo taken with my wife at the letter presentation, as I feared this could be used in the wrong way for publicity purposes, and perhaps make her more vulnerable by highlighting her link to me.

This all makes me sound like I was getting a bit paranoid and being overly cautious and protective but, in my view, that certainly wasn't the case. These were abnormal circumstances, and taking reasonable precautions seemed like the sensible thing to do. It might sound like a contradiction in terms, but I think a police officer is somehow less identifiable and exposed when performing their duties in uniform, even though they are more conspicuous. This is because most people probably see the uniform rather than the person wearing it. However, when you are dealing with something whilst dressed in civvies, your anonymity is compromised because you can no longer readily hide behind the uniform.

It is the individual person that's recognised – thus making your identity more palpable, and potentially putting you at greater risk of reprisal.

Anyway, I'm glad to report that there were no acts of retaliation inflicted on me, my wife or our property and, as time passed, any concerns soon evaporated; so we were then able to focus on cementing our relationship as a newly married couple. Mind you, that proved to be more of a challenge than either of us had anticipated and, within four years, our marriage was on the rocks and we were separated – not that I can in any way blame that outcome on the events that occurred after my off-duty arrest of the intruder. I suspect it was more to do with me not living up to her expectations; perhaps, not least, because when one of my fellow officer's told her I was affectionately known in police circles as a hobby bobby she might have misheard, and thought he said nobby bobby – which was not an expectation I met!

Many years after this particular event, I bumped into the intruder involved in this incident quite by chance in a local sports bar and he seemed to be a reformed character. Based on what he told me and his manner, which was much more subdued and conciliatory compared to his previous aggressive nature, it appeared he was no longer involved in criminal activities, had renounced violence and now lived a peaceful life with his family whilst earning an honest crust. This news came as a nice surprise because I always felt he lacked the quintessential moral fibre needed to go straight. Considering all the trouble he had caused me in the past, it was therefore good to know that maybe prison works for some, and it's even possible for a habitual offender to turn their life around – albeit, it had taken him until middle-age to recognise the error of his ways and do something about it!

During my 22 years of service, I recall there were about half-a-dozen other memorable occasions when I felt obliged to intervene while off-duty. One of these instances occurred when I was returning home in my car with some friends, following a night out in a nearby city, and spotted a couple of lads acting suspiciously outside a telephone box, which had clearly been vandalised. Amongst my friends in the car was Cassie, a police cadet. Cassie was a gem of a person, who was based at my local police station, and their behaviour had also aroused her suspicion. We both thought it was likely these lads could have been responsible for the vandalism, and we therefore decided to pull over to enquire whether they knew anything about the damage to the kiosk.

The two lads started to casually walk away in the opposite direction as we approached them but, once I'd announced I was an off-duty special constable and Cassie was a police cadet, and we just wanted a quiet word, they seemed happy to acquiesce with my request and, surprisingly, didn't attempt to run off. I explained that we'd noticed the telephone kiosk had been vandalised, and wondered whether they happened to know anything about it? As we'd not actually witnessed them doing anything wrong, I didn't want to sound too accusatory and, therefore, chose my words carefully when I questioned them about the damage. They completely denied knowing anything about it, and one of them stated that the call box had already been smashed up when they'd arrived at the kiosk with the intention of using it. So, at that stage, it was apparent that any evidence we had to take matters further was tenuous, and I was tempted to send them on their way without further ado, even though I sensed they'd probably been responsible for the vandalism. However, there was one little thing still niggling me.

I'd noticed that the lad who was taking the lead had a slight bulge under his anorak in the area of his midriff, and appeared to be clutching his stomach as though he was holding something, which seemed a bit odd. Without any concrete evidence to suggest something had been taken from the kiosk, I wasn't sure I had the power to insist on searching him; so, knowing that wasn't a clear cut option, I instead chose to nonchalantly enquire what he had under his anorak. Initially he made out there was nothing there but, after I'd lightly tapped the area of the bulge and felt something solid in that region, he changed his story, and tried to make out it was a bottle of booze he was taking to a party. I remarked if that was so, then he should have no problem showing me the bottle to put my mind at rest. At that point, he obviously realised the game was up and gingerly unzipped his anorak – and, low and behold, it wasn't a bottle of booze he revealed but an old-style telephone, which had clearly been ripped out from the kiosk.

Despite the incriminating evidence in his possession, he still attempted to deflect the blame for the vandalism away from himself and his mate by again suggesting the kiosk was already damaged when they arrived. As things stood, I still didn't have any hard evidence to prove otherwise, even though I knew this was likely a continuation of his cock and bull story. However, I had another offence up my sleeve that I could challenge them about because taking the phone could technically be classed as theft. I therefore cautioned the lad in possession, at which point he claimed he had only taken it as a souvenir – which was tantamount to admitting he was stealing it!

Rather than arrest the pair of them on suspicion of criminal damage or theft at that juncture, I instead decided to take their details so further investigations could ensue, and confiscate the phone as possible evidence. I thought this would make sense as I recognised the lead suspect and already knew his name. I also knew he was currently dating one of our sergeant's daughters, and it was going to be embarrassing for Cassie and I telling our colleague about this lad's suspected involvement in criminal activity. In fairness, when we did so, he took the news very philosophically and dealt with it as a true professional. He even got the lad and his accomplice to admit to the act of criminal damage. No charges were brought against either party in respect of theft but, when the criminal damage case went to court, both suspects pleaded guilty and were given conditional discharges. However, to compound the embarrassment for Cassie and I in regard to this matter, the magistrates did commend our actions, and compliment us on the tenacity we had shown in bringing the culprits to justice.

There was another occasion when I had to deal with a situation whilst driving home in the early hours following a night out, no more than a couple of weeks after this encounter with the two vandals. This time the incident I came across was a hit-and-run collision, where a pedestrian had been left prostrate in the middle of the road after being struck by a vehicle. I did well not to run over him again because, in the dark, I didn't see him lying there until the last second and only just managed to stop in time. The accident had occurred just on the brow of the hill near the town centre and, once I got out of my vehicle and approached the victim, a man in his thirties, I could tell he was in a really bad way. It appeared to me that whoever had knocked him down must have driven off knowing they were leaving the victim seriously injured or possibly dead.

I assumed I was the first person on the scene following the hit-and-run, and therefore the accident hadn't yet been reported to the emergency services. Consequently, I got one of my friends, who I'd been transporting home, to run to the nearest phone box to make a 999 call requesting an ambulance and the police.

The guy who'd been hit was covered in a combination of blood and oil, and it looked as though a vehicle had driven right over him. He was out cold, and as I checked for vital signs of life I thought there was every possibility he could already be deceased. I couldn't find a pulse and, if the victim was breathing, it was too faint to detect, so I decided CPR would probably be in order.

Before administering mouth-to-mouth resuscitation, I first placed him on his back, tilted his head backwards and checked his airway for any obstructions. While doing so, there was a gurgling noise and blood suddenly started to spurt out from his mouth. It came gushing out like a fountain – making me even more convinced he was a goner. Relieved I hadn't already started giving mouth-to-mouth, I instead focused on doing chest compressions, once I'd moved his head to one side – like you do when you're placing someone in the recovery position – to hopefully prevent him from choking on his own blood. I knew that if the bleeding did subside, then giving him mouth-to-mouth would be essential. This wasn't a prospect I relished, especially as I didn't have my plastic mouth-protector with me, which is designed for the purpose of preventing direct contact with a patient's lips when you administer this procedure. Before I got to that stage however, one of my full-time police colleagues and an ambulance thankfully arrived, probably within a minute or so of me starting to do chest compressions. I was therefore able to hand over to them, and then head home to clean myself up.

When I checked up on the casualty the next day, I was certain I'd discover this poor chap had died of his multiple injuries but, much to my amazement, I learned he'd survived and was doing really well. I also found out that I knew the injured party – a likeable rogue who'd often had dealings with the police – although, due to him having been covered in blood and oil when I'd come upon him the previous night, I'd had no idea he was someone with whom I was familiar. Anyway, I was delighted to learn that our fantastic colleagues in the NHS had been able to stem the profuse flow of blood, which had actually been emerging from his mouth due to a tear in an artery located in his throat – and, that following surgery, he'd now regained consciousness. The prognosis for him ultimately making a full recovery was also looking positive.

When the victim was fit enough to be interviewed about the incident, he declared that he couldn't remember the events of that night or recall what had happened – and the driver responsible for the hit-and-run was never traced. Intriguingly however, I did hear many years later that in regard to this so-called accident there was a real twist to the situation, which nobody had even considered at the time.

According to local gossip circulating long afterwards, our injured party had always known exactly who'd been responsible for running him down on that ill-fated night, and it certainly hadn't been accidental! Rumours were rife that it had likely been a case of attempted murder, and the victim had actually been targeted by a disgruntled husband, who was hellbent on seeking revenge after finding out about a steamy affair between this guy and his wife. If that was so, then our injured party was determined to keep it close to his chest and not reveal what really happened because the full facts never did emerge. He always stuck rigidly to his original story that he had no recollection of the incident or the events leading up to it. Without a detailed account from the horse's mouth, the only evidence available to the police was at best hearsay. This meant it would be virtually impossible to conduct a meaningful and thorough investigation to track down and charge the person responsible for nearly causing a fatality. Regrettably therefore, nobody was ever brought to justice in relation to this matter, even though the offence the driver had committed could well have been one of attempted murder as opposed to hit-and-run.

I vividly remember having to once more enter the fray whilst off-duty when I happened to witness a minor road traffic collision; an incident that then led to an act of road rage, with one of the driver's becoming violent and committing an assault. I was a bystander during the build up to this bizarre event, which subsequently unfolded in front of me.

Prior to witnessing the crash that occurred around mid-morning, I'd been shopping in my local town. I was just returning to my vehicle, which was parked in a cul-de-sac located close to the town centre, when I came upon a woman driver attempting to turn her vehicle around so she could exit the dead-end. Whilst in the process of undertaking this manoeuvre, she kept stalling the vehicle, and appeared to be getting quite flustered. She made a complete mess of her first couple of attempts to back her car into a turning point with a slight incline, and kept misjudging the distance she needed to go up the slope to effect the three-point-turn – which had become more like a 21-point-turn by the time she'd finished! Initially, I'd formed the opinion that perhaps she wasn't a very competent driver (an assumption that was nothing to do with her being a woman), or that she was just uncomfortable reversing and simply lacked confidence – and, therefore, I hadn't taken a lot of notice. However, that changed when things took a turn for the worse.

By the time I'd reached my vehicle, she'd finally managed to turn the car around and had headed off towards the T-junction at the end of the cul-de-sac. Briefly after I'd set off on my journey home, I caught her up at this junction where you pull out onto the main road. By this stage, another vehicle had come up behind her, so I naturally joined the queue at the rear. Where you exit this side road it is quite a steep gradient, and she again seemed to be encountering problems with her clutch control as she attempted to pull out. After her umpteenth abortive attempt at the manoeuvre she stalled her car, and it instantaneously rolled back into the vehicle behind her. The driver of the car she'd reversed into, a middle-aged man who I recognised as a resident from the cul-de-sac, got out to inspect the damage and have a word with the woman driver – and that was when a right old commotion erupted. Instead of the woman apologising and exchanging details she started shouting abuse at the shocked male driver, and remonstrating with him as though the collision had been his fault, which was clearly not the case.

In view of her irrational behaviour, I realised I would have to intervene but, before I'd even got out of my car, the issue had escalated further. In a flash the situation had also become more serious because, without warning, the deranged woman had then launched a vicious and unprovoked attack on the poor chap, giving him a mighty kick in the shins. Just as I approached the pair of them, she next struck another telling blow when she landed a nasty punch to the guy's face. The force of the punch knocked him off balance – making him reel backwards – and broke his spectacles as they went flying and fell to the ground. It also left him visibly stunned and sporting a nasty cut just above his right eye.

Instantly I shouted at her to stop and announced myself as a special constable. This at least had the effect of causing her to cease attacking the defenceless victim. I suspect it was also because her focus suddenly became escaping the scene before she was apprehended. She turned on her heels to run away but, before doing so, chucked her car keys into the river that runs parallel to the cul-de-sac; an action that I couldn't really comprehend, unless for some obscure reason she thought she'd be able to deny she'd been driving her car if she wasn't in possession of the keys. Anyway, she didn't get far in her attempt to flee, as I managed to catch up with her while she was running towards the town centre, and then detain her for assault causing ABH.

As soon as I was in close proximity, I could smell alcohol on her breath and see how dilated her pupils were; so much so, I could tell she was completely blotto – even without the benefit of a breathalyser to confirm this assertion. Therefore, I also advised her she was being detained on suspicion of drink-driving. She wasn't at all keen to accompany me back to the scene of the collision, and I knew she was going to resist my efforts to detain her. However, as luck would have it, a patrol car happened to drive by just after I'd apprehended her, and I was able to flag down the driver and enlist his support. My colleague, an experienced regular PC called Colin, immediately took control of the situation, but requested my continued assistance until further backup arrived as it was abundantly clear our prisoner wasn't going to take kindly to being placed in custody. Indeed, as we handcuffed her and put her in the back of the police car, she screamed at the top of her voice and did everything she could to escape our clutches, including trying to kick the car door open once she'd been locked in the vehicle.

While we awaited further assistance, so she could be safely transported back to the police station, we were able to turn our attention to the injured party and administer first aid. He was still in shock following the attack by the demented woman and we felt he should go to hospital to get checked out, especially as he may need a couple of stitches to his head wound. By now his wife had come out of their nearby house to investigate what was going on, so she was able to drive him to the local A&E unit rather than wait for an ambulance to arrive. As we left the chap in her care Colin advised him he'd be around later to take a victim statement and check on his welfare. Shortly after this Colin's sergeant arrived on scene to assist and my services were no longer required, so I was able to continue my journey home – and, as I drove away, I could still hear the woman shrieking at the top of her voice.

My involvement wasn't totally over because later that day I had to pop into the police station to make a statement and, whilst I was there, I also got an update on proceedings. That's when I discovered the woman I'd initially detained was already well-known as an alcoholic in another force area, and was in fact a disqualified driver, who was already wanted in connection with a number of driving offences. The offender subsequently got a 12-month custodial sentence after being found guilty of driving whilst disqualified, drink-driving and ABH.

There was a further occasion when it proved necessary for me to take action whilst off-duty when I encountered another drink-driver, who I thought posed a serious threat to other road users. I was on my way to visit a friend who lived in a nearby town, when a male driver came up behind me at a rapid speed and then overtook as we approached a blind bend, forcing an oncoming vehicle to swerve into the verge to avoid a head-on collision. In my mirror, I saw that the driver of the vehicle he'd narrowly missed had somehow recovered the situation without losing control and ending up in the ditch. Therefore, I didn't stop and continued my journey; effectively now in pursuit of the maniac that had nearly caused a serious accident. The offending vehicle was being driven erratically and the driver's speed fluctuated from excessive to really slow. It was also all over the road, so I already feared it was almost certain to be a drink-driver behind the wheel as I pursued him at a safe distance.

I was powerless to do anything to alert the police and, being off-duty in my own car, there was also nothing I could safely do to bring him to a halt. Therefore, as I followed, I just had to hope he would soon come to the end of his journey, or maybe pull over somewhere. That hope soon materialised because the suspected drink-driver suddenly pulled into a petrol station. I did likewise, and then endeavoured to stop him from leaving by parking my car across the forecourt exit, even though I realised he could still leave via the entrance.

It had been purely good fortune that he hadn't thus far caused a serious collision, so I intended to do my utmost to prevent him getting back on the road. I next ran into the service station lobby, alerted the forecourt attendant to my concerns and requested she phone for the police, which she duly did after I'd shown her my warrant card. Meanwhile, I went back outside to check on the state of the suspected drink-driver and make sure he wasn't trying to drive off.

The chap was out of his car, and looked unsteady on his feet as he wrestled with his petrol cap trying to undo it. I didn't approach him immediately – as

I didn't want to spook him – but, even from a distance, I could tell there was something seriously wrong with the guy, and he was either having some sort of funny turn or, more likely, was inebriated. Having finally undone his petrol cap, he attempted to stretch the hose to his car's filling point – except he'd pulled up so far away from the pump it was never going to reach. You could almost see his brain ticking over as he tried to fathom out why it wouldn't stretch far enough but, the obvious solution to his frustrating problem, which would be moving his car closer to the pump, clearly didn't enter his head. It suited me fine the longer he was baffled by this situation because I was playing for time, waiting for a police colleague to arrive so he could be breathalysed. After a short while pondering his predicament, and failing to work out why the hose wouldn't reach, the confused driver gave up on the idea of filling-up and returned the nozzle to its slot; at the same time using a few expletives to curse the pump. Perhaps he'd now worked out he needed to move his car closer to the pump, but I was worried he could instead opt to drive off through the unblocked entrance. That was something I had to prevent – so, at this point, I decided to approach him, even though I was out of my normal jurisdiction and didn't know how long I'd have to wait for assistance.

As soon as I got in close proximity the alcohol fumes were overwhelming – they were so over-powering you couldn't even smell the petrol. My suspicions he was likely a drink-driver had been totally founded. He appeared so drunk I was surprised he was still conscious, let alone able to stand up or, worse still, drive a car in that condition. The damage he could have done during his preceding journey didn't bear thinking about, and there was no way I was going to let this drunk get back behind a steering wheel. However, in order that I didn't panic him, I didn't initially explain my police connection. Instead, I deliberately played the part of a Good Samaritan who was concerned for his welfare.

I pointed out he looked unwell and may benefit from a rest before he continued his journey and, to my relief, he conveniently agreed with my suggestion. Rather than try to confiscate his car keys, I somehow persuaded him to obligingly hand them over to me, on the pretext that I could helpfully move his car to a parking space at the side of the garage for him – and, once I had them in my possession, I wasn't going to return them whatever demands he made. After I'd moved the car, I next managed to talk the driver into getting in the back to have a lie down; so I then felt increasingly confident I now had the situation well under control.

By the time a local PC arrived to deal with the issue about 15 minutes later, my drink-driver was out for the count. He was in such a deep sleep we couldn't even wake him up enough from his drunken stupor to administer the breathalyser. The PC therefore arrested him on suspicion of drink-driving, for being drunk in charge of a motor vehicle, and also for being drunk and incapable – with the intention of then getting the police doctor to obtain a blood test back at the local nick.

Therein ended my direct association with this matter; apart from once again having to find time to complete a witness statement. There was ultimately no need for me to attend the defendant's court appearance to testify as he sensibly pleaded guilty. However, I did learn that the judge acknowledged my part in helping to bring a serial offender to justice – as it was apparently the third time he'd been convicted of drink-driving, and the second whilst already disqualified. Hence why the sentencing took place in a Crown Court.

15 Clowning About

HITHERTO, WHILST CONVEYING STORIES about my time on the force, much of my focus has been on the serious side of police work, particularly some of the tragic and grim elements your encounter when performing your duties. However, as touched on before in some of my tales, life on the beat also incorporated fun times, especially when you were working alongside some of the renowned and eccentric characters of my era, who could inject a little humour into almost any situation. I think their ethic was 'work hard, play hard' and they certainly did both. As a result, there were occasionally light-hearted moments that occurred throughout my service. These could often be attributed to the assortment of mischievous bobbies with big personalities, who were engaged in the job back then – and I have nostalgic memories of working with some of them.

One of those inimitable characters was a delightful and charming PC known as Jaffa; an immensely funny cop who sometimes expressed himself comically in ways that perhaps wouldn't be tolerated in this day and age. He was a bit of a maverick, who could be a little controversial in his policing methods and some of the antics he got up to. Nonetheless, he was a shrewd operator and highly effective officer. In particular, he had a nose for sussing out when and where crimes were likely to take place, especially burglaries. He'd therefore developed a reputation for being an indomitable and exceptional thief-taker.

Of all the whimsical characters I came across during my 22 years as a special constable, Jaffa was probably the biggest joker in the pack. In addition to his reputation as an unorthodox, yet accomplished thief-taker, he was also known for his devilish sense of humour. He would never miss an opportunity to make light of situations or have a bit of fun, usually at someone else's expense when he felt it was appropriate to do so – or, more to the point, when he thought he could get away with it! When it came to carrying out pranks or taking the mick he saw everyone as fair game, including colleagues, members of the public, or even criminals for that matter (as he believed in equal opportunities!). As an exponent of practical jokes, some of which could be elaborate and innovative, he was something of a pioneer and an absolute legend. Figuratively speaking, he was therefore looked upon by many as being avant-garde in the way he devised and implemented such activities.

Jaffa not only got on well with colleagues, but also members of the public and those in the criminal fraternity alike. I think being such a likeable and gregarious chap, with a delectable nature and a lot of panache, enabled him to get away with far more than anyone else would ever have dared; including a number of spectacular exploits, which could easily have landed him in a lot of trouble. Although Jaffa's behaviour was not typical of most police officers, and could wrongly make him appear to be the complete antithesis of a respectable copper, this seemed to somehow boost his popularity with most people, and make him even more attractive to women – many of whom adored him and sought his attention. The fact he wasn't short of female admirers is probably not that surprising considering he was tall, blonde and handsome – and, according to such fans, looked dashing in a uniform! Even so, despite being a hit with members of the opposite sex, he was no philanderer, and rumours that sometimes circulated about his reputed success with the ladies were grossly exaggerated. They were probably started by someone envious of his obvious appeal, magnetic personality and infectious sense of fun – further traits that likely contributed to him avoiding any real backlash as a result of his escapades and practical jokes.

The most outrageous and audacious of these occurred when he was on night duty, and had arrested a well-known, hardened drinker for being drunk and disorderly. During the early hours this drunk was kicking up a fuss in his cell, demanding that he be put before the court immediately because he wanted to plead his case. He was very intoxicated, and other prisoners were complaining they couldn't sleep because of the racket the drunk was making by constantly shouting or banging on his cell door – so, ostensibly, Jaffa came up with a solution to deal with the situation and put a stop to the rumpus.

As things had gone quiet and there was a lull in the demand for officers to attend any incidents in the midst of the night, he decided that during his refreshment break he would grant the drunk his wish and organise for him to attend court or, moreover, a mock court in the courtroom adjoining the police station. Having appointed himself as the presiding judge, he set about roping in other colleagues to take part in his ruse, and co-opted the services of two probationary PCs to respectively act for the defence and the prosecution, albeit unwillingly. It was a Magistrates' court that was being utilised for his mock trial, but Jaffa reckoned it would give more authenticity to his planned proceedings if those running the show adorned gear normally associated with a Crown Court – and, somehow, he managed to obtain the type of wigs worn by judges and barristers, so they would all look the part when the poor unsuspecting drunk was put before the 'beak'.

Sure enough, the drunken prisoner therefore got his wish to immediately appear in the 'dock'. However, after he'd been found guilty of being drunk and disorderly, and been sentenced to 'a life behind bars' by 'Jaffa the Judge' for committing this 'heinous' misdemeanour, he most certainly regretted his demand for instant justice, or, injustice as it turned out. The irony of his sentence was lost on him because he clearly thought he'd been sent to prison for the rest of his natural days! Due to his drunken state, he apparently had no idea his appearance in front of the 'beak' had been a complete sham and, as he traipsed off back to his cell, he protested his innocence to those officers escorting him. He complained bitterly about the rough justice he'd received and how the sentence had been too harsh – as normally he just got a fine for this type of transgression.

Jaffa was sure the prisoner would have no recollection of his court appearance by next morning, and that the events of the night would be expunged from his memory following a deep, drink-induced sleep. This didn't turn out to be the case though. As soon as he woke he created merry hell and wanted to make a complaint about his miscarriage of justice, and the travesty of the 'life sentence' that had been dished out when he'd been put before the court. Fortunately, his memory remained somewhat blurry because it was apparent he still hadn't worked out that the whole episode had been a ruse. Consequently, Jaffa was soon able to pacify him and persuade the guy that the surreal court hearing had never happened and he must have had a nightmare. The poor chap was so relieved he wasn't being sent to jail for the rest of his days, and was about to be released on bail, he fell completely for Jaffa's explanation without ever latching on that he'd been hoodwinked – so there was no complaint and our mischievous colleague therefore got away with this malarkey.

With him just about managing to side-step any potential repercussions from his court case scam, it would have been understandable if he'd decided to rein himself in when it came to his jocular and fun-loving approach to life, but I somehow doubt that was the case. As he was a serial wind-up merchant, I suspect there were many other occasions where he continued to wreak havoc, and he could easily have caused his own downfall due to his famed sense of humour and outlandish behaviour. However, as instigating practical jokes and pranks was commonplace back in the day, and not all were done overtly, it wasn't always obvious who was responsible for them. It's therefore impossible to know just how many Jaffa was behind, or how many possible complaints he managed to dodge. Although he was certainly one of the leading lights when it came to creating comical incidents or exploiting potentially amusing situations in his self-appointed role of force clown, he certainly wasn't the only colleague who was practiced in this art – or the sole contender worthy of such a title!

Much of what went on was just harmless fun and playful mocking but, as some of the featured stories imply, there were occasions when it probably went too far, and crossed a line that wouldn't be tolerated in contemporary times. However, I think most of the antics that occurred were just horseplay, and the majority of wind-ups happened in-house and were aimed at fellow members of the Constabulary.

Senior colleagues were often the target of these high jinks and, while I was serving as a cadet, my first divisional inspector came in for regular stick. Our much-loved boss was built like a man mountain, and the sort of strapping bloke you would always want on your side whenever you found yourself in a tight spot. He had a loud booming voice, large ears and an excellent memory for detail so, rather predictably, he gained the nickname Jumbo – or, sometimes, he was unkindly referred to as Dumbo if he got annoyed and flew off the handle! His size, larger than life personality, rugged appearance and protruding ears did make him a prime target for some witty comments, but the one that sticks in my mind arose when a few of the guys were nattering about him as they came down the corridor towards his office. One of the PC's was bemoaning the inspector's decision to restrict overtime and, even though we were still some distance away and well out of earshot (at least for someone with normal sized ears!), a fellow colleague stated as quick as a flash:

'Keep your voice down mate, otherwise he's bound to hear you and get in a flap!'

Another officer then followed this up with:

'Yes, we don't want him hitting the roof if he flies into a rage!'

Another endearing operational inspector was also the target of some pranks during my time as a special – probably because he frequently set himself up for some mickey-taking due to his somewhat gung-ho and bombastic approach to policing. He always took it in good spirits though, and gave back as good as he got. Actual shenanigans involving our glorious leader included an unknown prankster tying a dustbin to his car bumper with a rope that exceeded 50 metres in length. This meant the unsuspecting inspector had no idea he was towing the bin until he'd left the police station yard and started heading up the road. It was at the end of a night shift so there was little traffic around, but a pedestrian on his way to work was a bit astonished to see a car pass by with a black bin in tow. For good measure, somebody also crept around to his house one night and replaced his prized doves with chickens – which he definitely viewed as a case of 'foul play' when he went out to the aviary to feed his birds the next morning.

On another occasion a colleague on night duty decided to surprise the boss by laying on a lavish breakfast for him in his office; so that when he arrived for duty the following morning it would be there waiting for him to tuck in. Our inspector had a healthy appetite to match his massive frame, and this 'kind-hearted' colleague clearly thought it would be a nice gesture if he provided him with a meal that would set him up for the day. He therefore paid the local abattoir a visit during the night and obtained a pig's head, which he placed on a large platter with all the trimmings and left as a surprise gift for his senior colleague. In his attempt to please the boss, the considerate colleague even went to the trouble of laying up the inspector's desk with cutlery, all the appropriate condiments and a bottle of Chianti to wash down his delightful treat – just to make it look like he would be dining out at a posh restaurant. I'm not sure if he appreciated the veritable feast that had been prepared for him, but he probably saw the funny side of this particular prank; which is more than can be said when it came to a couple of further practical jokes that were played on him.

There were two things in life that were sacrosanct for this inspector – his beloved dogs, and the pride he took in his appearance. However, that didn't stop someone from going too far and crossing those particular lines, by carrying out pranks that would impact on both of these sacred aspects that he deemed out of bounds.

Within his office, the boss had a treasured painting of his two adorable dogs, which was hung on the wall behind his desk, and a pair of black leather shoes that were bulled to perfection and ready to slip on whenever he received a visit from a high-ranking officer or other dignitary. In regard to the stunning painting, somebody thought it would be funny to replace it whilst he was away on leave. They chose a stuffed fish, mounted on a tatty piece of wood, to put up in place of his cherished picture. The fish looked something like a pilchard, and was about as ugly as it gets when it comes to this type of aquatic species – and, apparently, the inspector didn't think much of his new acquisition on his return to duty. I believe the acting-inspector got the blame and suffered his wrath, probably because his temporary replacement was keen on fishing. Despite the circumstantial evidence, this colleague denied all knowledge, and the identity of the culprit remained a mystery. Similarly, the bold colleague who had the audacity to sneak into his office prior to a visit by the Chief Constable and nail his perfectly polished pair of shoes to the floor was never traced. As you can imagine, the actions of this prankster caused uproar when the inspector rushed to slip them on just before the big boss arrived. In fact, I'm told you could hear his cursing throughout the station when he became enraged after realising what had been done to his best footwear!

Training sessions for special constables, which were usually fairly intense, and sometimes piecemeal and quite laconic by necessity, due to us all having day jobs that limited our availability, could still be a source of amusement and an opportunity for a bit of tomfoolery. The day we were being trained how to effectively utilise CS spray (subsequently replaced by PAVA) was no exception. An integral part of this particular workshop included officers being subjected to the spray, so they could appreciate the debilitating affects of coming into contact with this noxious substance. This was considered essential because, whenever the gas was administered, there was always the possibility the user, or any other colleague in close proximity, could be contaminated and incapacitated as well as the intended target. An officer affected by the gas would then be rendered ineffective until the effects had worn off. Bearing this in mind, it was felt that officers would gain an appreciation of how your body reacts, and be better prepared to deal with the impact of coming into contact with the gas, if they'd personally experienced being sprayed. Hence, once we'd been shown how to use the canister and apply the spray, I had the chance to undergo an unenviable encounter with the gas, along with my fellow special constables. We were all herded into a garage at the back of our nick, whereupon our trainer took great delight in testing our endurance when exposed to this substance.

Once the CS gas was sprayed into the garage, we had to see how long we could tolerate it before succumbing and making an exit – and, of course, nobody wanted to lose face and appear weak by being the first to make a dash for it. Therefore, after about 30 seconds, an unsuspecting colleague at the front was given an almighty push by someone who was stood behind, which had the effect of propelling this individual forward at a rapid rate and forcing him out of the garage. As this colleague shot out over the threshold following the shove from his fellow special, it naturally appeared as though he was the first person to give in and leave. This meant a mass exodus could then occur as the rest of us piled out; knowing our macho images were still intact and we'd preserved our reputations as tough, resilient constables – thanks to the unwitting scapegoat! I'm sure our trainer realised there was skulduggery involved, and knew exactly what had caused the first special to leave the garage in such a hurry.

Rookie constables, particularly those fresh out of training school, were always a good source of amusement for their more experienced colleagues – especially veteran officers like Jaffa or Paolo, who were always keen to have a little fun by exploiting their naivety. With them usually being gullible, and in awe of their more experienced colleagues, novices were generally ripe for practical jokes and considered fair game. A favourite was therefore putting new recruits through their cycling proficiency test in the station's backyard, where they would be set an impossible course to complete, which even a winner of the Tour De France would struggle to get around successfully. Inevitably, they all failed their 'mock test' – and were then informed they would have to undergo further lessons before repeating it, and meanwhile ride a police bike with stabilisers whilst on duty!

Another ploy involved the use of a false hand that looked very realistic, which a certain bobby would slip up the sleeve of his tunic just before he greeted a new probationary PC with a handshake. In advance of any such greeting, an unsuspecting new recruit would be suitably primed, and told by a 'helpful' colleague that a firm grip and vigorous handshake were the order of the day. Following such advice inevitably meant the fake hand would appear to have come off due to the level of force applied during the handshake, and the novice would be left grasping the false hand as the prankster nonchalantly walked away! The phantom 'one-handed bobby' had perfected this practice, so it genuinely looked like he was missing a hand once he'd released the fake one from his sleeve; thus ensuring anyone subjected to this prank would end up dumbfounded and suitably embarrassed.

Other more sophisticated pranks carried out at the expense of new recruits included removing a patrol car from outside the lodgings of a PC during his refreshment break, to give the impression it had been stolen, and dressing up a dummy so it would resemble a dead body when a novice constable came across it on his beat.

In regard to the 'patrol car theft', the young officer had just been approved to drive police vehicles and was on his first outing at the wheel of a Panda car. As he was on a day shift, he'd been granted permission to call in at his lodgings over the luncheon period. While he was tucking into his grub, an artful colleague used the spare key to move the police car elsewhere, so that when the rookie intended to resume his patrol he'd assume it must have been stolen. That is exactly what happened and, suffice to say, his accommodating colleague was instantly on hand to obligingly assist. He advised the fledgling PC there was no need to humiliate himself by notifying their sergeant about the 'missing Panda', as he would help him search for it. To make the ruse even more authentic and believable, his colleague also told him the patrol car had almost certainly been taken by joy-riders and would be found nearby. He then kindly drove him around for the next half-hour looking for it, until they conveniently came upon the vehicle parked up in a side road – exactly where this 'helpful' colleague had left it about 40 minutes earlier!

Moving on to the matter of the dummy that was staged to look like a dead body, an equally impressionable novice was the target of this particular stunt.

The 'body' was placed in some undergrowth in an area located on the youthful PC's beat, and he was then effectively led to it by his tutor constable, who was in on the practical joke and still accompanying him during patrols at this stage in his training. His tutor had no trouble convincing him the 'body' was a potential murder victim, and then told him to guard the scene whilst he went to get tape to seal off the immediate area. He also instructed him not to go near the 'body' under any circumstances for fear of contaminating any evidence. While the young PC was on his own awaiting the return of his tutor, another colleague briefly caused a distraction to take his attention away from the 'body'; thus enabling a further member of the team to creep up unnoticed and sneak away with the dummy whilst his probationary colleague was being side-tracked. So, when the tutor came back after a couple of minutes, the 'body' had of course mysteriously vanished, leaving the raw recruit not only somewhat stunned, but also completely speechless when he was asked to explain where it had gone!

16 'Lol'

IN ADDITION TO COMICAL EVENTS that were contrived, there were also a number of highly amusing episodes or odd incidents that arose naturally during the course of our duties. Frequently this seemed to happen whenever I was working with Ivan, and for some reason he always seemed to be present when nudity (usually involving the male anatomy!) or a sexually deviant event cropped up – as already highlighted when he was first on the scene during the infamous live sex show performed by the drugged-up couple on a mini-roundabout.

Two of the weirdest incidents occurred when Ivan and I were working one particular night shift. It was the middle of winter and bitterly cold. Ivan and I were out on foot patrol around 0100hrs and, as we walked by a derelict building, we heard the sound of running water, so went inside to investigate. We discovered a pipe had burst and that water was running down a back wall, creating a 'lake' in what used to be the lounge. The property was semi-detached and the adjoining house was still serviceable and occupied. Therefore, after radioing control to request the leak be reported to the Water Board, we decided to also notify the neighbours of the situation so they could take any necessary measures to prevent the water from leaking into their abode.

Ivan banged loudly on the door of the neighbouring house and, after an age, it was answered by a youngish guy in his mid-twenties. The chap looked a bit dishevelled, so we assumed we'd woken him up and he'd quickly thrown on some clothes before answering the door. Ivan apologised for disturbing him and explained the reason for our call. However, whilst we were stood there chatting to this guy, we both became a little distracted by something we couldn't help but notice. For some obscure reason he had a sock sticking out of his flies. Once we'd finished telling him about the leak next door and, before we bade him farewell, Ivan couldn't resist enquiring about the protruding sock. In response, the chap explained that he'd just started undressing when he'd heard the knock and, without realising, must have deposited the sock in his open trouser flies when unlocking the door. This explanation would just about have been plausible, but for the fact he still had both socks on – which made his storyline a little unconvincing!

Never one to miss the chance of making a witty or sarcastic remark when confronted by such a peculiar state of affairs, Ivan amusingly said off the cuff:

'Pull the other one mate, next you'll be telling me you're 'Jake the Peg' with the extra leg, but I can tell that's never a foot you've got in there!'

And, in response, the quick-witted 'sock man' replied:

'No, but it's a bloody good nine inches!'

We then went on our way without exploring the matter any further, so the mind still boggles.

Within an hour of experiencing this strange encounter, we got a call to attend a disturbance at the local park and, as we were in the vicinity, we started jogging towards this amenity. However, as we neared our destination, we were suddenly greeted by a sight that stopped us in our tracks. Around 100 yards away, stood in the middle of the road, was a man 'in all his glory'! Ivan and I looked curiously at each other – as if to check that our eyes weren't deceiving us – and then started running towards the guy who was naked from head to toe. As we approached, he presumably heard our footsteps because he suddenly hotfooted it towards the driveway of a nearby house. He made a beeline for the front door so, just before he entered the large detached house, Ivan shouted:

'Police, stop!'

Much to our surprise, he did as he was told and stood there bold as brass in the front porch waiting for us to catch up with him. His immediate comment to us was:

'Thank goodness you're the police. I was really fearful it was a couple of yobs chasing me.'

It seemed an odd reaction because the way he spoke gave the impression he thought it was perfectly natural for someone to be out on the streets in the middle of the night with nothing on – and that being caught red-handed by the police parading around outside in the buff was nothing to worry about. Ivan asked him to explain the reason for his odd behaviour, and he simply told us he'd heard a disturbance going on in the park opposite and had come out to investigate. This part of his explanation appeared genuine, since we were heading to the park ourselves to look into the cause of the rumpus, but that still didn't justify him being out in a public place completely naked. Nonetheless, Ivan decided just to warn him about his behaviour rather than report him for outraging public decency. He also advised our 'odd ball' that any future repetition of indecent exposure would have serious consequences, and then requested his details for our records. When naked man gave us his name as 'Mr Lonely' – surprisingly not an alias – we both instantly thought his response in itself spoke volumes!

Since we were on our way to investigate the disturbance in the park, we didn't have time to dig deeper into this chap's background on the night. However, Ivan subsequently made some further enquiries and was reasonably comfortable the guy was a harmless misfit, as he'd never previously come to the attention of the police. Anyway, once naked man had been suitably admonished, we went to deal with the rabble in the park responsible for creating all the noise in the early hours – although quite why they were there on a freezing night I've no idea. The din was down to a rowdy group of underage drinkers, who'd been overdoing it on the alcohol. Once we'd confiscated their illicit bottles of booze, disposed of the contents and quelled all the noise, they were duly advised to go home – which they finally did after much moaning and groaning about being sent packing.

The oddities we witnessed during that tour of night shifts didn't end there because the very next evening we came across another unusual sight. Shortly after we'd come on duty at 2200hrs we did a routine check on the local night-club. It had been snowing heavily throughout the day and, as we drove towards the car park at the rear of the facility, we spotted in the car headlights a naked backside sticking out of the snow. There was just enough of the posterior visible to make it look like one of those 'grooved slots' you'd park your pushbike in.

We immediately got out of our vehicle to investigate and, buried in the snow, we uncovered a young gentleman who was so inebriated that he'd passed out. Luckily, he'd only been there for a few minutes so hypothermia hadn't yet set in, and we were soon able to bring him around after we'd taken him into the night-club and got him warmed up. Once we'd tracked down some of his mates, we found out this lad was on his stag night, and had been taking part in a drinking game that had involved him downing a number of shots. As the loser of the game he'd been required to complete a dare, which entailed him performing a 'streak' around the car park – and that was how he'd ended up starkers outside in the freezing cold. Once the cold air had taken its toll, the guy had apparently collapsed face down in a snowdrift, and a few of his so-called friends, who were also drunk, had then decided it would be laugh if they buried him in the snow with just his naked bum sticking out. Clearly they had no idea of the potential consequences of their actions, so who needs mates like that. It was fortunate we came along when we did because their friend could well have come to serious harm due to exposure if he'd been left outside in the cold much longer – including suffering frostbite to a certain appendage!

A farcical event occurred the next time I had the pleasure of patrolling with Ivan. We were working a late shift and, around 1900hrs, we headed out to a village right on the boundary of the rural beat we were covering. It was once more a bitterly cold evening, and we'd gone to serve a warrant on an offender for the non-payment of a fine. When we got there, the chap was able to demonstrate he'd settled his outstanding debt with the court that day, so we didn't have to arrest him. This was just as well as it spared us a lot of embarrassment because, when we returned to our car, we discovered Ivan had managed to lock us out of it, having left the keys in the ignition. Luckily we did have a repeater radio with us and were able to call up for assistance – even though it meant we became the laughing-stock amongst our colleagues when they learned of our plight.

Our new section sergeant, who was on his first day working out of our police station, kindly agreed to head out to rescue us with the spare key, but we knew it would take him a while as it was some distance away and he was unfamiliar with the area. It therefore looked likely we would have to hang around in the freezing cold for the best part of an hour.

With us being out in the sticks, right on the outer edge of our disparate borough, there weren't many places for us to seek refuge, but Ivan suddenly had a brainwave. He remembered there was an old fellow who lived nearby that he knew. It was someone he'd met a few years before when attending a burglary at his house, so we decided to visit him on the off chance he was still in the land of the living and residing at the same address. To our relief, he was very much alive and kicking, and in residence at his primitive old cottage from the 'Dark Ages', which was located in the back of beyond. He was delighted to have some visitors and, after inviting us into his humble abode to join him for a cup of tea, led us into what was purported to be the dining area of his ramshackle house. It wasn't particularly warm but it was a step up from being stuck outside in the perishing cold. Once we'd joined him at his dinner table, the old boy took great pleasure in telling us we'd arrived just in time to see the end result of a project he'd been working on – the creation of a homemade table lamp.

Well, quite how Ivan and I managed to keep a straight face when he proudly presented us with the fruits of his labour I'll never know. The so-called table lamp turned out to be a complete monstrosity. It was comprised of a battered old biscuit tin, with a hole drilled through the lid for the wire, and an antiquated light fixture with a bulb screwed into it. The ancient light fixture wasn't even attached to the tin and was just hanging loose, so the bulb just flopped onto its side whenever the lamp was moved even slightly. However, this didn't appear to bother our host, who seemed chuffed to bits with his invention. In order that we didn't offend the old guy, we had to make out we were equally impressed with the result of his work by duly paying him appropriate compliments. At one point though, I had to make an excuse to rush to his toilet because I couldn't contain my laughter when Ivan commented he'd seen something similar on 'Antiques Roadshow'!

Also bordering on the farcical was the time I was working with Gavin, a PC just out of his probationary period. Whilst on mobile patrol early one Saturday evening, we were sent to investigate a burglar alarm activation at a branch of ATS on the local trading estate. The key-holder had been alerted and was due to meet us there. Upon our arrival, we did a quick recce around the outside of the building and could see no sign of a break-in. However, once the key-holder arrived, we needed to go inside the premises to check nothing untoward had happened, and also so the alarm could be switched off and re-set. The manager of ATS was the registered key-holder but it was actually his wife that attended with the keys, along with appropriate instructions of what to do. She had come because when they'd received the call at home, alerting them to the alarm activation, both of them had been in the midst of getting ready for a night out, and she'd somehow beaten him to it – which she admitted had been a first and something of a shock to her hubby!

Once we'd accessed the main building and the good lady had de-activated the alarm, we then set about checking the rest of the premises for anything that might have caused it to go off. Our check included entering a large store at the rear of the main warehouse, and that was when we found ourselves in a compromising situation. The wife unlocked the door to the store and then followed us in, leaving the keys in the lock the other side. Almost instantly, a draught caused the store door to slam behind us and, with it being one of those automatic locking devices, we suddenly found ourselves trapped in the back room with no means of escape. We therefore had to radio control to explain our predicament and await the arrival of the husband to rescue us. This outcome left Gavin and I feeling like a right pair of wallies, even though it wasn't technically our fault we'd ended up as 'prisoners'!

My own stupidity almost led to me ending up in a not dissimilar situation when I was once out on my own doing foot patrol in the town centre around 0100hrs. I remember it was a midweek night and the town centre was deserted, so I was focusing on checking shop doors were secure, although I wasn't really expecting to find any unlocked. Naturally, the rear entrances of shops are generally more vulnerable and, therefore, where it was possible to check them I did so – and that was how I suddenly found a wide open back door belonging to a local bookmaker. The first thing I should have done was alert the control room but, for some inconceivable reason, I chose to ignore protocol and enter the building without doing so. I simply assumed the door had either been left open accidentally, or hadn't been shut properly and had blown open – because these seemed the most likely causes, especially as there were no signs of a forced entry. However, I had the shock of my life once I'd tentatively walked into the premises.

Just after I'd stepped over the threshold of the doorway and taken a couple of paces into the shop area, the door was slammed shut behind me. Unbeknown to me, somebody else was already in the bookies, presumably an intruder, who must have heard me coming and hidden behind the door until they had the briefest of opportunities to make their escape. In that split second, I recall I heard the faintest of noises, and glanced over my shoulder to catch the merest glimpse of someone as they bolted out of the premises, shutting the door behind them.

It all happened in a flash and, as I only spotted the intruder out of the corner of my eye, I had no chance to register what this person looked like, or even what they were wearing, especially as it was dark. Within a couple of seconds I'd gathered my thoughts and instinctively raced outside with the intention of pursuing the individual but, much to my dismay, there was no longer any trace of the intruder I should have caught red-handed. It was as if this person had vanished into thin air. I therefore hoped my mind had been playing tricks on me and the intruder had never existed but, deep down, I knew this wasn't the case – and whoever it was had managed to flee the scene due to my ineptitude and inexplicable action. I belatedly notified control about the insecure premises and the near miss I'd had with an intruder. When the key-holder arrived shortly afterwards, and advised me nothing of value was kept in the bookmakers overnight, I was at least able to console myself with the knowledge the intrepid trespasser would have left empty-handed.

Certain colleagues were a constant source of amusement with their witty remarks, but perhaps the funniest of all the amusing comments I heard during my service was a classic remark made to Spud by a member of the public during a village festival. Whilst we were on duty together, Spud got roped into taking part in an exhibition of Morris dancing; an experience that he found quite humiliating, mainly because participating in such an activity didn't suit his sombre, macho image. He also had two left feet when it came to dancing and was totally out of synch with his fellow dancers throughout the routine. This compounded his embarrassment, especially as the bemused audience found his performance hilarious. Having spectacularly made a fool of himself, he was therefore mightily relieved when the session came to an end and he could cease being the centre of attention. It was at this point a villager came up to him and said:

'Well mate, after witnessing you Morris dancing I reckon there's no chance you could be circumcised!'

Spud was understandably confounded by this villager's odd comment and replied:

'As it happens you are right, but what makes you say that and how did you know?'

To which he mockingly got the response:

'Because I knew that only a complete prick would ever do something like that!'

The range of weird or comical things that happened to police officers during the course of their duties never ceased to amaze me. These included the time that Royston, a very posh village bobby, got sent to deal with a herd of cows that had wandered onto a road close to his patch while he was working a night shift. Upon his arrival, he assumed they must have escaped from a nearby field because he spotted the gate to this particular meadow was wide open. Being pitch dark in the middle of the night, he realised it was important to get them off the road as quickly as possible. Therefore, to get them out of harms way, he took the decision to usher them through the open gateway – believing they had most likely come from this field and, if not, he could investigate to whom they actually belonged the next day.

Once he'd got the cows back into the field, and closed the gate behind them, he returned to his police vehicle to notify control the matter had been resolved and write up his notebook. While doing so, he thought he briefly heard the distant sound of chinking glass coming from nearby but, at the time, it hardly registered and he believed his ears must have been deceiving him; well, that was until he was awoken by someone banging angrily on the door of his village police house early the next morning. When he opened the door still half-asleep, since he'd only recently taken to his bed, Royston was greeted by an irate farmer complaining about the state of his crop of strawberries, which had apparently been partly destroyed and partially devoured by a herd of cows overnight. Royston rapidly came to his senses, and soon realised the cattle the farmer was referring to must be the same ones he'd rescued from the road – and the faint sound of chinking glass had been caused by them trampling through the strawberries and knocking into some jam jars, which had been strategically placed around the field on poles to frighten birds away. Yes, the field he'd ushered them into was undoubtedly this farmer's prize strawberry patch, which had been almost ready for harvesting until these uninvited overnight guests had taken it upon themselves to tuck into his luscious crop!

Unsurprisingly, our eminent colleague decided there was nothing to be gained from telling the farmer exactly what had happened the night before, so played dumb about how the cows had ended up on this former fruit bearing pasture. However, he did helpfully promise to carry out a thorough investigation into the matter, and make every effort to identify the culprit who'd been responsible for allowing these gluttonous and destructive animals to graze on his land!

Quite early in my service as a special constable, I was once working with Nev on mobile patrol covering the town centre when we decided to park up and go for a wander around a housing estate. There was nothing unusual in that, except this particular part of town was a bit run down, and perhaps not the best place to leave a police vehicle unattended for too long – which was exactly what we did when an elderly couple invited us to join them for a cup of afternoon tea. Having done our bit for community relations, we returned to our police car about an hour later, and neither of us noticed anything wrong with the vehicle. We therefore happily continued patrolling for another couple of hours, until it was time for us to return to the police station prior to signing off. As we pulled into the station car park, one of our sergeants was coming out of the main entrance and, on spotting us, he turned into a carbon copy of the 'laughing policeman'. Initially we had no idea why he was roaring with laughter but, once we exited the patrol car, it soon became clear.

Somebody had been tampering with the police sign on the patrol car roof, which now ran from front to back rather than from side to side – and it now looked more like an ice-cream van or pizza delivery vehicle than a police car! Just how neither of us had noticed this obvious change in its appearance when we'd returned to it following our earlier foot patrol is baffling. Clearly our powers of observation must have completely malfunctioned, meaning we once more deservedly made a mockery of ourselves – not only amongst our colleagues, but also any members of the public who'd clocked us driving around town.

Occasionally, the opportunity to have a laugh whilst on duty would simply fall into your lap, and that was the case when I was once on foot patrol with Simmo, a tall, dark and handsome PC who was in his second year of service. It was a Saturday evening and, as we were patrolling the town centre, we suddenly attracted a lot of interest from a coach load of nubile young ladies who were out on a fancy dress hen party, and about to head off to enjoy the night-life in a nearby city. Simmo had a beautiful girlfriend that he adored – so, in spite of his good looks, he didn't have an eye for other ladies and was no lothario; even though he was something of a woman magnet and some of them certainly had the hots for him. But, on this occasion, he nevertheless thought it would be amusing if we boarded the coach, and made out we were a couple of kissograms that had been booked for the night out. It sounded like a good idea at the time, and we were welcomed aboard with open arms by members our newly acquired fan club – and there was much whooping and catcalling as we were eagerly ushered to the rear of the coach to take a seat with the chief hen. However, that was when things started to get a little awkward.

It soon became clear that our hostesses, most of whom had already consumed a significant amount of alcohol, honestly thought we were part of the entertainment for the night and were therefore loath to let us leave the coach. So, when the driver started up the engine and was about to head off before we'd convinced the party of ladies that we were genuinely police officers and would not be joining them on their trip, the situation became a little dire and called for drastic action; especially when a few of the hens actually attempted to bar our exit. Fortunately though, Simmo kept a cool head.

He quickly got us out of our jam by playfully slapping the chief hen in handcuffs to make out she was being arrested, which had the effect of making the other partygoers think it was all part of the game, and thus play along with us. As a result, those barring our exit stepped aside and instead cheered their friend as we took her into 'custody' and led her off the coach. And to say we felt relieved once we'd made our escape intact, and then freed our 'prisoner', would be an under-statement. Undoubtedly it would have been impossible to rationally explain how two members of law enforcement had managed to get themselves 'kidnapped' by a bunch of women, while on active duty in full uniform, and then taken on a night out miles away!

It was also Simmo I was paired up with for a prisoner escort the following week, when we discovered in the khazi of this prisoner's cell what could only be described as the largest ever toilet deposit known to mankind! The prisoner was due to be taken for a court hearing, and when we went to collect him from his cell he complained that he couldn't use the latrine because it was blocked – and it appeared the blockage had in fact been created by him producing a download the size of a log. Just how a human being had ever managed to pass something so enormous through their back passage was a complete enigma to Simmo and me because doing so must have been akin to going through childbirth. Without hesitation we instantly decided it was a job for 'Dynarod' to clear the blockage as neither of us felt inclined to tackle a problem of that magnitude!

Amusing episodes continued to crop up intermittently as I went about my police duties, and there were certain quick-witted colleagues who had the ability to see the funny side of anything and often create humorous situations, sometimes deliberately, but ordinarily just by chance. My best friend and colleague Ivan probably stood out more than anyone else with his warped sense of humour, and he could turn virtually any given situation into a farce. He was a natural when it came to exploiting opportunities to do his job with a smile on his face, or equally adept at making a fool of himself – and, if 'acting the goat' was classed as an art form, I'm sure he'd be worthy of a place on 'Britain's Got Talent'. That said, he was still a brilliant, innovative and very capable copper; someone you could totally rely on whatever challenge you faced, even in perilous situations. As a result of his somewhat unconventional approach, he was also everyone's go-to colleague for getting uncommon or odd tasks completed, and he occasionally used offbeat methods to do just that. In that regard, I recall two occasions when he contrived to get a court summons issued to individuals who'd been eluding the police, one of them a famous comedian renowned for having a pop at the 'Old Bill' during his performances.

Colleagues from the Met had been trying to issue a summons to this particular celebrity for several weeks, but he had managed to outfox them and evade their attentions. However, they were aware he would be performing at a theatre in our town so contacted our Constabulary for assistance, and it fell upon Ivan to do the dastardly deed whilst this comedian was in the locality – although they probably weren't expecting him to do so in the middle of his live performance, which is exactly what happened. Ivan strode onto the stage, much to the comedian's surprise, and duly served the summons before he had a chance to even realise what was going on. I'm sure the audience probably thought it was all part of the act, and the recipient took it in good spirits; perhaps because he was so taken aback by Ivan's audacity.

In another not dissimilar situation, Ivan also walked out to the middle of a cricket pitch whilst a match was in full swing in order to issue a summons to a guy who had been avoiding him for some weeks. This lad frequently committed driving offences but was difficult to track down, and always seemed to be giving the police the run-a-round, so Ivan once more used his ingenuity to get the job done. Ironically this lad subsequently became a good friend of both Ivan and I. Now he is much older and wiser, he looks back with fond memories on the time Ivan resorted to interrupting a cricket match to serve him with his summons – and fully appreciates why he went to such lengths to finally get him before the court.

Before returning to more serious matters, I must briefly mention a number of other mildly amusing incidents that cropped up during the course of my service; like the time Beth was persuaded by a group of youths to let them give her a push on a park swing one evening whilst she was on duty. Of course, once she was on the swing they took advantage of the situation by pushing as hard as they could, and then refusing to stop when she wanted to get off. In the end she had no choice but to call up on her radio for assistance and, when she did so, all we could hear was her squealing over the airwaves and embarrassedly shouting she was trapped on a swing in the local park. By the time we'd come to her rescue, the young yobs had finally run off, leaving her as a quivering wreck who would never again go near a swing!

Equally bemusing was the occasion when a novice WPC took a statement from a shopkeeper who'd been the victim of a violent attack during a robbery, which had resulted in him suffering a broken arm. His right arm was patently in plaster for all to see, but the young WPC asked our victim in all seriousness:

'And which arm was it sir that got injured during the assault?'

Once again it was the same young officer that ended up red-faced when she got in a muddle with her words as she was giving evidence in court. She was presenting her findings in a case against a gentleman she'd witnessed indecently exposing himself, and inexplicably told the court the defendant's penis was of uncertain size!

On hearing this remark her tutor constable had to quickly intervene and say:

'I think what she means Your Worship is that the accused was uncircumcised!'

It probably came as no surprise to her tutor when shortly after this slip-up she also gave the wrong call sign when they found themselves confronting a violent prisoner. Instead of calling for urgent assistance she gave the call sign for 'going off-duty', which perhaps isn't such a bad shout if you want to avoid a confrontation!

This WPC's foolhardy acts seemed almost insignificant compared to the naïve behaviour of one of her novice male counterparts. He succeeded in making a complete wally of himself when he encountered a couple of local miscreants who were having difficulty starting 'their' car. When it came to cock-ups, you could argue this rookie constable excelled in this department because the two lads were actually attempting to steal the vehicle, and somehow persuaded him to help push the car to get it started. The obliging probationer, who'd never met the two brazen young tearaways, had no idea he'd been hoodwinked as the pair of them thanked him for his help and waived farewell as they drove off in the stolen car. The penny only dropped for the green PC a short time afterwards, when a message came over the radio to look out for a vehicle that had been taken without the owner's consent – which just happened to have the same registration number as the car he'd helped them to steal. He probably thought he'd been doing his bit for community policing by lending them a helping hand, and was mortified when he realised he'd been fooled into aiding and abetting a crime – not that his colleagues showed him much sympathy as they constantly reminded him of his faux pas!

Knowing the two car thieves in question, I can understand how they managed to con the unfortunate constable involved in this incident, and you have to admire their barefaced cheek. During their youth they were constantly up to no good and frequently leading the police on a merry dance, but they did exceed all expectations once they finally grew up, and even ended up going straight and running a legit business after years of offending behaviour. Anyway, the novice PC involved in this particular mishap, who ended up feeling like a complete imbecile, didn't appear to learn his lesson as a consequence of the car theft incident because, just a few days later, he went on to further excel in the art of making a fool of himself.

He came across what he presumed was a car on fire, and bravely dragged the driver and passenger from the vehicle before it became a burning wreck, and then summoned the fire brigade to the scene. However, once he'd completed his daring rescue act, he then embarrassingly discovered there was no fire. What he thought was the car going up in smoke was simply steam coming from an over-heating radiator, and the couple were just sat in the vehicle waiting for the breakdown recovery service to arrive – still, better safe than sorry!

The occasion one of our sergeants arrived slightly late at a court hearing and tried to creep in unnoticed, didn't go as planned. An appointment with his optician to collect his new glasses had been the reason for his tardiness and, as he crept into the courtroom, he certainly made a spectacle of himself. Probably because his eyes hadn't adjusted to his new specs, he missed the top step at the entrance to the court and went hurtling down the rest of the stairway, gathering speed as he attempted to recover his balance and not fall flat on his face. He probably looked a bit like a hapless and bumbling Norman Wisdom in one of his comedy films as he made his grand entrance in anything but an inconspicuous manner! Not that I can say much because, just a few weeks later, I effectively followed in his footsteps when I arrived late at the same courtroom for a training session. Like him, I was trying to creep in without drawing attention to myself, but ended up doing the complete opposite when I stumbled down the steps – in my case, I couldn't blame it on having new glasses as it was down to me still being in a daze after oversleeping.

I think it was probably Paolo who got the award for being the coolest operator at our station because, when a group of us got stuck in a lift during a night out at our HQ, he certainly kept his cool in a sticky situation. About 15 of us had arrived for the do being held in the Divisional HQ's social area, situated on the top floor of the building, and we all piled into a lift that was only meant for a maximum load of eight people. As you can imagine, we were crammed in like sardines, and the inevitable happened with the lift breaking down and getting stuck between floors. There was an emergency tannoy button in the lift for raising the alarm in the event of a malfunction, but initially nobody answered our call.

In a short space of time it began to get mighty hot and conditions became extremely claustrophobic with so many of us being trapped in such a confined space. To make matters worse, one of the passengers was heavily pregnant and became fearful that she may go into labour. Her level of panic increased with each passing minute as the atmosphere slowly worsened and it became harder to breathe. This had the effect of making nearly everyone feel a little frantic – the exception being Paolo. He was stood right next to the two-way tannoy when someone finally answered the emergency line and enquired what was wrong. His immediate response wasn't to explain our plight and state we needed urgent assistance but, instead, to calmly tell our possible liberator he was starving and would like to order fish & chips. Paolo's attempt at wit at such a fraught time didn't exactly settle the nerves of our pregnant friend, and I think she would have throttled him if she'd been close enough to get her hands around his throat! Luckily, the person answering the call didn't just hang-up, and stayed on the line long enough to learn the lift had jammed and we needed to be rescued – but, even so, it was still a while before the engineer arrived and we were finally extricated.

Paolo's reputation for being a cool dude did eventually suffer a body blow when he once overdid it with the alcohol and made of a mug of himself. Generally, if you need directions, I think most people would agree with the old adage, 'then ask a police officer'; however, that didn't apply in regard to Paolo after his drinking exploits one night. Following an evening out at the police bar he'd left a little worse for wear around 11pm to make his way home – all of 100 yards away from the police station. Then, around an hour later, he stumbled back into the police bar covered in mud, having never made it home. Tongue in cheek, he informed his colleagues he'd wanted some fresh air and had gone for a walk, but the truth was that he'd become well and truly lost after heading off in the wrong direction and getting completely disorientated – despite his house being just around the corner. Opposite the nick was a school, and he'd plainly spent the last hour staggering around their playing fields in the pitch dark and, by the state of his clothes, had clearly spent more time scrambling about in the mud on all fours than he had on his feet!

Relaying all these amusing anecdotes could falsely imply that fun times were plentiful in my day, and policing was dealt with in a light-hearted manner, but that was never the case. Although there were elements of fun, such aspects never detracted from the fact police work was rightly viewed by officers as a serious business – and always treated as such by those colleagues I worked with throughout my time on the force. Above all else, delivering a quality service was seen as paramount, and their professionalism always shone through whatever challenges they encountered.   Likewise, their incredible ability to respond effectively in a crisis never ceased to amaze me and constantly earned my utmost respect.

17 Lack of Domestic Bliss

RESPONDING TO DOMESTIC DISPUTES was probably my least favourite task when it came to carrying out police duties, principally because you often had to deal with distraught and unpredictable people in volatile situations – which I'm sure is something that will resonate with anyone who has been engaged in law enforcement. I'd grown up seeing home as a safe haven, and once I became involved in upholding the law I rapidly realised this wasn't the case for many people. For some, home could be a nightmare; a place where they inexorably faced abuse and the imminent threat of danger on a daily basis.

Attending domestics, as we called them during my days of service, even though this term didn't really capture the true horrors of what often went on behind closed doors, was something that occurred frequently during most shifts and formed a huge part of each frontline officer's overall workload. No doubt this still remains the case nowadays. With some domestic incidents, the worst aspect was becoming aware of the awful things affecting members of that particular household, and then not being able deal with them in the way you wanted. Whilst protecting anyone at risk of enduring harm was always our main aim during such interventions, we also had to be mindful we were actually encroaching into the personal lives of those impacted as soon as we stepped over a threshold into their domain – and therefore needed to be suitably respectful of that situation. Equally, it was important to realise that in some instances ambivalence could play a big part in volatile relationships – and also that any form of love/hate relationship, which a victim possibly had with their abuser, could create a degree of ambiguity, and influence how they wanted you to deal with matters.

Although you primarily arrived at the scene of domestic incidents as a peacemaker or arbitrator, invariably that could change in a flash, especially if it became necessary to remove or arrest an aggressor. In such circumstances, you could easily end up being viewed as public enemy number one in the eyes of those you were trying to deal with or help, instead of being looked upon as a welcome redeemer. Consequently, it was commonplace for those present to suddenly gang up against us – including the victim in some instances.

In addition to those domestics I've already alluded to elsewhere in my memoir, there are many others I still vividly remember for a variety of reasons. The first of these I attended with Nev soon after I'd joined the Special Constabulary, and it was another of those situations that combined serious undertones with an element of farce, due to some of the behaviour verging on the absurd.

Nev and I were covering response during a weekday night when we were sent to deal with a domestic disturbance at an address on a local council housing estate. Upon our arrival we could hear there was a bit of a commotion still in progress and, once we'd entered the property, we discovered this was due to an ongoing dispute between a mother and her teenage son. What had likely started as a noisy confab had developed into a full-scale quarrel, and they were hurtling abuse at each other as the slanging-match ensued. From what we could ascertain between the abusive exchanges, it appeared the argument had arisen because the lad had woken everyone up after noisily coming into the house following a late night out. He had been berated by his mother for doing so and had taken exception to this.

Our initial attempts to calm the situation down seemed to fall on deaf ears as they continued to scornfully spit venom, with the mother at one point referring to her boy as 'parasitic scrounger'. Nev therefore had to lay down the law and threaten to arrest both parties if they persisted in screaming at each other – and this briefly had the desired effect of shutting them both up. However, it didn't last for long. The mother informed us that her miscreant son had become increasingly out of control since starting to take drugs; so the teenager then decided he'd get revenge on his mum for being a snitch by grassing her up. He retorted she was also a lawbreaker because she'd been claiming benefits to which she wasn't entitled. For the mother this was transcending a forbidden line and like a red rag to a bull – so, without warning, she flew into a rage and went berserk. She armed herself with a poker and started chasing her son around the house trying to hit him over the head with her improvised weapon.

Within a split second all hell had broken loose, and a situation we thought we had under control had descended into a fiasco. Immediately Nev and I sprung into action. We attempted to catch the mother to prevent her from doing her boy some serious damage – and, after several laps of chasing her around the downstairs rooms as she pursued her son, we finally managed to apprehend her.

Fortunately, we'd been able to disarm her before any of her attempted blows had connected with her son's head, and things then calmed down. With no injuries having been inflicted, Nev decided he would caution them both about their behaviour rather than take them into custody. As part of this process, he stressed once again that any repetition of their totally unacceptable behaviour would result in them being arrested. This time it had the desired effect as they heeded his advice and then went to bed as suggested; meaning we got no further calls to that address during the remainder of our shift. Ultimately it was a good outcome, and heartening to know our intervention had likely prevented a vicious crime being committed. However, when I reflect on the farcical situation we encountered, with the pair of them running around the house, followed by Nev and me in hot pursuit, I imagine it would have looked like one of those comical law enforcement scenes from a silent movie, rather than a serious matter that required the attendance of real police officers.

The next really memorable domestic I attended I was working with Gavin, once again supporting on a night shift. We'd been on mobile patrol for the first half of our Saturday night tour of duty, and I recall it had been unbelievably busy with us dashing from one job to the next. Around 0100hrs, we were just returning to the nick for our refreshment break when we were asked to respond to a 999 call reporting a disturbance at a residential address, so we hastily made our way to the location we'd been directed to attend. A worried neighbour had reported the emergency after hearing shouting and banging coming from the house next door, but otherwise the information we had was minimal and we didn't really know what to expect upon our arrival – which is often the case where domestics are concerned.

When Gavin and I arrived we discovered the front door was wide open and we could see two chaps in the kitchen, so we announced ourselves as police officers and entered the property. One of the chaps was massive and he had the other guy, who was much smaller, held tightly in a bear-hug. This was actually a relief because the smaller fellow was clutching a large carving knife in his right hand, and threatening to stab another man in the house with it – who at this point was not known to us, but turned out to be his stepfather. As the much larger chap, who appeared to be something of a gentle giant and police-friendly, seemed to have the situation under control, we were able to focus on getting our knife-wielding adversary to release his grip on the weapon, which he duly did after some gentle persuasion. We then attempted to ascertain what had been the cause of the fracas by calmly talking to the agitated young man, whilst the bigger guy continued to restrain him.

It transpired the young man had got married the previous afternoon, and that following the wedding ceremony a small reception had been held within this council house occupied by his mother and stepfather. The married couple were now spending the night here before heading off on their honeymoon the following morning. Occupants at the house that night also included the groom's younger brother, along with several other close family members who were staying over. In total there were nine people in the property and, bar our friendly giant who appeared to be sober, they'd been drinking to excess.

Seemingly, a blazing row had begun when the stepfather had allegedly made an offensive remark to the groom's mother, to which his stepson had taken exception. Things had then escalated to the point where the enraged young man had picked up the knife and used it to threaten his step-dad – at which point our able 'assistant' had intervened, and tried to stop the situation from boiling over by restraining the groom in a bear-hug. It emerged that there was not a lot of love lost between the stepfather and stepson and they shared a mutual dislike of each other. This had clearly surfaced more than normal once they'd become embroiled in an argument whilst under the influence of alcohol.

Anyhow, once things had calmed down and we had the situation under control, we then reasoned with the newly married young man to get him to take on board his behaviour had been totally unacceptable, and accept that any further repetition would result in him spending his wedding night in the cells. After much coaxing, it appeared we'd won him around because he reluctantly acknowledged he had been out of order and it was now time for bed – where he would hopefully sleep things off. Next, we turned our attention to the other family members and tried to convince them it was time to draw a close on the matrimonial celebrations and retire for the night. Following a little cajoling, they also agreed to comply with our proposal, so we hoped it would now be appropriate for us to make our exit – albeit we appreciated this had been an explosive situation, which could easily and rapidly deteriorate once more after our departure. And indeed that proved to be the case.

Certain aspects of policing inevitably involve officers making judgement calls, and therefore things don't always turn out the way you hope. Where people are concerned, the level of unpredictability understandably increases when you are dealing with dysfunctional families or those affected by alcohol, drugs or mental health conditions – and, in regard to this particular volatile situation, we knew at least two of these factors were clearly in-play. Bearing this in mind, Gavin and I naturally had reservations about leaving the groom in the house for the night, especially in light of the aggression he'd been displaying. However, as his stepfather hadn't wanted to press charges against him (perhaps because he was loath to see him arrested on his wedding night), the conclusion we'd reached on balance was that we would have to risk it, and hope he'd calmed down enough for us to do so. Both of us were therefore wondering whether we'd done the right thing as we walked down the garden path after leaving the house. As it turned out, we didn't even reach the garden gate before things suddenly went pear-shaped and we knew the decision we'd felt compelled to make, mostly against our better judgement, had backfired on us big time.

Gavin and I were instantly galvanised into taking action when we heard a blood-curdling scream, followed by a piercing shriek, which alerted us to the fact trouble had once again erupted. As we re-entered the property to investigate what had caused the renewed commotion, we discovered a tumultuous scene. The kitchen was a bit like a battle zone with blood splattered all over the floor and walls. The stepfather was on the floor with blood oozing from a gaping wound on the side of his head, and the groom was stood over him holding a kitchen chair, which he'd used to assault his victim.

As the assailant raised the chair above his head with the intention of smashing it into his stepfather for a second time, Gavin and I rushed forward and jointly tackled him to prevent him from committing another assault and inflicting further injury. The force with which we piled into him caused the three of us to go tumbling through a doorway into the lounge, and collapse onto a sofa – so at least we had a soft landing. At this point the offender was still gripping onto the kitchen chair and we had to wrestle with him to get it out of his hands. Luckily, Gavin and I had ended up on top of the violent groom, so this gave us the upper hand as we endeavoured to get him under control. It also meant that Gavin was able to use his radio to call for urgent assistance. This was just as well, since other members of the household had taken umbrage at our efforts to place the violent offender in handcuffs and were now siding with him – thus negating the slight advantage we had from being on top of the assailant.

Of those that interfered, the most vociferous and aggressive of these was the bride, who started to lay into Gavin after she'd unsuccessfully tried to pull him off her husband. Thankfully assistance arrived rapidly, and the first officer to join us at the scene was Ivan. He immediately grabbed the wife with the intention of dragging her away from Gavin. However, the groom took offence at Ivan's action and lashed out at him with his right leg, striking him with a forceful kick to the nether regions. The agony caused by this kick made Ivan see red and, in self-defence, he threw a punch at the perpetrator of his assault – only to miss and instead strike Gavin a fearsome blow on his right shoulder! To any onlookers it would probably have looked like a comical scene out of a 'Punch & Judy' show, even though this unnerving experience was anything but.

Dealing with any type of brawl or physical attack can be daunting, and when it occurs in someone's home you are presented with additional challenges. Not only is the problem compounded by the fact you are trying to operate in a confined space, meaning it can be tricky to regain control and expediently remove the main cause (or causes) of the threat from the scene, but also because you can face extra hostility from anyone else present. This was one of those instances, and it wasn't until we had three further officers arrive to assist us that we were finally able to fully get the upper hand and complete the arrest of the groom. Once we'd removed him from the house and placed him in the waiting 'Black Maria' – or, to be factually correct, a police transit van – the paramedics were then able to take over administering first aid to his stepfather. That more or less brought a close to this incident, but we did end up also having to nick our prisoner's younger brother. He had to be apprehended when he objected to us arresting his older sibling, and exhibited his displeasure by banging on the windows of the police van with his fists and then launching a karate kick at its back door.

In terms of the overall outcome, you could argue that the groom deservedly suffered the wedding night blues when he had to spend his first night as a married man alone in jail contemplating his lot, instead of sharing a bed with his bride and blissfully enjoying his nuptials. The following day he was charged with GBH, and subsequently he received a custodial sentence, so hopefully he used the time to reflect on the repercussions of his behaviour, and how his downfall had been self-inflicted.

Both Gavin and Ivan were left feeling a little tender following their respective involvements in the arrest of the main aggressor – Gavin as the result of the 'friendly fire', and Ivan as a consequence of the kick he'd received to his 'Crown Jewels' – but there was no lasting damage and the pair of them were ok to continue their duties. And, in Ivan's case, I did hear on good authority there was actually a plus side because, when he got home after his shift and revealed the injury he'd sustained to his wife, she was for once quite impressed with the swelling in that part of his anatomy!

There was no time for Gavin and I to ponder on the events that had led up to the stepfather being injured, and any soul-searching had to be put on ice because as soon as we'd finished dealing with the groom we got a shout to attend another domestic. Having to respond to urgent incidents one after another isn't that unordinary, and can be par for the course where policing is concerned, but this particular night shift was especially frenetic – so demanding you needed to be like some sort of ubiquitous superhero in order to cope with the volume of emergencies. This latest call was to a neighbourhood at the other side of town and we hastily made our way there.

The request for police attendance had once more come from a concerned neighbour, who'd been woken up in the middle of the night by yelling coming from next door. However, by the time we got to the house in question things seemed peaceful, even though the downstairs lights were on and members of the household were clearly still up and about. In spite of the apparent state of serenity, it was nonetheless necessary for us to investigate that all was now well, so we therefore knocked on the door and made it known it was the police calling. Shortly after doing so the door was answered and we were greeted by a well-built, respectable looking gentleman, who was probably aged in his mid-forties. We explained that we'd received a report of a disturbance coming from this address, and his immediate response was to apologise for putting us to any trouble. According to his version of events, there had been a 'minor row' between himself and his wife, but everything was now sorted and they were fine. He also informed us that they'd been out at a party that night and a slight disagreement had arisen just after they'd returned home around 2am – which had perhaps become a little heated due to them both being under the influence of alcohol.

This explanation seemed reasonable, but we pointed out that for peace of mind we still needed to check that his wife and anyone else residing at the property were ok, and able to corroborate what he'd told us. We half expected him to go on the defensive at this stage, but he remained affable and obligingly invited us in so we could have a word with his wife and teenage daughter. As we were ushered into the lounge to meet them, it was immediately obvious they had both been distressed prior to our arrival, and were frantically trying to recover their composure and wipe away the tears that had clearly been flowing. Gavin once more explained the reason we were there and, without being unduly invasive, sensitively enquired if they were ok – to which they both responded in the affirmative. To Gavin and I it was evident there was probably more to this situation than we'd been told. However, it seemed there was no way they were going to break ranks and reveal more details about the altercation, or divulge anything else about a potential lack of matrimonial bliss. This was despite requesting the man of the house leave the room while we speak to his wife and daughter – so they'd have a better opportunity to be open with us if something more untoward had occurred.

As so often happens in this type of circumstance, those who likely need help decline to say anything that would enable the police to take appropriate action. Therefore, although we sensed something was probably amiss within this home setting, we were unable to do anything more, especially as there were no visible signs either of the female parties had suffered physical violence. Consequently, this was an instance where you hoped police intervention would act as a deterrent if the gentleman was prone to be controlling, abusive or violent towards his loved ones.

A couple of other domestics left a lasting impression on me for contrasting reasons; the first because our presence probably prevented any bloodshed – and the second because a significant amount of blood had already been spilt.

In regard to the initial incident, I was working on a late shift with a rookie constable known as AJ when we were asked to attend the home of a middle-aged couple, whose 26-year-old son had threatened to stab them. The threat had been made during a row over the phone and the son was purported to be en route to their home. Our instruction was to join his parents at their house and remain with them so we could intercept the son, who had a history of mental health problems that sometimes made him unpredictable. Once there, the parents told us that their son had phoned them from the pub about an ongoing dispute and become abusive. This apparently wasn't unusual once he'd consumed a copious amount of alcohol. The call had culminated in him making the threat to stab them, which they'd taken seriously since he had a tendency to become violent after drinking.

During our conversation with his parents, I also discovered I'd been to school with their son – and actually been in the same class for several years. However, I hadn't realised I knew him because he'd changed his name via deed poll since our school days. Once I became aware we'd been at junior school together, I recalled that even then he sometimes posed a threat and was frequently in trouble for bullying. Based on what his parents told us, I suspected he'd subsequently developed into a bully at home since becoming an adult, and been a handful for them to manage.

As the time ticked by and he still hadn't arrived, you could sense they were getting increasingly agitated – especially the dad, who at one point lit a cigarette the wrong way around and amusingly set the filter alight, which did create some light relief. I think whilst AJ and I were present they appreciated we offered them some degree of protection, but they understood we couldn't play nursemaid for an indeterminate amount of time, and would soon have to assume their lad wasn't going to turn up imminently. Indeed, once an hour had elapsed, AJ came to that conclusion and explained we would have to resume our patrol, but would give passing attention in case their son was in the vicinity. We also advised the couple to immediately call 999 if he did come around after we'd left.

Upon exiting the house, we did a quick reconnaissance of the immediate area just in case he was lurking somewhere in the shadows and, sure enough, discovered him not far away hiding behind a car. No doubt he'd spotted our police vehicle parked up the road from his parents' house and, having assumed there were officers visiting his mum and dad, was waiting for us to leave before he made his move. In addition to being under the influence of alcohol, he was also in a distressed state and, far from threatening to do harm to his parents, he seemed more intent on causing himself damage as he kept telling us he wanted to end it all. A search revealed he was not currently in possession of a knife – possibly because he'd disposed of it on spotting the police vehicle. In the circumstances, AJ decided the most appropriate course of action would be to detain him under the Mental Health Act for the sake of his own safety, and that of his parents, with a view to getting him sectioned on the basis he was threatening self-harm. This seemed a sensible approach, especially as his parents were not keen to press charges against him for threatening behaviour, and felt he needed help addressing his issues relating to alcoholism and anger management. After successfully pursuing this course of action, we subsequently informed his parents. They were suitably relieved, and then able to retire to bed for a good night's sleep in the knowledge that any immediate threat to their welfare had been removed – and also that their son, who clearly harboured suicidal thoughts, would now be getting the help they'd been craving for some time.

This was an example of police intervention leading to a positive outcome for all parties. It not only prevented any bloodshed and gave the parents some peace of mind, but also ensured the young man would now have the chance to embark on a path to recovery. Therefore, once we'd done a quick search of the peripheral area to check a knife hadn't been discarded in close proximity, we were able to move onto our next task knowing we'd done our best to address the situation we'd encountered.

The second of these contrasting domestic incidents also involved a young man, this time the teenage son of a single parent. In this instance, the mother had locked her son out of the house after he'd been out drinking and failed to return home by a stipulated time. Her decision to bolt the door had been taken to teach him a lesson because he'd ignored a midnight curfew, which had been imposed after he'd repeatedly come home late drunk, and woken his mother and younger siblings by doing so. Upon discovering the door locked, the young man had flown into a rage. After much swearing and banging, he'd then smashed a pane of glass in the front door with his right hand in an attempt to reach the lock and undo it. As a result, his fearful mother had phoned the police to request assistance, believing he could be violent towards her if he gained entry. However, what the mother didn't know when she summoned the police, was that her son had sustained a serious injury to his hand as a result of breaking the glass.

On the night this happened I was part of a small taskforce, comprising of six special constables and a regular officer named Scotty, who was the acting-sergeant in charge of proceedings during this shift. We were occupying a crew bus and our unit was being deployed in the town centre to combat anti-social behaviour, but we'd been diverted to deal with this domestic-related incident because Simmo, who was covering response, was already committed at another job – where a wife had allegedly stabbed her husband.

Our biggest concern upon arriving at the reported disturbance was the physical state of the young man. There was a considerable amount of blood pouring from wounds to his right hand, most of it coming from his middle finger, which had a six-inch shard of glass sticking right through it. The drunken lad was in an emotional state and, despite the severity of his injury, almost seemed oblivious to it. Our main aim was to administer first aid, but that wasn't straightforward because all the agitated lad wanted to do was gain access to his home and go to bed – which was a non-starter considering the damage he'd done to himself. Rather than call an ambulance, Scotty decided we would transport him immediately to the local A&E department to get his injury dealt with as a matter of urgency. During our journey it was necessary to restrain him because his behaviour was erratic, and he kept trying to remove the shard of glass from his almost severed finger – which would undoubtedly have done more harm than good. We also had to keep him under control whilst a doctor removed the glass and applied appropriate treatment. This included inserting around 30 stitches to his wounds. By the time the doctor had finished, the effects of the alcohol our patient had consumed had started to wear off, and he'd become increasingly aware of the immense pain he was in – and he was clearly feeling sorry for himself. Having transformed from a 'lion' to a 'sheep', and ceased being so churlish, his mother decided not to press charges against him for criminal damage. Instead, she agreed he could return home now he'd been patched up and was showing remorse for his actions – thus bringing this situation to a close in terms of it being a police matter.

Whilst dealing with this incident, we'd also been hearing regular updates over the radio from Simmo about the domestic he'd attended, where a man had been stabbed in the stomach during a row with his wife. He'd reported that the husband was bleeding profusely from the stab wound, and he'd arrested the wife on suspicion of committing GBH. With the husband having suffered life-threatening internal injuries, it sounded like it was a tense situation that could develop into a very serious crime scene, so CID officers had joined him at the location.

It was heartening to learn later that the injured party did ultimately survive, as the knife had just missed connecting with any vital organs or piercing any arteries. However, I was surprised to discover he'd been so fortunate because, once we'd returned to the police station after our patrol, I'd seen the size of the carving knife used in the stabbing, and just how far it must have penetrated. The end of the blade was considerably bent, presumably from striking a bone – perhaps the rib cage or pelvis – and, based on the length of the curve, I anticipate it must have gone in a good four to five inches, so he was indeed a lucky man.

My final account of a domestic incident outlines what happened when Ivan and I responded to an emergency involving another threat to kill. Without doubt, this was the most haunting and moving of all the domestics I ever attended throughout my service.

On the occasion this occurred it was late at night and we were operating as the active response unit. While patrolling the town centre we suddenly got an urgent call over the radio, and the first thing the control room operator checked was that we were double-crewed. Upon hearing this, we intuitively knew we were about to be asked to respond to something deemed quite serious. From the tone of the operator's voice, you could also work out it was going to be one of those incidents that may place us in considerable danger – well, more than you'd normally expect to face during the course of your duties! So, instantly our adrenaline levels became raised.

A 999 call had been received from a young girl, who'd apparently fled her home along with her younger brother. She'd indicated that her father had been threatening to kill their mother and, from what the operator had gleaned about the situation, it sounded like he could be in possession of a firearm. We were informed the children would be waiting for us outside the telephone box the young girl had used to make the emergency call, and instructed to make our way immediately to rendezvous with them – but to then assess the risk before intervening further. With haste being crucial, we blue-lighted it to the location we'd been given. There we spotted the two young children standing on the pavement outside the telephone kiosk looking absolutely terrified. It was a freezing cold night and the pair of them were stood in their pyjamas shivering, while desperately awaiting our arrival.

Our primary objective was to manage their welfare and protect them from harm. To make sure they were safe, we therefore placed them in the back of the police car, suitably wrapped in an emergency blanket to help them warm up. The girl was probably aged around seven or eight, and her little brother was no more than five-years-old. Understandably, they were both extremely upset. Between her sobs, the distressed young girl was able to tell us that she'd been woken up by her father shouting at their mother – and, that when he'd angrily said he was going to shoot their mum, she'd been so scared she'd grabbed her younger brother and run out of the house. This had been an amazingly brave and sensible thing to do when faced with such an alarming situation. Once out of the house, she'd then had the wherewithal to go to a nearby telephone box and phone for the police; an equally admiral action for someone so young.

It melts your heart when you see little children having to contend with something that causes such anguish. Consequently, when the young girl pleaded with us to not let her daddy shoot her mummy, Ivan and I felt compelled to do whatever we could to prevent any escalation of the incident – even though we appreciated this would mean us entering the home from which the children had just made their escape.

Having secured the children in the police car, we proceeded with extreme caution as we approached their home and knocked on the door. We knew we could be putting ourselves in a precarious situation, and there's nothing like an unknown threat to heighten one's awareness and put you on your guard. Whilst awaiting an answer, Ivan therefore advised we should stand back from the doorway, just in case someone brandishing a weapon confronted us. As we stood there feeling some degree of trepidation, I wondered whether we were being courageous or plain stupid in our actions. On reflection now, I don't think either really applied. Ultimately, it was just another judgement call, based on a combination of what we knew about the situation from talking to the children and our human instincts. Besides, exposure to an element of danger is an intrinsic part of the role where police work is concerned – it always has been and always will be – and how we dealt with this specific incident wasn't about us being gung-ho, brave or naïve. It was simply the way things were, and historically how the job got done at that particular time; so, in terms of our response that night, every police officer would have done the same thing during that era.

Anyway, it was an anxious couple of minutes as Ivan and I patiently waited for someone to come to the door. We didn't know what to expect or what type of reception we'd receive – or whether we'd end up having to force entry if nobody came to let us in. After what seemed like an age, someone finally opened the door and, much to our relief, it wasn't the father greeting us with weapon in hand, but a lady dressed in her night attire. As she looked at least 60-years-old, we presumed it wasn't the mother of the children we'd left in the police car. She appeared to be in a state of shock and very pleased to see us. We didn't need to explain why we were there and, during a quick conversation on the doorstep, we ascertained she was the maternal grandmother.

Immediately she was forthcoming about what had happened. Quickly she told us that her daughter and son-in-law had been having a blazing row in their bedroom, and their raised voices had awoken everyone in the household, including herself and her grandchildren – who, as we already knew, had been so scared they'd fled the house. She also informed us that the row had escalated rapidly and culminated in her son-in-law threatening to shoot her daughter. Furthermore, she importantly went on to say he possessed a firearm, but she didn't think it was a real gun – and she therefore presumed it had been an idle threat when she'd heard him say he was going to shoot her daughter. Naturally, we needed to know as much as possible about what we were dealing with, and she also helpfully revealed that, other than herself, it was only her daughter and son-in-law in the property at that time – since the children had of course already made their escape.

Once armed with all this intelligence, including that the daughter and son-in-law were likely still in their bedroom, Ivan shouted up the stairs that we were police officers and ordered the couple to come down with their hands in the air. The woman did as she was told and soon emerged at the top of the staircase. After she'd descended the flight of steps and joined us downstairs we could see she was in a distraught state, but physically unharmed. She insisted everything was ok and that her and her husband had settled their differences following a 'tiff', and police involvement was not required.

This is what frequently happens when dealing with this type of matter but, on this occasion, there was no way we could leave it at that, bearing in mind the impact the so-called 'tiff' had disturbingly had on the children, and the fact that a firearm might have been involved. We were therefore adamant we needed to speak with her husband, and would also need to check whether he possessed a firearm. In response she told us he did own a gun, but it was just a starting pistol and he hadn't threatened her with it.

As her husband still remained upstairs in his bedroom, having not complied with Ivan's instruction to come down, we had to decide whether to go upstairs to confront him or call for armed backup. Taking into account the information his wife had given us, we opted to do the former. After announcing we'd be coming up the stairs we tentatively did so, and then entered the guy's bedroom once we'd persuaded him to get out of bed and put his hands out to show us he wasn't holding a weapon. In the circumstances, it seemed strange that the chap was still in his bedroom acting as though whatever had been going on didn't involve him. He was the type of man you'd perhaps describe as nondescript because he was relatively small in build and looked as though he wouldn't say 'boo to a goose'. I therefore had to remind myself that bullies and abusers come in all sorts of forms, shapes and sizes as there is no stereotypical contender who behaves in this manner – and that even someone with Walter Mitty characteristics, and a stature that makes them appear timid and unassuming, could still pose a serious threat.

Firstly we checked where he kept the starting pistol that his wife had advised us he possessed and, without hesitation, he confirmed he did have such a firearm and it was in a box under his bed. Although it was not illegal to possess such an item, Ivan stated we would need to check it was indeed only a starting pistol and not some other lethal form of firearm. Considering he hadn't initially responded to our command to come downstairs, he now seemed compliant and accommodating because he instantly showed Ivan exactly where to locate the box containing the starting pistol, which was stored under the bed – and then agreed to voluntarily hand it over for us to take away, even though he vehemently denied using it to threaten his wife.

In situations where a 'weapon' has been used in a threatening manner it would naturally be confiscated. However, as it appeared doubtful the chap's wife was going to make a complaint against her husband, which would enable us to make an arrest, seize the pistol and subsequently charge him with an offence, we knew it could be a grey area. It was therefore helpful when he chose to hand it over willingly, and agreed the police should take possession – whereupon it could be destroyed. This was especially important bearing in mind the children had been subjected to such a high degree of fear. They would have experienced huge anxiety knowing it had likely been used to terrorise their mother – and we certainly didn't want any repetition of the poor little mites being scared witless or having further emotional trauma inflicted upon them.

Just as we'd anticipated, the wife did continue stating the situation hadn't been as bad as we'd been led to believe. She attempted to minimise the impact of the whole affair, by insisting the children and her mother must have been mistaken when they thought they overheard her husband threatening to shoot her. Even though she admitted her husband had raised his voice during their row, she stressed this outburst was out of character and he'd never done anything like it before. She also assured us he wasn't a violent man. Without her making a complaint, or at least confirming her husband had made a threat to kill, we were powerless to deal with this matter in the way we wanted – which would be to arrest him in light of his suspected threatening behaviour.

With the wife's corroboration being the key to us taking any positive action, and knowing a charge would never stick in the absence of such testimony, Ivan did try a different tactic in order to get her to support a case against her husband. We strongly suspected she wasn't telling us the full story and, most likely, was sticking by her husband out of fear, or because she was trying to protect him out of misguided loyalty – and either way we understood her reasons for doing so. However, in a last-ditch effort to get her to admit there was an issue at home, Ivan highlighted the matter of her children and the adverse affect this incident would have had on them. He hoped that if he focused on their wellbeing, and emphasised just how scared and upset they'd been when we'd found them sobbing their hearts out, it might get her to see things differently. From her body language you could see this really hit home and presented her with a dilemma. Therefore, as she struggled with this torment and wrestled with her conscience, Ivan and I wondered if her obvious concern for her children's welfare would be enough to tip the balance and get her to be more candid.

To anyone who hasn't been exposed to living in an abusive relationship or a volatile environment, or been in a role that has brought them into contact with such situations, I'm sure it could seem like this should have been a simple decision for her to make. But, however perverse it might appear, that is far from being the case when someone has endured a traumatic and turbulent lifestyle, where they've had to go through each day being wary and judicious over a sustained period. Often those trying to survive in such circumstances are living in a revolving nightmare, and there are all sorts of complexities that come into play when someone has persistently undergone this type of experience and likely feels trapped. Consequently, it came as no surprise to us when ultimately the wife wasn't swayed by Ivan's tactics and resolutely stuck to her story – and declined to make a formal complaint.

Whilst disappointed at this outcome, because her refusal to do so meant we were stymied when it came to taking any robust action, we entirely understood her reluctance to substantiate any allegations against her hubby, and the reasons for her decision. Moreover, we also appreciated that her reticence didn't mean she was being complicit. Neither did it infer she was being accepting of the sorry state of affairs that her family faced so, as always in these situations, we remained non-judgemental. However, with us being unable to persuade her otherwise in regard to pressing charges, one frustratingly sensed the police would likely be back sometime soon.

Having reached this impasse, despite coming tantalisingly close to getting the mother to change her mind, our primary concern remained the welfare of the children – as we knew it would now be necessary to return them to their home. Before doing so, we explained to them what had happened as a result of our intervention, and made sure they were comfortable going back inside the house. We told them no harm had come to their mummy and, upon giving them this news, we could visibly see their relief. From their reaction it was also apparent they were both desperate to get back home to have a cuddle with her.

Despite our reservations about the environment they were living in, it was important at this stage that we told them things were now ok so we didn't cause them to worry too much, or burden them with our concerns. However, at the same time, we made it clear they'd done exactly the right thing in calling the police, and should call us again if they ever experienced anything similar that made them frightened. Naturally we didn't want to go into any detail about the starting pistol but, to put their minds at rest, we did assure them that their daddy didn't have a gun and wouldn't be shooting their mummy – which technically was the truth, since it wasn't a genuine firearm and was no longer in the house.

Whilst we had to do everything we could to give the two young children peace of mind, both Ivan and I still had grave concerns about their future welfare. We knew we'd almost certainly just been dealing with a dysfunctional family unit, where there was likely to be an underlying endemic problem, which would need to be brought to the attention of Social Services. I have little doubt that when Ivan alerted them to the matter, he would have discovered this family was already on their radar.

It played heavily on our minds that we'd had to leave the children in a potentially perilous situation, due to us not having the necessary evidence to justify removing them. However, if nothing else, we hoped our attendance should act as a warning to their father, and possibly make him consider the implications of his alleged unacceptable behaviour – particularly the devastating impact it had clearly had on his children. The outcome in this instance wasn't ideal, but at least we knew we'd done our best to minimise the likelihood of anyone in this household coming to harm based on the legal powers in place at that time – which often made it virtually impossible to take things further against an offender suspected of domestic abuse without the victim pressing charges. Again, after confronting this heart-rending situation, we didn't have the luxury of giving it too much thought before having to deal with the next emergency call.

These accounts of domestics represent just a small proportion of the overall number of incidents of this nature that I attended throughout my service, but they typify the issues, difficulties and highly charged emotional situations that were regularly encountered when dealing with such unpredictable matters. Frequently such incidents featured domestic abuse, often committed by those who were under the influence of alcohol, or sometimes drugs. Predominantly, but by no means exclusively, the aggressors we encountered when dealing with situations involving domestic abuse were male and, as highlighted before, it was common for their aggression to be re-directed at the police when officers encroached into their private lives or tried to intervene.

18   Wayward Driving

Responding to road traffic collisions (RTCs) understandably features prominently as part of police work and I attended my fair share of such incidents during my time on the force. Driving can put anyone on the wrong side of the law at some point during their time on the road, and also at risk whenever they get behind a wheel or astride a motorbike. In terms of innocent people losing their lives or being seriously injured in the UK, vehicles are statistically far more lethal than guns and knives combined – and, in the wrong hands, can become a deadly 'weapon'. This was something I used to occasionally point out to bolshy, indignant or uncooperative drivers who thought the police ought to leave motorists alone and focus on catching criminals. Maybe such people would find it an enlightening and sobering experience if they had to witness and deal with the devastating scenes of utter carnage that bad driving can bring about – scenes that can resemble a battlefield. I won't go into detail about some of the horrific sights that you come across at traffic collisions but, needless to say, it can be very gory, especially when there are multiple serious injuries or fatalities involved. Perhaps seeing such tragic events first-hand, and the pain and despair they can cause, accounts for the contempt I therefore felt towards speedsters, or anyone who endangered innocent road users by recklessly taking to their vehicles whilst under the influence of alcohol or drugs.

Dealing with RTCs often went hand in hand with encountering drink-drivers, and that was the case when I accompanied Sian (an experienced WPC) to a serious collision. It had occurred just outside a picturesque village on the outer fringes of our patch, and apparently involved two vehicles, which were now completely blocking the road having collided on a narrow bridge running over a river. A 'Good Samaritan', who'd stopped to administer first aid, had also advised control it was a head-on crash between a saloon car and a campervan, and that significant injuries had been sustained by the occupants of the car – a mother and daughter. In light of this, we rushed to the incident on blues and twos. En route we learned the driver of the campervan had left the scene, having possibly done a runner, and that our sergeant for the shift, along with Spud who was paired with him in a patrol car, had also been despatched to help deal with the collision. This latter part of the update was good news, since the incident had been classed as a high priority, after taking into account that two of the parties involved had suffered serious injuries, and it had the potential to develop into a fatal accident (FATAC).

An ambulance arrived just as we got to the scene, so we were able to concentrate on securing the area and making it safe whilst the paramedics got to work on the injured mother and daughter. Thankfully, they'd not been trapped in their car, despite the severe damage it had incurred after being struck head-on. Also, once their injuries had been assessed by the paramedics, it was heartening to learn that although serious, they weren't after all deemed to be life-threatening. Upon hearing this news, our sergeant decided he would return to the borough and leave Sian, Spud and me to deal with the incident – and also to search for the missing campervan driver.

As there were no independent witnesses to the collision, we would ultimately have to rely on the occupants of the two vehicles to piece together the cause of the accident – but we appreciated that wasn't going to be feasible yet, with the campervan driver having gone AWOL, and the injured mother and daughter currently being in no fit state to explain what had happened. We'd established the missing driver was likely male and had disappeared immediately after the collision – thus far though, we'd not discovered his whereabouts. However, with there being a lot of blood in the camper, we assumed he was probably in a bad way and had suffered a significant wound; so urgently needed medical attention. We thought he might have wandered off in a daze due to a head injury and being in shock, or possibly run away because he was intoxicated – but, whatever the reason, it was essential we located him without delay.

An enquiry via the police national computer (PNC) to obtain the campervan driver's details revealed the registered keeper was indeed male, and a subsequent person check informed us this individual was wanted by our colleagues in the Met – having been identified as a possible suspect in an attempted murder case they were currently investigating! On the basis of this information, we presumed the owner was most likely the driver, and therefore the wanted person – who, according to records held on file, had links to the capital's 'underworld'. He was also described as a dangerous criminal with a string of convictions for committing a range of violent offences. This revelation upped the ante considerably, and meant we had to intensify and widen our search, especially as we hadn't managed to locate him after a quick recce of the surrounding area. We therefore requested assistance from a dog handler, and luckily didn't have to wait long for such a colleague to arrive.

The handler had been in the vicinity and monitoring our radio transmissions, so he was almost instantly available to assist. Upon his arrival he set his dog Fido to work. It immediately picked up a scent, but the trail rapidly went cold once Fido came away from the narrow bridge where the crash had taken place. In the circumstances, the handler soon reached the conclusion the suspect driver had either been transported away from the area by someone in another vehicle or, more likely, had entered the water. Our colleague thought the guy might have jumped into the river and could actually be hiding under the bridge. Therefore, he cunningly suggested that if we discreetly made it look as though we'd given up the search and retreated from the scene, maybe the suspect would emerge.

By this time the ambulance had left and the damaged vehicles had been towed away, so he anticipated it would look quite natural to the absent campervan driver if we were to now leave as well, having seemingly failed to find him. We duly complied with the dog handler's cunning plan and headed off, with one of us driving his police van to make it look like he was on his way as well – whilst, in actual fact, he remained, appropriately hidden out of sight with his hound. It didn't take long for our astute colleague's theory to bear fruit. Within a couple of minutes we got a radio call from him to say he'd apprehended the suspect. Sure enough, he had been hiding under the bridge and had come out from his hidey-hole immediately after we'd departed and the coast had appeared to be clear. In a wet and bedraggled state he'd then clambered up the river bank to the road – where he'd been greeted by the welcoming long arm of the law in the form of a ferocious looking Alsatian! Bearing this in mind, he'd wisely opted to come quietly and was in handcuffs by the time we arrived back at the bridge.

Having been identified as the wanted man, and placed in custody on suspicion of attempted murder, our mysterious suspect was also further arrested for drink-driving after providing a positive breath test. Sian, Spud and I then had the undesirable task of transporting him to the nearest custody station in our district, once we'd dressed a large gash just under his chin. During the course of our journey, we not only discovered our prisoner had indeed leapt from the bridge immediately after the collision – because he knew he was wanted back in London and was trying to evade capture – but also that he was every bit as vile as his police record suggested. He was a fiendish and fearsome looking man with very distinct features, and to me he resembled a cross between 'Rasputin' and 'Fagan'. His devilish look was further enhanced by a glint of evil in his piercing eyes, the pungency of his unpleasant odour and his unkempt appearance. The blood that had been oozing into his straggly beard from the wound to his chin also did nothing to improve his looks!

To describe this 'charming' chap as foul-mouthed would be an understatement. Throughout our trip to custody, he constantly talked at us like some sort of deranged monster. He informed us he was in cahoots with the devil, with whom he'd made a covenant so he could act as the 'Grim Reaper', and then menacingly described in detail the macabre acts he was going to perform on our respective anatomies in retribution for his arrest. The disparaging comments and hideous threats were incessant, even though we'd done our best to make him comfortable by dressing his wound, and then wrapping him in a blanket to keep him warm until his wet clothes could be removed and replaced on reaching our destination.

As an aside, I'm glad to say our revolting adversary didn't manage to exact his revenge; otherwise I'd now be missing certain vital body parts and talking in a squeaky voice!

By the time we arrived at the custody suite we'd had enough of escorting this misanthropic character but, much as we feared, the custody sergeant refused to accept our prisoner until he'd been patched up – so we then had to traipse off to the nearest hospital A&E department to get his chin wound stitched. The ragged cut required about 20 sutures and this procedure was carried out by a very tolerant casualty nurse, who remained notably professional and focused throughout, despite our prisoner being an obstinate cuss. Regrettably, she also had to put up with this detestable man continuing his demented tirade of abuse and evil ranting and raving, although it was mostly aimed at the police rather than her.

Whilst the 'devil's disciple' underwent his treatment, Spud and I had to take it in turns to be handcuffed to him to keep him under control and make sure he didn't try to make a bolt for freedom. This had the effect of accentuating his particular brand of recalcitrance, and made him even more verbally abusive towards us as he vociferously and proudly spouted his disdain for the law and shared with us the satanic doctrines he'd espoused. At one stage, while Spud was taking his turn in the hot seat, our prisoner took particular exception to his close attention and threatened him. He gleefully told my fellow SC he'd be exacting his revenge by thrusting a red-hot poker where the sun doesn't shine if he didn't let him go; to which my normally sombre and straight-laced colleague quick-wittedly replied in the vernacular:

'Ok mate, but I should let you know that we don't usually get perks in this role!'

It's never enjoyable having to be up close and personal with anyone you consider to be so repugnant, let alone when they are undergoing a delicate medical procedure; however, I can say with authority that being shackled to a crazy and deluded prisoner whilst they are having stitches is still more preferable than being handcuffed to someone when they are undergoing a stomach pump, which is something I also experienced. In this instance, a prisoner we'd arrested on suspicion of burglary informed us he'd taken an overdose of painkillers and needed medical intervention – and, as he had a history of attempting daring escapes from custody, we were taking no chances. Hence, yours truly had the unenviable task of remaining handcuffed to him whilst his stomach was pumped. And, for anyone who doesn't appreciate what that entails, I can affirm it is not something you really want to witness close up. For those unfamiliar with this process, the term pump in this context means inserting a tube into a patient's stomach via their mouth and throat, and then pouring in copious amounts of a saline solution to flush out the system – and I can assure you it has the desired effect, as the entire contents of the stomach soon emerge back up the tube and into a waiting bucket!

Anyway, in regard to our 'Rasputin/Fagan' look-alike, he was eventually discharged from hospital around 0200hrs, and we finally got him booked into the custody suite and banged up in a cell an hour later. Relieved to bid farewell to this obnoxious prisoner, we then made our way back to base, whereupon we had to draft statements and make up our pocketbooks – some six hours after we'd first attended the RTC.

Later that day our irresponsible driver was charged with drink-driving and, following further investigation into the cause of the collision, dangerous driving was also added to the charge sheet. Next he was transferred to our colleagues in the Met so they could pursue their enquiries into his involvement in the case of attempted murder. It came as no surprise when Sian subsequently enlightened me she'd found out this pernicious wrong-un was heavily into the occult and devil worship. Back in London he had even acquired the nickname of 'Beelzebub' due to his wicked look and iniquitous behaviour. This nickname was quite apt in view of the profanity and evil raging that Sian, Spud and I had experienced during his blistering verbal assaults – which definitely contained sinister undertones. You get so used to having disparaging comments aimed at you when you're out in uniform that after a while it becomes like the norm and has little affect. However, the tone, ferocity and duration of this 'delightful' chap's abusive diatribes and threatening outbursts were on another level, and undoubtedly the worst I ever had the misfortune to endure. In fact, if this loathsome man had any redeeming qualities, and most people do, even those with a particularly nasty or unpleasant streak, then they didn't surface during the time I spent dealing with him.

One evening, not long after the RTC involving 'Beelzebub', I accompanied a novice WPC to another crash scene. This one had taken place on a country road just outside of town. It was a non-injury collision involving a single vehicle, which had skidded on a bend and collided with a telegraph pole – but, what started out as a fairly innocuous incident, could so easily have turned into a serious accident with tragic consequences.

Inexplicably, my colleague parked our patrol car well beyond where the damaged vehicle had ended up, without perhaps realising it wouldn't therefore be visible to any vehicles approaching from the other direction around a blind bend, even though it had the blue lights flashing. She'd dropped me off just prior to reaching the crash scene so I could put out the police slow signs and then carry out traffic control on the other side of the blind bend but, before I'd had a chance to do either, the situation became markedly precarious.

The light was already fading, so I sensibly had on my reflective jacket and carried a flashing torch. However, as I walked towards the blind bend, a male driver coming in my direction still didn't see me. I remember that as he came around the curve of the bend, I frantically waived my hands in an attempt to get his attention but, by the time he spotted me, it was too late for him to take evasive action – and he would have ploughed into me if I hadn't leapt aside at the last second. Luckily I was fine, but that wasn't the end of this saga.

The recovery vehicle had beaten my colleague and I to the scene of the RTC, and the maintenance guy was already in the road sweeping up the debris. Having just missed me, the oncoming car next went careering towards him and, to avoid being mowed down, he had to spectacularly launch himself headlong into the hedge on the verge of the road!

After nearly hitting me, the startled driver had probably spotted the crashed vehicle that blocked his path looming in front of him and, in the nick of time, he'd hit the brakes and swerved away. However, as a result his car had gone spinning out of control and straight towards the maintenance chap, forcing him to take the evasive action outlined for the sake of his own salvation. The poor fellow suffered some superficial scratches to his face and hands, due to his brush with some brambles in the hedgerow, but otherwise seemed fine. Therefore, once I'd pulled him out of the bushes and he'd recovered from the shock of his life, he actually saw the funny side of this calamitous ordeal – which luckily ended up as a near miss rather than a catastrophe.

From my colleague's perspective what happened was a learning curve and, having experienced how dangerous crash sites can be, she rapidly came to appreciate the importance of carrying out a risk assessment when you arrive at the scene of an RTC. Not that I'm one to speak, as I once nearly caused a major incident during a road-cycling event whilst undertaking traffic control. It wasn't entirely my fault, but again a simple risk assessment could well have prevented a collision arising between one of the cyclists and a car.

For this event a number of officers were required to police potential traffic hot-spots along the route – in particular covering junctions where traffic control would be needed to ensure the smooth progress of the contestants. I was detailed to oversee traffic flow at a T-junction in a village a couple of miles out of town, and had duly been dropped off by the road traffic unit that would be leading the procession of cyclists throughout the duration of the event.

During our briefing, I'd been informed my personal police radio wouldn't work out in the sticks, so I'd need to stay alert and look out for the lead police vehicle that would be travelling around 150 metres in front of the convoy of cyclists. In effect, this would be my cue to stop any vehicles at the T-junction, which could possibly hinder the cyclists or cause a bottleneck if they were heading the same way. This all sounded simple enough – but things didn't go according to plan.

I'd been given a rough idea what time the cyclists could arrive at my location on their first circuit, and advised the contestants should have thinned out a little by this stage. However, neither the estimated time of arrival, nor the suggestion the cyclists could be quite dispersed, proved to be accurate. To make matters worse, the police escort vehicle was no longer at the head of the leading pack of around 30 bikes when they suddenly descended on me, several minutes before their expected time. This in itself wasn't a problem because, when they came into my view about 300 metres away, I still had a few seconds to react and stop any traffic at the T-junction – but what happened next did cause a big issue.

Just prior to the T-junction there was a driveway and, whilst my back was turned, a car had emerged from it onto the main road. To my horror, this vehicle then stopped right next to me waiting to turn right. The old chap at the wheel clearly hadn't seen the pack of cyclists hurtling towards him, and had pulled out into their path just a couple of seconds before they reached the point where I was stood halting the traffic. I reckon, at most, he'd left a gap of about a metre between his car and the nearside kerb for the fast-approaching cyclists to somehow squeeze by his stationary vehicle. In the split second I had to compute what was likely to happen, all I could visualise was a massive pile up. Indeed, there was a big bang, which I assumed had come as a result of several bikes colliding with the back of the elderly gentleman's car. Much to my amazement (and relief!) though, it had been caused by just a single cyclist smashing into his rear end. Miraculously, all the others had somehow managed to get by on the inside unscathed – with some of them actually mounting the pavement at considerable speed. Quite how they averted a disaster I'll never know, but it was a tribute to their cycling skills that they achieved this feat. The bike of the one unfortunate rider who'd not been so lucky was a crumpled wreck but, mercifully, he was uninjured.

What happened next again defied belief. In spite of the noise from the impact, the car driver seemed completely oblivious to the crash he had caused and started to nonchalantly drive away. It was like everything was happening in slow motion, so my immediate reaction was to start running after the errant driver, whilst also yelling for him to stop. To onlookers it probably looked like a scene from the 'Keystone Cops' as I chased after the vehicle on foot. I made a mental note of the car's registration number as I anticipated my pursuit would be futile but, much to my delight, the driver headed off so slowly I actually managed to catch up enough to bang on the car boot – which finally got his attention and caused him to pull over. I then briefly told the mystified driver his vehicle had been involved in a collision that I needed to talk to him about, and instructed him to wait while I first checked on the welfare of the cyclist.

As indicated, the cyclist had remarkably survived the scrape without sustaining as much as a scratch and, although the same could not be said for his bike, which had likely been damaged beyond repair, he appeared quite accepting of the situation. To his credit, he even acknowledged that encountering hazards during road races was a natural phenomenon, and one of the risks you have to occasionally face when participating in this type of sport. He was therefore happy to exchange details with the car driver, so he could pursue an insurance claim and get recompense for his wrecked bike – but, beyond that, he didn't want to cast blame or see the driver being prosecuted for driving without due care and attention. I felt this was magnanimous of him, and it certainly made life easier for me in terms of the way I could deal with this non-injury RTC, which technically didn't require police involvement. Keeping things low key also suited me, as I really didn't want to acquire unwelcome renown amongst my colleagues for being the officer who'd overseen this debacle; not that the freak accident had been my fault because there was little I could have done to prevent it.

To be on the safe side, when I spoke again with the car driver involved I did still caution him, and advise he could be reported for his traffic violation. This was just in case the cyclist changed his mind after further reflection, and decided he would like to see the matter taken to court. I also reported the incident to the chief inspector who was supervising the event, so he could decide whether the matter warranted further investigation or action – but he was happy with how I'd dealt with it up to that point, and determined it would be 'case closed' unless the cyclist made a complaint. In fairness, I think this was probably the correct outcome because, in the driver's mitigation, you could argue that the pack of cyclists coming towards him certainly weren't observing the speed limit for a built up area. That was the end of this particular matter and I was able to move on and forget about it, which was fine by me as it meant news of this disastrous duty never did become common knowledge, and I escaped the calamity with my untarnished reputation more or less intact.

RTC's that I attended included another head-on collision, and this one happened in town when I was working with Nev on a Saturday evening. It involved two cars and, bizarrely, by the time we arrived at the scene both drivers had disappeared, having abandoned their respective vehicles. However, a sole eyewitness to the crash was still there. He told us one of the drivers was a lad, probably aged in his mid-20's, and the other a young woman of similar age – and that neither had been physically injured. Although he reckoned both drivers had been adhering to the speed limit, he felt it was the male driver who'd been at fault, because his vehicle had drifted into the path of the young woman for no apparent reason. As a result, he wondered whether the young man had been drinking. Helpfully, he informed us the lad had disappeared immediately after the collision, whilst the female driver – who seemed to be in a state of shock following the crash – had subsequently been given a lift to the police station by a passer-by she appeared to know.

A PNC check of the vehicles revealed details of the respective owners, and it transpired they were actually known to Nev and I – with the guy turning out to be one of Nev's rugby playing mates, and the young lady a former girlfriend of mine! We soon managed to track down the young man, who had returned to the nearby clubhouse of the local rugby team. Subsequently, we also met up with the young lady back at our police station, where someone had indeed dropped her off. When breathalysed, the male driver tested positive and was duly arrested, but we knew this was unlikely to lead to a prosecution as he would likely claim it was down to the alcohol he'd consumed after the RTC (to 'calm his nerves' as he put it), and it would be virtually impossible to prove otherwise. However, during interview he did admit he'd been responsible for the accident – as he candidly told us he'd been distracted whilst fiddling with his car radio, and had drifted over to the opposite side of the road. Consequently, he was reported for driving without due care and attention, which nowadays is referred to as careless driving. As for my ex-girlfriend, it was clear she was blameless and could be exonerated. Nevertheless, to ensure we did everything by the book, we did breathalyse her, which was understandably embarrassing for both parties. Much to her relief the test proved to be negative, so at least the outcome didn't result in her having to be arrested. I was equally relieved as it's not unheard of for drivers who weren't the cause of an RTC to blow positive, in which case the penalty for doing so can still be a ban.

Perhaps the most horrendous RTC I ever witnessed was also the most incredulous and wondrous because it ultimately had a happy outcome. When it occurred, I was in my own car heading to the police station to start a shift and was waiting at a crossroads controlled by traffic lights. They were on red for vehicles travelling towards the town centre (like myself), and similarly for those approaching from the opposite direction. However, for some unaccountable reason, a car driver coming from the town centre failed to notice his light was showing red and went straight over the crossroads into the path of an HGV vehicle that was travelling west to east. The lorry hit him full-on broadside and the impact of the crash sent his car hurtling out of control towards the adjacent pavement, where a young mother was walking along pushing a pram containing her week-old baby. The car mounted the pavement and smashed into the pram, ripping it from her grasp, before crushing it up against a pub wall. This all took place within a split second and created total pandemonium. Understandably, the distraught mother, who amazingly hadn't been struck by the car and was unhurt, started screaming – whilst another much older lady, who'd been an eyewitness to this horrific incident, became hysterical and then fainted due to shock.

I jumped out of my vehicle and ran over to survey the scene and to see what I could do to help. There, I was instantly joined by several other motorists who'd pulled over and come to assist – including the lorry driver involved in the collision. He was naturally shaken by what had just occurred, but was at least physically uninjured. Between us, we just about managed to drag the crashed car away from the trapped pram enough to release it. The pram was a mangled wreck and had been squashed to about half its normal size, and we all held our breath as we checked the condition of the baby. I feared the worst but, much to my astonishment and delight, it appeared completely unharmed, and it was a heart-warming feeling to be able to hand over the little bundle of joy to its much relieved and grateful mum – whose tormented sobbing immediately turned to tears of joy.

Next on the agenda was turning my attention to the car driver, whose vehicle had been hit by the HGV, to check on his welfare, and then the bystander who'd passed out after witnessing the accident. At this stage both seemed ok, but I still wanted an ambulance to attend to ensure everyone involved was given the once over by someone with medical expertise, not least the mother and her baby. As I wasn't officially on duty, I also requested my colleagues attend to deal with the car driver. He had clearly committed an offence when he'd run a red light – and, at the very least, his driving had been careless, if not reckless.

This was one of those rare occasions when a serious RTC happily had a positive ending, but sadly that is often not the case. Regrettably, many of them result in tragedy, including a really dreadful collision a road traffic cop from another force once told me all about – although, after I'd learned what had happened, I wished he hadn't!

From the first part of his explanation it didn't sound like the outcome of this incident was going to be too devastating, but what he ultimately revealed certainly epitomised the true horror of what can happen when things go drastically wrong on the roads. He told me he'd been patrolling the motorway on a foggy morning and been sent to an RTC involving two boxed-container type lorries. Based on the information he'd received, he'd assumed he would be dealing with a fairly routine and typical event for a motorway, particularly during foggy conditions, where one vehicle had run into the back of another. However, upon his arrival, he'd discovered it was more than just a shunt. It appeared the rear driver had failed to stop in time after the lorry in front had been forced to rapidly slow down due to a queue of traffic ahead. Although they'd been travelling in the slow lane, there had been a significant impact at a relatively high speed, resulting in the cab of the rear lorry becoming embedded in the boxed compartment of the HGV at the front. My colleague further explained the fire and ambulance services were already in attendance, so he'd rapidly been updated. He'd found out the driver of the rear vehicle was trapped and had suffered a nasty head injury, which had caused him to lose consciousness; whereas the other driver was completely unharmed but in shock.

At this stage, everyone involved from the emergency services had no reason to think they were dealing with anything other than a serious, but reasonably straightforward, RTC – but how wrong this outlook proved to be. Once the fire brigade had managed to free the trapped driver, and he had been shipped off to hospital, still in a very groggy state, the recovery team were able to set about pulling the two damaged vehicles apart and removing them from the crash site; evidently, this was when a truly horrifying discovery was made. Unbeknown to everyone present, there had been a motorcyclist travelling in between the two HGVs – so nobody was prepared for the shocking and gruesome sight that therefore greeted them. Clearly the only person that would have known there'd been a motorbike involved in the tragic accident was the unconscious lorry driver, who'd been in no fit state to inform anyone about its presence. Hence why it had come as a bombshell to those at the scene when they'd unexpectedly discovered the crushed body of the rider amongst the wreckage, along with his mangled bike. Rightly, the traffic officer didn't go into the gory details, but then he didn't need to be too graphic for me to know that the ghastly sight he witnessed that day would have churned the stomach of even the most hardened emergency worker.

Anyone involved in dealing with the most unpleasant aspects of life, which entails seeing first-hand the injuries sustained by casualties of serious accidents or victims of atrocities, has to find a way of coming to terms with it and develop a coping mechanism. Nobody is immune to the adverse impact that dealing with trauma can have on your psyche. However, as previously mentioned, although you never get used to witnessing awful sights, or being up close and personal with people who have suffered some of life's worst experiences, you just have to learn to put it to the back of your mind and not dwell on it. Deep down you feel the pain, sorrow and anguish that come from seeing your fellow beings having their lives ended or shattered, and I can assure you that seeing people with catastrophic and sometimes fatal injuries does take its toll. Professionalism, along with a durable constitution and a degree of bravado, generally keeps you going regardless and gets you through when faced with adversity, even though human nature means you would rather avoid having to deal with the consequences of such traumatic events.

Despite the obvious impact that witnessing sickening scenes can have on one's inner self, perhaps the most harrowing and stressful aspect of dealing with incidents that result in a fatal outcome, is then having to be the bearer of devastating news. Confronting any situation involving a fatality is bad enough, but having to inform the deceased loved ones can, in some ways, feel even worse – perhaps because you know the tragic and life-shattering information you are imparting will forever impact their lives. Delivering death messages relating to children could be especially telling. There was never an occasion where I had to take direct responsibility for doing so but, during my first stint in the police, I did once have to accompany my inspector when he went to inform the parents of a young lad that their son had sadly perished following an accident. It was a heartbreaking experience that left us both feeling crestfallen – and to this day it remains an agonising memory.

As a special constable, I wasn't subjected day in day out to some of the worst things life can throw at you, and I think that helped me to effectively look after my mental wellbeing, as did the ability to 'compartmentalise'; a process that my first sergeant taught me all about when I initially joined the cadets (as previously indicated). Equally, I believe the comradeship and camaraderie I shared as part of a tight knit group were also key factors that helped me to maintain a healthy and balanced mind – although I'm sure some of my family and friends might have a different opinion in regard to my assertion that I have managed to retain my sanity!

19 Stake-Outs

THE TERM STAKE-OUT CAN SOUND EXCITING and full of intrigue but, in reality, carrying out covert operations involving observations was generally the complete opposite, and mostly laborious – there were, however, a few exceptions that come to mind.

One such duty that wasn't boring occurred when I was part of a small team designated to carry out observations on retail premises in a local shopping precinct. Intelligence from a reliable source suggested a smash & grab raid may be carried out on a shop in our town's main precinct, but the informant didn't know which outlet would be targeted. On the night in question, eight officers were in the team that had been delegated to take part in the operation, with four of us acting as lookouts in observation points. The remaining members of our crew, including the DS running the show, were parked up nearby in an unmarked police car waiting to pounce if and when the raid took place. I was paired with Simmo, who was back temporarily from his attachment to the Drug Squad to assist with the operation. He was familiar with the city-based gang that had been identified as the probable perpetrators, so would hopefully recognise them if they arrived on the plot. Simmo and I were using the local electricity board building as our observation point, whilst Dai and Spud were in the adjacent sports shop. Between us we had a good view of all the precinct's shops, and would be able to spot any suspicious activity.

As with most stake-outs, time can drag whilst you are waiting for something to happen, but Simmo and I were keeping ourselves amused by watching a young drug dealer ply his trade. Simmo instantly recognised him, and since the adolescent 'entrepreneur' had no idea of our presence he was being totally blasé as he openly dished out drugs like they were sweets, largely to teenage customers. In the time he was distributing his wares, which was less than an hour, the dealer did a roaring trade and had in excess of 30 customers. For a small town it was dealing on an epic scale, and shocking to see so many youngsters utilising his services. Simmo desperately wanted to apprehend him but knew that doing so could blow our cover, and potentially wreck the whole operation, so he just had to make a mental note to pursue him on another occasion.

Once the drug dealer had shut up shop around 2300hrs little else happened for the next couple of hours. However, as the time approached 0100hrs, Simmo suddenly spotted a bloke nonchalantly ambling towards us, who he thought resembled one of the gang members we'd been primed to look out for as a suspected perpetrator of ram-raids. As he got closer, Simmo was able to confirm he was definitely a criminal he recognised – a burglar with a host of convictions, including previous for smash & grabs. This guy's actions soon convinced us he was sussing out the situation, and checking the area was clear before his accomplices joined him to carry out the planned raid. It was also apparent he was showing considerable interest in the sports shop that Dai and Spud were occupying – and these premises could possibly be the target! Simmo radioed other squad members to let them know he'd identified a likely suspect and it could soon be all systems go; thus putting everyone on high alert. Adrenalin levels rose as the tension mounted – not least for Dai and Spud.

This event happened before the days of the extendable baton (ASP), CS Spray or Taser so none of us were particularly well equipped to defend ourselves if things turned nasty. Being in plain clothes, Simmo and I didn't even have our truncheons with us. Dai and Spud, who looked like they could be first in the firing line, were likewise 'unarmed'. Anyway, things moved on rapidly, and once the initial gang member had completed his recce and given the all clear, it wasn't long before an estate car containing two other males drove slowly into the precinct and backed up towards the sports shop – indicating it was almost certainly the planned target! As soon as the occupants of the car got out Simmo instantly recognised them, and was able to advise they were also known to him as members of the criminal gang mentioned in the tip off about a possible ram-raid. He was able to inform our team that the trio had been suspected of being participants in a number of such crimes within our force area.

It now looked odds-on that a raid was on the cards, and we were going to finally catch them in the act and get the chance to take down three hardened criminals. One of the gang jumped back into the car and started revving it up, presumably preparing for a quick getaway. The other two lifted the boot and pulled out a scaffolding pole, which we assumed they were going to use to smash the window of the sports shop. Everything suggested the smash & grab was imminent and tensions rose further as we awaited the call to strike – at least, that was until something happened to spook them! Just as the two suspects tasked with smashing the window reached the shop-front the getaway driver suddenly beeped his horn, which caused his associates to stop in their tracks, do an about-turn and put the scaffolding pole back in the car. Understandably, those of us located in observation points had been focusing our attention on the raiders and, consequently, hadn't noticed that the local beat officer had driven into the road leading to the precinct and parked up his Panda car no more then 100 yards away. However, the getaway driver had immediately spotted the police vehicle and, therefore, sounded his warning to call off the raid.

What had looked like a dead cert, in terms of our operation coming to fruition, had instantly become a non-event. The DS running the show, who was in the standby car waiting in the wings along with three other plain-clothed colleagues, had to rapidly make a decision about how we should respond as the gang members packed up shop and started to drive away. There was the option of pulling the suspects over and arresting them for going equipped, but he knew the chances of pursuing a successful case against them on this basis would be tenuous. Instead, he aborted the mission and gave the order for everyone to stand down. He came to the conclusion they would 'come again' at some stage, and any intervention would simply serve as a warning that the police were on to them – thus making them more difficult to catch in the future.

Following a 'post-mortem' into what had gone wrong, it soon became clear that nobody had thought to brief the night crew about the covert operation that was taking place; hence why the town centre beat officer had innocently strayed onto the patch in the midst of the raid. No doubt someone was left suitably red-faced as a consequence of this oversight, because the resultant outcome had been more akin to the experiences of the hapless sheriff in the 'Dukes of Hazard' than members of the 'Flying Squad' in 'The Sweeney'!

The most bizarre undercover operation I took part in during my time as a special was a stake-out at a block of public conveniences in our town centre – and there was nothing attractive or glorious about participating in a clandestine mission in such an unappealing environment. Observations at this location had become necessary because a notorious and dangerous paedophile had been spotted hanging out there. He'd recently moved to the area and, according to local intelligence, was suspected of trying to entice young boys aged around 12 to 14 years to this particular toilet block to participate in acts of gross indecency – which would naturally be viewed as non-consensual considering their age, and therefore classed as sexual assaults.

Understandably, his predilection for underage males caused a high level of consternation, as it was feared this prolific offender could be a serious threat to any young lad with whom he came into contact. His attempts to lure children who met his preferred profile to his 'den' – driven by his perverted desires – needed to be urgently addressed and stopped, using whatever legitimate means were available to law enforcement. Taking into account the severity of the situation, and the need to prevent anymore potential victims being exposed to his lurid behaviour, the highly unusual action outlined was approved without any hesitation. Doubtless, the police's duty of care, and need to protect the welfare of youngsters at risk of being accosted by this active, registered sex offender were key to local bosses reaching this decision and giving the go ahead. They would have been seen as overriding factors, which outweighed the inevitable invasion of privacy that would arise as a result of the police conducting covert observations at the said public convenience. With permission granted, a team of officers were consequently able to proceed with a series of targeted operations, despite the impact this may inadvertently have on the civil liberties of innocent parties who were using these lavatories for their intended purpose.

Was it not for the seriousness of this situation, due to the nature of offending and the risk this paedophile posed to young boys, you could be excused for thinking that performing observations in this type of facility would normally be something you'd associate with a comedy sketch show, rather than a serious, necessary and essential police operation – which it certainly was, based on all the evidence. However, any reasonable person would still appreciate why the ends would hopefully justify the means in this case – and also why the police were prepared to go to such lengths to prevent this individual from carrying out the type of grievous and sick acts of depravity he was known to commit.

I wasn't personally involved in the first round of observations, but those colleagues that did take part were astounded and horrified by what they encountered. The targeted sexual predator didn't make an appearance during the initial operation – but, much to the surprise of the officers carrying out observations, six other adult males did engage in a range of lewd activities. Some of these constituted acts of gross indecency in a public place; albeit their actions were consensual and everyone involved was over the age of 18.

Nobody had anticipated a public convenience would prove to be such a den of iniquity, or that a small market town would have such a latent problem when it came to sexual deviance. The number of blokes caught in the act so to speak was quite overwhelming, and it was equally shocking when several of them turned out to be eminent businessmen, who were reputedly well respected in the local community. I'm sure that trying to uphold their long established and favourable reputations, once they'd appeared in court and been found guilty, would have been a challenge – and it disappointed me to learn so many men were prepared to risk tarnishing their good names by behaving in this abhorrent manner. Still, at least the outcome of that first stake-out justified the hierarchy's decision to sanction the initial operation. Also, as the original objective had not been met, it enabled them to permit the process to continue. Another attempt to catch the known paedophile was therefore planned for the following week and, although the target was once more a no show, the team did catch two further sexual deviants.

During this second operation I was part of the team that took part in the surveillance. I was paired with PJ, who at that point in his career was on attachment with our local CID branch and, whilst the two of us were taking our turn doing obs, a couple of guys met in the toilet and performed sex acts on each other. They were duly arrested by other members of the team once we'd fed-back information over the radio from our covert position, and subsequently charged with committing two acts of gross indecency in a public place. Again, one of the men involved was someone well-known in the local community, and not the sort of respectable person you would anticipate catching in this type of compromising situation. He owned a company and lived in an affluent area in a nearby idyllic village, so understandably he was desperate to preserve his good reputation by any means. I guess that's why he elected to go for trial by jury rather than agree to his case being heard by local magistrates, especially as he vehemently denied having done anything wrong and was indignant about being charged with behaving indecently.

Right up to the last minute he stuck to his guns and was planning to plead not guilty. However, as the final reckoning fast approached, something caused him to accept ignominious defeat and alter his plea to guilty – therefore, PJ and I got a message to stand down just before we were due to appear at Crown Court. Presumably, his barrister must have advised that the CPS had a strong case and would be presenting compelling evidence detailing his acts of depravity, so he should accept his fate; especially as the other defendant implicated in this criminal behaviour had already admitted his part in the sex acts and pleaded guilty.

Whatever the reason for his change of heart, PJ and I were relieved when we learned we'd be spared from taking the stand because it can be a nerve-racking experience. We'd been expecting a tough grilling when we testified, despite it being a relatively straightforward case where we would have been corroborating each other's evidence. When it comes to testifying you are under no illusions, and anticipate you will get a hard time during cross-examination – even though all you are doing is giving a factual account of exactly what happened, based exclusively on your statement of evidence. Having your version of events contested when presenting evidence is perfectly understandable, and you would expect nothing less of a good defence barrister. Nonetheless, when you're in the witness box having your integrity called into question, it can sometimes make you feel like you're in the dock rather than the defendant – so you can appreciate why it was always a blessing when a defendant chose to plead guilty.

In all probability, these unexpected cases of sexual deviancy, which arose during the undercover operations, might have prevented us from catching the paedophile we were actually targeting. This was because once the offenders had been convicted, and reports of the court cases had appeared in the local press, it had become public knowledge they'd been caught 'fraternising' in the toilet block. No doubt our primary target would therefore have got wind of our operation and likely gone to ground. Anyway, whatever his reason, he never did show and all our efforts were in vain – in terms of the team achieving its main objective.

On a positive note though, the operation did hopefully stop him committing further assaults on young males in our locality. The action taken also enabled us to close down a broader network of deviant males who'd been convening in a public place to engage in sordid behaviour, albeit involving consenting adults – so clearly our time hadn't been completely wasted. As far as I know, the convicted paedophile we were targeting vanished from our area shortly after our attempts to catch him had failed to materialise. Worryingly, having escaped our clutches, he no doubt became another community's problem. Although, once our force had traced his whereabouts, the relevant Constabulary would have been alerted, and the job of monitoring this predatory pariah's behaviour would have become their responsibility.

At one point during my service the opportunity to take part in covert observations almost became like a weekly event. I recall several weekends on the trot when my Friday and Saturday nights were spent with Spud on the rooftop of the town's shopping precinct looking out for a prolific burglar who was targeting retail outlets. Within our borough there was a hostel for male ex-offenders who'd been recently released from prison, and at any one time there were usually up to a dozen of them housed at this complex. Having just completed their custodial sentences, the majority of them were on licence and were being monitored by the Probation Service – and, in fairness, some of them didn't cause too many problems. However, there were others who were more troublesome, and one in particular who became the scourge of our town and the bane of local police officers due to his constant offending.

His litany of prior convictions demonstrated he was a successful career criminal who had total disdain for the law of the land. Records showed that wherever he went on his release from prison there was always a considerable increase in the number of burglaries in that vicinity – not just a spate of such crimes, more like a tsunami! He was like a one-man crime wave, and he generally targeted shops and other commercial properties. The guy originated from Wales but soon got to know our local area, and seemed to have an uncanny knack for picking out vulnerable premises where there were easy pickings. Although he was only in his late twenties, he was already a streetwise and proficient career criminal who had honed his burglary skills to perfection. As a thief, he was right up there with the best of them and, metaphorically speaking, definitely Premier League, so catching him was proving to be a real challenge. His favoured means of gaining entry was through skylights – hence the need to stake-out rooftops – and his speciality was shimmying up drainpipes, which he managed to do very deftly being wiry and of small stature. He was incredibly difficult to track as he had the ability to go about his business unnoticed, usually operating in the shadows in the midst of the night. Discreetly trying to follow him was also a challenge because he was always very alert, and soon got wise to anyone that was attempting to do so. This was another reason why we ended up covertly keeping an eye on selected premises (more in hope than expectation!) on the off chance he may be spotted attempting a break-in whilst they were under surveillance.

Our local head of CID was sure this prolific thief was responsible for the vast majority of burglaries in our area because, since he'd been residing at the hostel for ex-offenders, the crime rate in our town had soared – making it vital that he was taken off the streets as soon as possible. Over a lengthy period, numerous attempts to bring him to justice had failed and it felt like he was waging war on our town, with a record number of break-ins occurring in just a couple of months. There were several occasions when he was nearly caught, but he always seemed to be one step ahead, and somehow managed to evade detection. I recall one such night in particular when it appeared his luck was about to run out and he'd be captured in the middle of a job.

A team of officers, including myself, were doing obs at a large range of locations all over town. By forming a cordon of observers we'd set a trap, and it looked odds-on we were on the cusp of making a breakthrough, and finally going to catch our formidable opponent in the act because, between us, we could view the rooftop of virtually every town centre building.

I was working with Kathy, a WPC with about five years of service, and we'd been designated to use the attic room in the local library as our observation post as this vantage point would give us an extensive view of about a dozen shop rooftops. The night didn't start well for us because when we arrived at the library for our shift we couldn't get into the building. We were able to unlock the door but, for some reason, we couldn't get it to open and, therefore, had to summon assistance from a fellow officer who'd previously accessed the library to do observations. As soon as he arrived and opened the door with ease we felt like a right pair of nincompoops! Neither of us had realised it was a sliding door, which was of course why it hadn't opened when we'd tried pushing and pulling it in traditional fashion after undoing the lock. Although we didn't make fools of ourselves again that night, it probably was a bad omen that set the tone for the shift, as the crafty burglar once more eluded us, even though it appeared promising at one point that he'd possibly fallen into the trap that had been set for him.

In the early hours, Kathy spotted someone on the roof of a well-known retail outlet that sold car accessories, which was one of the tallest buildings in the town's shopping precinct. It was some distance away and too dark for her to definitively identify the person as our target, but everyone involved in the operation knew there was a strong possibility it would be him and was on red alert as we surrounded the building. The key-holder was requested to attend so the premises could be searched for signs of a forced entry on the roof – and, hopefully, an intruder inside. However, much to everyone's dismay, the elusive burglar was nowhere to be found during the ensuing search; despite it being clearly evident someone had tampered with the skylight in an attempt to gain access.

Having been unable to capture our suspect in the act of breaking-in, infuriatingly meant there was nothing concrete to go on, especially as he was far too astute and forensically aware to have left behind any compelling evidence, such as fingerprints or DNA. The absence of anything conclusive connecting the daring burglar to the attempted crime, except our intuitive suspicions it was almost certainly him, also meant we were effectively back to square one, even though we'd probably come tantalisingly close to catching him. Quite how he escaped our clutches on that occasion I'll never know, but Houdini comes to mind, and our suspect's vanishing act was like a carbon copy of one the famous escapologist's amazing performances. What had looked like being a euphoric result had been snatched away from us at the last moment – and instead we were left feeling frustrated after working tirelessly to apprehend him, and potentially coming so close to finally catching our 'prey'.

If we had indeed missed catching our target by a whisker, it clearly didn't bother him because, during the next few weeks, the number of burglaries in our area reached epic proportions. The bulk of them bore his hallmark, and the need to catch him became so pressing the Regional Crime Squad (RCS) were ultimately brought in to spearhead the investigation, in a concerted effort to end his crime spree. Unlike local officers, they had the advantage of being unfamiliar to him, which increased their chances of being able to blend in and track him without being noticed. This hadn't been achieved so far as he seemed to recognise virtually everyone based at our station – even when they were in civvies – making it impossible for them to remain inconspicuous whilst pursuing him. The RCS were also used to going up against tactically aware and cunning criminals, such as our persistent burglar, and knew how to meticulously adapt their game plan accordingly. Equally, no matter how complex, they were adept at gathering, analysing and utilising intelligence from a variety of sources to inform covert ops and identify offending patterns. Approval to implement this resource intensive and costly operation by the RCS was no doubt a last resort, predicated on the theory this unrelenting burglar would continue targeting rich pickings in our town until he was brought to book.

Having been tasked with the mission of bringing down our town's tormentor, the RCS set up a major operation to achieve this objective, and they succeeded in doing just that after several painstaking days of watching him like a hawk. This wasn't surprising because they not only had the additional resources and expertise needed to focus on such an operation, but were also practiced in surveillance tactics and the art of covertly pursuing streetwise criminals. Fortunately they caught the offender whilst he was in the process of carrying out a burglary, which ensured he would have no wriggle room when the matter went to court. As a consequence, he also decided to have a significant number of other similar breaks-ins (or 'conquests' as he saw them) taken into account when he was charged with the offence; I believe it was more than 50 in total! Unsurprisingly, the local crime rate dropped considerably once this prolific cat burglar was back in custody. This reduction confirmed the well-founded view of many police officers that this savvy criminal had been responsible for the vast majority of burglaries, which had occurred in our town over the preceding six months.

I dread to think just how many more victims would have suffered at the hands of this repeat offender, and how much more misery he would have inflicted if his crime reign had continued unabated. Granted it involved a substantial amount of police officer hours to catch him, but I think it was time well spent as bringing this burglar's relentless campaign of offending to an end meant that local business owners and townsfolk could at last sleep easy once more.

Although it was a good feeling for embattled members of law enforcement to finally bring him to justice, there was no real rejoicing. I think that was because officers appreciated just how much mayhem he'd caused whilst leading everyone a merry dance – and how his offending had gone on for far too long before he was eventually caught, even though they'd been doing their utmost to bring him to book.

Whilst this particular crime spree was almost entirely attributable to this sole offender, and it was great to see his crusade of pillaging come to an end

– albeit after he'd left a trail of devastation – the soaring crime rate our town endured throughout that era regrettably continued. In part, that was due to the previously mentioned hostel for ex-offenders being located in our area because, coincidentally, the rate dropped substantially once it closed down. It did fluctuate, depending on who was living at this facility at any given time, but overall I reckon it went up around tenfold whenever the worst offenders happened to be residing in our town.

During the course of my service I took part in a number of other surveillance operations. These included one where reliable information suggested there could be a robbery at our local football club, and another where it was feared there was going to be an armed raid on the town's main post office. In regard to the anticipated robbery at the football club, I was initially earmarked to join a regular in the back of a covert van that had been strategically sited close to the clubhouse – where those hiding inside would have a good view of the most likely access points. However, as this deployment would mean me remaining in a prostrate position in a confined space for several hours, and it was my first duty after a lay-off due to a bad back, it was deemed prudent for me to switch with another colleague. Instead I became part of the 'strike team', which would be lying in wait in a crew-bus parked nearby, and ready to pounce in the event the robbery occurred. I didn't object to this change of role, as the prospect of lying in an uncomfortable position for some considerable time wasn't very appealing. Unfortunately, in spite of all the planning, and the tip off coming from a reliable source, we all spent a fruitless night waiting for something that never happened, leaving us all feeling a little deflated.

Regrettably this can be the case when you are acting on intelligence that turns out to be flawed. Alas, the outcome was the same in respect of the anticipated raid on the post office – not that I'm complaining as I had no desire to come to face-to-face with armed raiders! For this particular operation I was paired with Gavin in a marked police car, and we were tasked with covering one of three possible exit routes from the town centre. Likewise, two other double-crewed mobile patrol units had a visible presence, and they were given the job of watching the remaining escape routes that fleeing robbers may use.

Apparently, the intelligence about a possible armed raid on a post office had come as a result of a conversation being overheard by a local 'busy' (colloquially speaking) at a pub in Liverpool, and the information our northern colleague had got wind of had been a little vague. Our town hadn't specifically been named during the conspiratorial conversation, but certain details mentioned about the location of the planned raid had implied it could be the target. And hence why a counter operation was mounted to coincide with the night this suspected robbery may occur, just in case the information received by our Constabulary from their Lancashire counterparts did relate to our town's post office. Based on the inconclusive and somewhat scant information that had come to our force's notice, I suspect a full-scale operational plan probably couldn't be justified, and it was felt that a limited response to this possibility was reasonable and proportionate.

Those of us involved in the 'observational' aspect of the operation were informed our role was purely to keep a watchful eye on the vicinity, just in case the balloon went up – and we were given strict instructions not to intervene if the raid did materialise. It was also stressed that under no circumstances should we make an attempt to stop any vehicles leaving the scene in the event a robbery occurred, due to the strong possibility the perpetrators would be carrying firearms. Our primary function was to act as spotters, and then report in immediately if we identified a suspicious vehicle potentially containing the raiders. However, we were told that we could follow a suspect vehicle from a safe distance until it was intercepted by the roaming armed response team that was on standby in the area.

This all sounds fine but, in practice, such situations don't always go according to plan. The reaction of criminals to the presence of police officers can be unpredictable, so there was no guarantee they would respond in the way we hoped in the unlikely event we did end up pursuing them at a safe distance – especially as their emphasis would be on making a clean getaway, possibly at any cost. Knowing they may not adhere to our way of thinking if we did cross their path, didn't make me ecstatic about doing this particular duty, but needs must; although I have to say I was relieved when the raid didn't happen.

Not long before I decided to finally call time on my tenure as a special constable, I was approached by two full-time colleagues who were hoping to secure my help in an investigation they were taking the lead on. The suspect in the case they were investigating had recently moved to our town and was known to be a prolific drug dealer – and it just so happened he lived in close proximity of myself and my family; in fact only a few doors away! Due to the position of this suspect's house, which was located at the end of the close where I lived, it had been impossible for my colleagues to carry out surveillance on his activities without drawing attention to themselves – so they'd hatched a plan, which effectively entailed me becoming their 'eyes and ears'.

They explained it was necessary to gather vital intelligence that implicated the suspect, before they could proceed with a raid on his property. Therefore, they wondered if I could assist by casually and discreetly observing any visitations to this house and recording relevant details – such as the time a person arrived, the number of visits made by each individual and their vehicle registration where appropriate.

Since this suspect had moved in, along with his girlfriend and another chap (who I subsequently discovered was the alleged dealer's sidekick), I'd frequently witnessed a string of known 'users' regularly visiting this property. As a result, I'd already presumed my new neighbour and his associates were likely running an illicit 'joint enterprise' from their abode. Moreover, they appeared so casual in the way they were dealing, it didn't seem like they trying to operate under the radar by concealing what was going on. Instinctively, I therefore knew these occupants were bad news – particularly the prime male suspect – and it came as no surprise when I learned from my colleagues that the 'main man' was suspected of being more than just a small-time player in the world of drug dealing. However, what did come as a bit of a shock was just how high up the food chain they thought he might be when it came to such unscrupulous criminal activity.

I could appreciate where my fellow officers were coming from when they asked for my assistance. Being the suspect's neighbour, I was ideally situated to do some observations, without it being too obvious I was keeping tabs on the occupants or anyone coming and going. On the surface at least, requesting I keep an eye out for any suspicious activity didn't therefore sound unreasonable; however, in spite of the way it was presented to me, I did find their proposal disconcerting on two counts.

Firstly, with the dealing happening virtually on my doorstep, it was all a bit too close to home for comfort for me to become heavily involved. Consequently, I was worried about what the possible implications could be for my partner and children, in the event this suspected drug dealer found out I'd effectively been spying on him – especially as he would know exactly where I lived! Secondly, with it being implied this suspect was seriously connected, and likely had links with organised crime, I was also concerned about just how far such associates may go to protect their business interests.

Naturally, I also felt it would be wrong to turn a blind eye and completely ignore the law breaking that was going on in my neighbourhood, and the turmoil this was causing. Therefore, although I declined to become officially involved in any covert surveillance, I tentatively agreed to keep an eye on the situation and log anything going on, which I happened to witness by chance. And it didn't take me long to spot a few disturbing things happening, which increased my anxiety about the seriousness of the situation that was starting to unfold in our normally peaceful and quiet street.

In addition to the abundance of visitors calling at the suspect's home, no doubt to get their fix, I also noticed on two occasions a vehicle parked up nearby containing two sinister looking blokes, who were clearly intent on closely watching the drug dealer's property. Their car index number revealed they were from the London area, and the vehicle was linked to an organised crime gang based in the capital; so it was evident someone involved in serious criminal activity at a high level was likely taking an active interest in our local dealer – and indeed that transpired to be the case.

Within days of noticing the two unsavoury looking strangers lingering in their car for the second time, the dealing that had been going on at this neighbour's house came to an abrupt end, and it seemed the 'main man' had done a disappearing act. At the time I could only surmise why this might be, but I subsequently found out the probable reason. One of my colleagues informed me our suspect had gone on the run because he'd apparently been stepping on the wrong toes and fallen foul of an established crime lord who, according to gossip, viewed him as a duplicitous renegade and was now out to exact revenge. This doubtless meant he would be fearing the worst and expecting to suffer some serious harm. Quite what he'd done to get on the wrong side of this feared gangster nobody knew for sure, but rumours suggested he'd possibly gone rogue and been double-dealing – and his life could even be in danger.

On hearing this worrying news, I was not only concerned for this chap's welfare, but also relieved I hadn't become too involved in the investigation and, as a result, perhaps come to the attention of this organised crime boss. I was already aware of one young woman who'd ended up residing in our town on witness protection after being asked to do similar surveillance on a neighbour – so I could just imagine how my family would have felt if the same thing had happened to us. It's not a prospect they would have relished, and I don't think they would have been thanking me for the opportunity to move somewhere different!

I know this all sounds a bit far-fetched, and that such an outcome would be a worst-case scenario. However, in this type of situation, it's important to realise there is always a faint possibility something like this can happen – and to consider what the repercussions might be if things go drastically awry whilst you are closely involved and somehow upset the 'wrong people'. Thank goodness, in this instance, that wasn't the case and everything moved on rapidly before I'd had a chance to gather any meaningful information, which could be used as evidence in a future prosecution of the drug dealer or his accomplices. Therefore, with the drug dealing having ceased, I was just pleased things could now return to normal in our small neighbourhood, and my 'bit part' in the investigation was over.

Some months later I was updated by another colleague on what had become of the suspected drug dealer, and I'm afraid it was grim news. He'd been arrested elsewhere on drug-related charges and placed on remand but, before he'd been apprehended, he'd apparently suffered a significant wound to his leg. From what I was told, during the time he was on the run, after getting on the wrong side of the organised crime boss for allegedly going off script, he was constantly fearful he'd become a target. Therefore, when he felt at greatest risk, he would keep a shotgun tucked away down his trouser leg for protection. But, you could say that doing so had ultimately backfired on him because, on one such occasion, the gun unfortunately went off accidentally, which resulted in him suffering some catastrophic, life-changing injuries. Next, whilst he was in prison awaiting a trial date, effectively convalescing as he recuperated from his self-inflicted wounds, his life had tragically come to an end in mysterious circumstances.

His demise was due to hanging and, as far as my colleague was aware, it had been concluded that he'd committed suicide. Nevertheless, there were those who thought otherwise and questioned whether his life really had been taken by his own hand. Bearing in mind what had gone before, they believed something untoward had occurred, and someone else had played a part in bringing about his premature death.

Rumours were therefore rife that he'd come to a sticky end as a consequence of foul play, and could have perished as a result of a contract killing ordered by a 'third-party' – which had then been covered up to hide the truth. However, in the event he was 'eliminated' on behalf of someone who'd put out a contract, then they'd clearly done a good job in covering their tracks as nothing had surfaced to indicate this was so. In the absence of any evidence to conclusively demonstrate there'd been any subterfuge, interference or obvious third-party involvement, the coroner had therefore declared the inmate's death was due to 'misadventure' – in other words, as a result of suicide according to my colleague.

Despite this outcome, suspicions and theories about the cause of death apparently continued to circulate, with some people petitioning for an 'open verdict' because they still felt it was implausible he'd died by his own hand. To my knowledge though, nothing was ever uncovered to show another person might have played a part in bringing about his untimely parting from this life; so I think that was the end of the matter and it was case closed.

20 Caught 'Bang to Rights'

It's not often you are fortunate enough to catch someone red-handed committing a crime but, when you do, it's an exhilarating feeling. Similarly, when you uncover really compelling evidence linking a perpetrator to a particular offence it can be equally satisfying. I was personally lucky to experience both these outcomes on several occasions.

The first time this happened I was working with Gavin and it was around 2300hrs on a Friday evening. We were keeping an eye on people out enjoying the night-life as we cruised through the town centre in the response car, when we were suddenly interrupted by a taxi driver who flagged us down. He seemed a bit stunned as he told us he'd just spotted a young guy smash his way into a nearby supermarket. Seeing this crime being committed had clearly unnerved him, but he said he would show us exactly where the incident had occurred, as long as he didn't have to come too close because he thought the burglar looked aggressive and had already clocked him witnessing the break-in.

We immediately summoned further assistance as we followed the taxi driver to the scene of the suspected break-in. Once he'd directed us to the point of entry, he then hid around the corner waiting to see what happened. There was a gaping hole in the glass panelled front door of the supermarket where the intruder had broken in and, as we approached, the audacious 'late night shopper' came stumbling out of the premises carrying a wire basket laden with bottles of alcohol. His haul included a variety of spirits and, as he stepped through the hole in the glass with his overflowing basket full of bottles, several of them tumbled to the floor and smashed on hitting the ground. Oddly, as our brazen thief exited he seemed more concerned about losing some of his bootie than he was regarding our presence.

Trying to escape our clutches would have been futile, but once we'd collared him he came up with a couple of lame excuses for his blatant looting. Firstly, he informed us he thought the shop was open because it was accessible through a big hole in the glass entrance, which he claimed was nothing to do with him and must have been caused by someone else. We of course knew this explanation was nonsense as we had a witness who'd seen him smashing his way into the supermarket. However, his paradoxical efforts to justify helping himself to an array of alcoholic beverages didn't stop there. Next he told us that he fancied getting something to drink to quench his thirst – or, more likely, to indulge in a heavy bout of drinking based on the volume of bottles he'd taken – and he hadn't planned on stealing the goods, but there was nobody at the check-out to take his money. Again it didn't need a detective of the calibre of Sherlock Holmes to question the veracity of his explanation for nicking a large quantity of liquor, or to recognise that he was telling another porky.

In spite of his rash behaviour, I suppose you could say he was trying to think on his feet as he came up with these ridiculous excuses for his pilfering; however, that would be a contradiction in terms because he could barely stand up, having already had a skinful. In view of the pungent odour emanating from his clothes, and the fact his pupils were dilated, it also seemed likely he'd been on the 'whacky-backy', even though a search didn't reveal he was in possession of any dope. Anyway, being tanked up and high probably accounted for his petulance as he wasn't exactly helpful when we asked him for his name. With a wry smile on his face, he said:

'I'm Arthur Daley and that's all I'm telling you, so just f... off and leave me alone!'

He possibly thought he was being a smart cookie with this response, but it wasn't the most original fictitious name, and definitely not an alias we were going to believe considering the character 'Arthur Daley' was the well-known chancer in the 'Minder' series; a popular TV show of that era. As we attempted to put him in handcuffs, the well-built young thief became even more obstinate. He told us we couldn't arrest him because 'we weren't wearing our helmets' – a common myth amongst some lawbreakers but, of course, a complete fallacy. Likewise he became increasingly stroppy and bombastic when we tried to place him in the police car. However, by that time backup had arrived in the shape of Ivan and PJ. With their help we soon got him under control and into the vehicle, so we could ship him off to the custody suite.

Whilst all this had been going on, the taxi driver who'd alerted us to the break-in had wisely been keeping a safe distance, and occasionally peaking around the corner to make sure we'd detained the lone raider. Then, as we drove off from the scene, he put his thumb up to acknowledge we'd successfully arrested the suspect. The poor chap looked as white as a sheep, but all credit to him for not just cowering away in his taxi and instead hanging around in case we needed help to restrain the intruder.

Next morning, once the dozy burglar had sobered up, he reluctantly admitted to being the culprit who'd broken into the store. This was hardly surprising since he faced indisputable evidence that proved his guilt, not least that he'd been caught on-the-job as he went on his late night 'shopping spree'. He accepted it had been a pretty dumb thing to do right in front of an eyewitness, but then, figuratively speaking, he wasn't the sharpest knife in the drawer considering it should have been obvious he'd never get away with this crime. Despite his stupidity, he still had a cockiness about him, which was even perceptible when he appeared in court. In view of his temerity and brash manner, I therefore doubt the six-month prison sentence dished out by the magistrates acted as a future deterrent or wiped the smirk off his face. It's also unlikely it caused him to change his ways because he never showed any remorse for his actions.

This wasn't the only occasion I attended this supermarket when someone had been spotted stealing some goods, but the circumstances relating to this next incident were certainly different. At the time I was working a Saturday afternoon stint in the company of a new sergeant called Des, when we got a call requesting our attendance to deal with a shoplifter who'd been detained by the store detective.

As a deterrent, this supermarket chain operated a zero-tolerance policy when it came to such crime, so always tended to prosecute anyone caught shoplifting. However, Des was clearly a little uncomfortable about them taking this path in respect of the young woman who'd been apprehended for stealing some essential household items, including baby food and nappies, until we knew more about her personal situation.

She was in her early thirties and a first-time offender with no record of committing any type of crime in the past, so he wanted to explore what had made her succumb to temptation on this occasion. As a result we discovered that she'd recently lost her husband, currently had no form of income and was in dire straits with nobody to turn to locally for help, having only just moved to the area. Her late husband had passed unexpectedly within the last couple of weeks, shortly after they'd come to our region and, due to some financial issues he'd encountered prior to his death, of which she'd been blissfully unaware, she was unable to access any accounts – meaning she was effectively destitute. Being in a desperate situation with a young child and baby to feed, she'd ended up helping herself to some vital supplies, with the intention of paying the supermarket back at a later stage. However, having been caught in the act, her world had now come tumbling down.

Understandably Des took pity on her once we'd found out what had caused her to resort to shoplifting and the motive for her indiscretion – even though she willingly admitted the offence. In these exceptional circumstances, when clearly she was grief-stricken and had acted out of character, having fallen on hard times, he felt there was no way her problems should be compounded with a criminal conviction; he therefore did his utmost to persuade the supermarket manager to drop the charges and not make an example of her.

You couldn't help but be touched and swayed by the woeful plight of this young woman, and Des was so convinced by the validity of her credible explanation, along with her impassioned and persuasive plea for leniency, he even offered to pay for the items that she'd taken. However, once the manager knew the reason for the theft, and realised the 'shoplifter' had only recently lost her husband and been suffering extreme hardship, he not only withdrew the supermarket's threat to pursue a prosecution, but also chose to donate the items to the woman and her family.

That wasn't the end of the matter, as we next contacted Social Services on behalf of the young widow to ensure she got the help and support needed. We also put her in touch with a local charity that would provide immediate access to essential items – at least until her situation was resolved and she'd overcome the financial difficulties she faced.

There were several colleagues who rather cynically thought that maybe the compassionate and benevolent side of Des had only surfaced because he was dealing with an attractive young woman, and wondered whether he would have done the same if this hadn't been the case – but I felt they were wrong and being grossly unfair, and that he did exactly the right thing. And, as I got to know him well over the ensuing years, I knew for sure that he was a kind, caring and empathetic individual with a benign manner, who always did his best for everyone and treated people fairly whatever their gender, and also whatever they looked like!

It's rare that opportunities to bring criminals to justice simply fall into your lap, but I was fortunate to once experience such an outcome. This arose mainly due to luck, although I'd like to think that perhaps my investigative skills and policing instincts also played a minor part in bringing about this result. On the day this happened the town was celebrating its carnival, and I'd been on duty since lunchtime policing a junior parade that was taking place during the afternoon in advance of the main evening procession. Once the afternoon parade was over, I decided to spend a couple of hours patrolling the town centre before returning to the station for the evening briefing – and, whilst doing so, I bumped into a young man I knew vaguely, both through my day job and policing activities. It was this chance encounter that effectively kick-started a series of events, which ultimately led to me arresting an active burglar who'd somehow managed to evade the attention of police up to that point.

Jamie, the young man that I bumped into, had been involved in some petty crimes, but was always friendly whenever I came across him, and I would describe him as a likeable rogue. He happened to be with his older brother Trevor, so he introduced me to his sibling. Trevor also came across as sociable and police-friendly. I'd never met him before and it emerged he'd only recently moved to the area – and up to this point hadn't been on our radar. During a convivial chat, Trevor told me he'd never been in trouble with the police and that he didn't have a criminal record, and I remember him jokingly saying that was because so far he'd never been caught! It could well have just been kidology, but when I discreetly checked his details for any previous convictions or outstanding warrants the results were negative – so who knows.

Later that day, following the evening carnival procession, a number of officers, including myself, were directed to patrol the town centre to maintain public order amongst the crowds of people who were continuing to celebrate their night out on the town – many of whom had flocked to the fair and the pubs. At 2300hrs, a call went out over the radio for someone to attend a disturbance that had kicked off at the rear of a town centre inn and, as my good self and Kathy – who I was paired up with that night – happened to be closest to the venue when the message came through, we acknowledged we would respond. Other officers in the vicinity advised they would also assist, which was good to hear considering we didn't know how many people were involved in the disturbance. However, due to our close proximity to the inn, Kathy and I were first on the scene.

Upon our arrival it was evident there'd been a scuffle between a small group of drunken lads, but they'd already settled their differences. As nobody had sustained an injury or wanted to make a complaint, that was essentially the end of the matter, but then there was a twist to the situation. It turned out one of the lads who'd been involved was Trevor – the young man I'd met by chance earlier in the day – and he wanted a quiet word with me. He insisted on speaking with me in private because he had something he needed to get off his chest, which he didn't want to talk about in front of Kathy. The mind boggles in that situation, but Kathy reluctantly agreed to leave us to chat once I'd explained we had history – albeit a brief one, having only met him for the first time earlier that day.

Trevor, who was clearly intoxicated, then proceeded to tell me about a car theft he'd committed a few days ago, which he now felt bad about. The details he could recall were minimal, so I thought it was either a wind-up or the drink talking when he embarrassedly explained he'd decided to come clean. However, after weighing up the situation, I came to the conclusion the best course of action was to initially arrest him for being drunk and incapable, based on the fact he could barely stand up, and then also on suspicion of car theft, just in case there was an element of truth in his admission. I therefore cautioned him, undertook a preliminary and somewhat cursory search to make sure he wasn't concealing any weapons or illegal substances about his person, and then called up for a mobile unit so he could be transported to our local nick.

The astonished look on Kathy's face was a picture to behold when I suddenly walked by her escorting my prisoner to the police car I'd summoned. At that stage, she had no idea how an innocuous event that we'd attended together, and sorted to her knowledge, had now led to me taking this young man into custody. She must have been wondering what on earth I was doing, and no doubt thinking my decision to arrest this young man would mean I'd taken leave of my senses.

Later on, I was able to explain to Kathy exactly what had happened but, in the meantime, things had moved on rapidly and there had been further revelations. Once I'd searched Trevor more thoroughly after arriving at custody, I'd discovered he was in possession of a significant number of credit cards that clearly didn't belong to him. Things then got even better when a search of his accommodation uncovered a large hoard of stolen property! The value of these stolen goods exceeded several thousand pounds, so I guess you could say my hunch to arrest him, on the off chance there might be some truth in his admission about a car theft, had fortuitously paid off big time. To be honest, I had no inkling that Trevor had been so heavily involved in illicit activity, or that my decisive and somewhat intuitive action that night would enable us to uncover a major player within our local criminal fraternity – although some of my colleagues understandably thought luck had definitely been on my side. I certainly couldn't argue with that viewpoint, and have to agree that subsequently uncovering the stash of stolen items was down to good fortune rather than any prophetic powers on my part.

During Trevor's interview the following morning, which had taken place once the effects of the alcohol had fully worn off, there'd been no further mention of a stolen car on his part – and, even when asked outright about it, there'd apparently been a blank expression and complete denial. However, there was little he could do to deny his culpability regarding the dodgy credit cards found in his wallet, or the substantial haul of stolen goods stashed away at his abode – so at least it had been possible to charge him with possession of all these illicitly obtained items. Whether he was just a fence involved in unlawfully and wittingly handling stolen property, or the person actually responsible for stealing these items, we couldn't tell without firm evidence or a confession – hence why he was only charged with possession rather than theft. Overall though, it was still a positive outcome, which – as highlighted – had essentially arisen out of nothing but a stroke of good luck. And, bearing in mind he'd brought about his own downfall, he probably rued getting inebriated that night and letting his tongue runaway with him during his drunken ramblings.

I will never know whether it was just the drink talking when he disclosed details of his involvement in the unconfirmed theft of a vehicle, or if he felt the burden of guilt deep down and needed to clear his conscience by divulging this information. Either way, it unintentionally opened a can of worms for him, and meant several victims of burglaries became the beneficiaries of his alcohol-induced loose talk – as a number of stolen items could ultimately be returned to their rightful owners. This included re-uniting an old lady with a treasured heirloom, which was especially pleasing.

Another remarkable and somewhat comical instance of a burglar being caught bang to rights is also worth mentioning, even though I wasn't personally involved. The young thief impacted by this incident had broken into a local boutique and had used a skylight as his means of entry. Unfortunately for him, he'd slipped as he'd climbed through the skylight after forcing entry, and had landed awkwardly on a revolving clothes rail located immediately below. This had resulted in him becoming impaled on the central pole – which had penetrated his left armpit – and being stuck there until someone came to his rescue. He'd broken into the store sometime on the Friday night but wasn't actually discovered until the following morning, when a female member of staff arrived to open up. She didn't initially realise there'd been a break-in because the shop comprised of two floors, and it wasn't until she heard someone calling for help from upstairs that the stunned shop assistant went to investigate. To her horror, she then came across the interloper impaled on the clothes rail – just hanging there like a Christmas tree decoration! Suffice to say, she was more than a little taken aback at what she discovered and instantly called the emergency services, including the police.

I subsequently heard that when the first officer on the scene asked the trapped burglar what had happened he allegedly replied:

'I thought I'd just drop in and hang out for the night!'

If that was indeed the case, then fair play to him and you have to admire the poor chap's laid-back attitude and sense of humour, especially as he must have been in considerable pain and lost a significant amount of blood. By good fortune, once he'd been released from his predicament by the fire brigade, and shipped off to hospital for treatment on his damaged armpit, he went on to make a full recovery. Following his recuperation he then of course had to face a court appearance for the act of breaking and entering; although, in many respects, you could argue that divine intervention works in mysterious ways and had already played a part in ensuring justice had been served. It transpired this break-in was the young man's first attempt at a burglary so, after this painful and laughable initial experience, which had culminated in abject failure, you could appreciate why he was fated to then go straight.

A case of a woman seemingly being spotted helping herself to something turned out to be anything but a fair cop. When this occurred I was working with Rosie, a WPC who'd just finished her tutorship period, and we were on foot patrol together on a Saturday afternoon policing a street fayre in the height of summer. The pervading atmosphere was jovial and cordial as we mingled with the crowd of people that were attending the event. However, as we made our way along the main thoroughfare, where the majority of shop traders had outdoor stalls, the ambient mood and pleasant tone instantly changed when we were accosted by an irate shopkeeper, who wanted to make a complaint about someone stealing a scythe that he'd had on display outside. He informed us he knew the culprit, a middle-aged woman, and he wanted her arrested forthwith.

According to the shop owner, who was known to the police for being quite volatile, having once attacked a motorist's car bonnet with a sledgehammer after an altercation, this woman had deliberately taken the scythe without paying for it. Based on his explanation, it initially sounded like a cut and dried case of theft, until he let it slip that he hadn't personally witnessed the woman taking the item, but his 17-year-old Saturday assistant had indeed done so. The proprietor went on to say that this member of staff had been minding the stall when the woman had 'pinched' the scythe and, because he also knew the alleged perpetrator by sight, he'd been able to identify the so-called culprit.

As the belligerent shop owner was intent on raising his voice whilst making his allegations, the resultant commotion had attracted the attention of anyone passing by, meaning a large throng of people had rapidly gathered around the stall and started to earwig. One of these people turned out to be a good friend of the lady that was being accused of this 'crime', and she took exception to the way the shopkeeper was casting aspersions and started to defend her buddy – so, before we knew it, a slanging-match had ensued between the two of them.

Given the situation, Rosie and I decided we needed to take matters off the street before things escalated. Therefore, we got the two parties to come inside the shop where we could carry on a discussion with some degree of privacy. We discovered that the accused lady had gone home because she wasn't feeling well, and her friend kindly offered to fetch her back so she could speak for herself and explain her side of the story. This seemed like a sensible course of action since she only lived a short distance away. Consequently, despite the protestations of the shopkeeper, who insisted the woman had blatantly stolen the scythe and demanded we go to her home to effect an immediate arrest, we agreed that inviting her to return to the shop would be the most helpful option.

Within a matter of minutes, the woman at the centre of this controversy returned to the shop selling antiquities, and told us she was horrified at being accused of theft. She explained her side of the story. According to her, the scythe had been propped up in a litter-bin next to the stall, so she'd enquired with the young shop assistant if it was there because it was presumably being thrown out – and if she could therefore take it. In her view, he'd then acknowledged it must have been placed in the rubbish as it wasn't wanted, and it should be fine if she took it.

Her explanation caused a right old furore. The proprietor stated in no uncertain terms that her justification for 'stealing it' – on the pretext it had been thrown out – was nonsense. He claimed she knew perfectly well it was for sale because she'd enquired about purchasing it earlier, and maintained his stance that he wanted to pursue a case against her. And when the young sales assistant could only state for sure that the scythe had been propped up in the litter bin, and not corroborate whether the woman had asked him if it was ok to take it – because he couldn't recall the precise details of their conversation – Rosie reluctantly decided she had no choice but to arrest the poor woman for theft.

I totally understood her reason for doing so, especially as the turgid nature of the shop owner meant he came across in a bullying manner, but I wasn't comfortable with this outcome. The woman we'd taken into custody was in a distressed state, clearly wasn't well and seemed unlikely to have deliberately stolen the item. I thought it was more likely she'd mistakenly taken the scythe after genuinely believing it was being chucked out, and felt the custody sergeant would almost certainly refuse a charge in the event we took her back to the station. Besides, I also anticipated the matter would never stand up in court in the improbable event it ever got that far. Knowing the background of the proprietor, and that he had a tendency to be vindictive, I additionally sensed his motives for wanting her arrested were dubious; especially as it had become apparent he disliked the accused and there was bad blood between the opposing parties.

I therefore shared my misgivings with Rosie – including the information about this shop owner once severely damaging a car after a driver had parked outside his premises partially blocking his doorway – and asked her to hold on briefly whilst I had another chat with the owner of the business to put forward an alternative resolution. As he'd now started to calm down a little, I managed to persuade him to drop the charge against the woman, as long as she immediately returned the scythe and apologised for the misunderstanding – which seemed a much more logical and palatable way of dealing with this dispute. I think in part, he was swayed by my proposal when he realised that a lot of his time would be taken up giving a statement and getting embroiled in other aspects of litigation – all for a case that would have virtually no chance of succeeding because it would likely be declined by the CPS before it progressed to any futile court proceedings. Having secured the shop owner's agreement to accept the solution proposed, which the alleged defendant also agreed to abide by, Rosie was able to de-arrest her prisoner; enabling us to then depart the scene knowing that we'd done the right thing, albeit after a prolonged, challenging and contentious period of interaction.

For a police officer to catch a criminal in the midst of carrying out a crime is one thing, and there are of course risks associated with coming across this type of situation, which go with the territory. However, when it comes to a member of the public facing this scenario it can be even more parlous, and the outcome can be catastrophic, especially when prevailing circumstances give the innocent party little alternative but to confront the person engaged in the crime. This was exactly what happened to a housewife when she came home and discovered not one, but two burglars ransacking her house.

She lived in the countryside and had just returned home from a shopping trip when she disturbed the two brazen burglars going through her things. It was the middle of the day and she had absolutely no idea the intruders were in her home until she walked in on them. With the isolated cottage being in a remote area, I suspect the two burglars anticipated it would be easy pickings when they targeted the property after checking nobody was at home, and were banking on getting clean away without being disturbed. I therefore doubt they were expecting the owner to come back anytime soon and catch them in the act, let alone put up some resistance. Anyway, as a result of the housewife's untimely return, the situation she encountered rapidly turned into an incident of aggravated burglary, which culminated in the poor lady being seriously injured when she was hit over the head with a brick.

It was subsequently discovered she had been attacked after she'd verbally challenged the two intruders and informed them she was going to call the police. Apparently she'd been more incensed than intimidated by their presence, and wasn't going to back down in spite of their threatening manner. Consequently, when the feisty housewife had tried to block their exit and picked up the phone to follow through with her threat to dial 999 as a very brave act of defiance, one of them had carried out a vicious assault by striking her a fearsome blow over the head. They'd then fled the scene, taking with them a number of valuables, including her purse and bank cards, whilst leaving their victim unconscious on the kitchen floor lying in a pool of blood.

By the time the husband returned home several hours later, had found his wife on the floor and called the Emergency Services, her condition had deteriorated further. She was rushed to hospital, where the initial prognosis didn't look good and suggested she may not recover from the trauma. With it being touch and go whether she would survive, initially it even looked like this incident could well become a murder case. Mercifully though, this plucky homeowner's heroic actions didn't result in her losing her life and she went on to make a full recovery. Also, once she'd come out of her coma after 24 hours, she was able to give a good account of what had happened on that fateful day and a detailed description of her attackers.

I wasn't directly involved in responding to this aggravated burglary, but I was engaged on the peripheral of the subsequent investigation when I was asked to work with Stevie, an experienced uniformed PC, to undertake routine enquiries in the surrounding area. This entailed us stopping any motorists in the vicinity to see if they had witnessed anything suspicious around the time of the offence, or noticed anyone who looked out of place in the locality. The spot-checks didn't result in us picking up any useful leads, although a couple of locals that we pulled over did have a vague recollection of seeing a car parked up the lane near where the cottage is sited on the day the break-in took place – but, regrettably, couldn't remember much about the vehicle. Stevie and I spent almost our entire shift in the area, and our spot-checks were followed by some house-to-house enquiries in a nearby village, which proved to be equally unproductive.

Despite our enquiries not yielding any clues, and an extensive investigation by local CID officers not identifying any leads, ultimately the perpetrators of this dreadful crime were apprehended. As luck would have it, two possible suspects were subsequently caught on camera attempting to use the victim's bank card at a cashpoint in London. To crown this breakthrough, they were also spotted trying to fraudulently use her card at various retail outlets when officers trawled through CCTV of shops in the vicinity of the cashpoint in question. These individuals were well-known to police as prominent burglars, so they were hunted down and taken into custody. Therefore, you could say that our London colleagues effectively got 'two for the price of one', thanks to both perpetrators foolishly being caught on camera. Upon their arrests, searches of their respective abodes revealed further evidence linking them to this offence, meaning they were charged accordingly and then convicted of various offences connected to aggravated burglary, including GBH. This, in turn, meant they deservedly ended up receiving lengthy custodial sentences.

21 Public Order

ALONGSIDE DEALING WITH DOMESTICS and missing persons, devoting time to keeping the peace and attending public order incidents also featured prominently during most tours of duty. Of all the tasks associated with police work, maintaining public order probably took up the majority of time and caused the most aggro. Whether it was going to calls relating to anti-social behaviour, policing events, controlling unruly or hostile crowds, dealing with drunken yobs or responding to any type of incident that involved violence, they all had the potential to wreak havoc and demand the attention of a considerable amount of resources. Sometimes our arrival at such scenes, or attempts to intervene to stop things getting out of hand, could even act as the flashpoint for more bystanders to get involved – especially when alcohol was involved and certain people watching on didn't understand or like the reasons for our actions. I recall this was so when an attempt to arrest one individual for breach of the peace instantly got out of hand, and we suddenly found ourselves completely outnumbered and facing what I can only describe as a mini riot.

I was working a night shift on a Saturday and was out on foot patrol in company with PJ. We were in the town centre keeping tabs on the pubs at closing time as night-time revellers spilled out onto the pavement. The vast majority of them were dispersing without causing any problem, and either making their way home or to their next port of call, which tended to be the town's main nightclub or one of several fast-food outlets located in the vicinity. Also on duty in the area were two other officers who normally served in a different town within our borough. They were supporting us over the weekend in question, and one was acting as our sergeant for this particular shift. Although these colleagues had been on mobile patrol, they'd decided to park up and go for a walk around the town centre as the pubs emptied. Naturally, a visible presence of police officers will often act as a deterrent, in terms of preventing instances of law breaking, so they were reasonably thinking that flying the flag would make sense. As mentioned however, sometimes it can have the opposite effect, especially where drunk and disorderly behaviour is concerned – and this was one of those occasions.

The pair of them were on the opposite side of the road to PJ and I when they were approached by a drunken yob who took exception to their presence. He started shouting and swearing at them and, when he failed to heed their advice to stop doing so and go home, he was duly arrested for breach of the peace. PJ and I immediately went to assist, and the four of us attempted to usher the prisoner into the back of the police car, but our efforts were to no avail. The well-built chap refused to get in and, as you can imagine, when someone is resisting being put into a relatively small space it's virtually impossible to get them to comply without manhandling the individual using reasonable force.

Within a very short space of time our endeavours to get our prisoner into the vehicle had attracted a lot of attention, and a large, jeering mob had appeared out of nowhere and completely surrounded us. Members of this crowd were being egged on by our prisoner, who was yelling at them to intervene and stop us from arresting him. You could see the hostility in the faces of those who were siding with him, and sense the febrile atmosphere as our plight rapidly became dire.

Overall, it was probably the scariest situation I encountered during my 22 years of service, and I reckon the crowd numbered in excess of 80 people at its peak. Although only about half-a-dozen of them probably posed a major threat, the aggressive posturing, along with the intensity of the provocative goading and taunting by almost everyone present, made it an incredibly intimidating and frightening experience. In this type of circumstance, a mob mentality and animosity can quickly pervade throughout such a mass gathering, and even those who wouldn't normally be that aggressive or blatantly anti-police can soon become emboldened, particularly when they are being riled up by the actions and behaviour of the more unruly element of a hostile crowd.

Assistance had been requested as soon as it had become clear trouble was spreading and things were getting rapidly out of hand, and within minutes every available officer in the area was on scene – which meant three further colleagues had joined us just a few minutes after things had turned ugly. However, even though it was a luxury and highly unusual for our station to be able to muster seven officers for a night shift, this was never going to be enough to quell a frenzied, rampaging mob of this size, or to regain complete control and restore order. Additional help was therefore urgently sought from further afield and, in the meantime, our backs were very much against the wall – quite literally in some respects!

Our inspector was one of those who had responded to our initial call for assistance, and he had come in the police van, which meant we now had a better chance of placing and securing our uncooperative prisoner in the back of a vehicle. While the two arresting officers did just that, the inspector ordered the rest of us to form a cordon around the rear of the van and to face the crowd in a defensive stance to stop them intervening. We were also directed to draw our truncheons – for me this was only the second time I ever did so during my entire service! In the event it became necessary to defend ourselves, we were instructed to target the ringleaders and main aggressors that were trying to instigate trouble and initiate violence. This worked, perhaps because none of the unruly mob wanted to be the first to make a move and risk being struck with a baton; however, the combative posturing continued and certain members of the crowd carried on baying for our blood and making threats.

The standoff felt like it lasted for an age, but once we'd finally managed to get our prisoner into the vehicle and he'd been transported away from the scene, things finally started to calm down a little; enabling us to restore some semblance of order. Even so, full order wasn't restored until we were joined by a task force of 12 additional officers sent by Divisional HQ. They arrived about 30 minutes after the incident had begun, and we were then able to track down and arrest some of the other individuals who we'd identified as being involved in the affray – and ensure they were duly charged with public order offences and brought to justice.

As indicated, this particular incident was one of the most menacing confrontations I endured whilst performing my duties, and all seven of us directly involved were lucky to come through it unscathed, thanks to the very thin blue line just about holding. Encountering thuggish behaviour during a weekend late shift was nothing strange, and something you expect to happen regularly where policing is concerned, but the speed at which we'd found ourselves surrounded by a marauding crowd was not so commonplace and did come as a bit of a shock.

A yobbish element had been at the forefront of the rabble that descended on us so quickly, and it felt like they were showing all the signs you might associate with pack mentality as they were drawn to the scene. I suppose the behaviour of a certain element was reminiscent of the type of soccer hooliganism that permeated across the land and blighted the country during the 70's and 80's, and this experience certainly made me realise just how vulnerable you can be when things turn nasty in an instant. It also taught me how self-preservation becomes your primary instinct when you are backed into a corner and things get a bit hairy, and also just how much courage and fortitude every officer is expected to display in this type of situation – because, once you've been forced into taking action, you simply cannot back down, or be seen to capitulate in the face of mob rule. Violent events are extremely terrifying, but adrenaline generally kicks in at the time and helps to get you through them – and, in some ways, it can feel scarier afterwards when you have the opportunity to reflect and digest.

The previous story highlights how certain acts of disorder or anti-social behaviour are often synonymous with a culture of excessive alcohol consumption, and the significant part drunkenness plays in people losing self-control. However, even when drink is not a factor, anything involving a large crowd of people, combined with a tinderbox atmosphere, has the potential to create major difficulties from a policing perspective, particularly when emotions are running high and there is potential for civil disobedience. That was certainly so when I was involved in crowd control during a march protesting against the introduction of the Poll Tax back in 1990, at a time when the nation had become polarised by this emotive issue. It was at the height of national protests against this hated tax, and to police this event all available special constables based at our station had been mobilised, which meant there were seven of us taking part in this duty, along with one regular who'd also been assigned to this task.

This march and mass gathering was part of a nationwide campaign taking place on the Saturday in question, and a phenomenal amount of police resources were being dedicated nationally to overseeing the protests and keeping the peace. Overall there were more than 20 marches within our force area alone, so it was clear we were going to be stretched to the limit, especially as a number of officers who normally policed more rural parts of the district had been diverted to cover the Constabulary's larger cities. It had been anticipated that if trouble brewed it was far more likely this would occur in urban areas, as opposed to sleepy market towns, which seemed like a reasonable assumption.

The march in our town was scheduled to take place at 1100hrs, and beforehand we were required to attend an extensive briefing. This was run by the borough's inspector and he gave strict instructions about how to police the event. We were advised there would be two assembly points for protesters, one at the southern end of the town and the other at a more northerly location. Consequently, we were split into two groups of four, so we could police both contingents of protesters during their respective marches. I was informed I would be part of the detail allocated to safely escort those protesters gathering at the northern meeting point, which was located in the grounds of the local cricket club. Organisers of the march had notified the police that both contingents of protesters would initially march to the town centre, so they could then merge into one large group before moving on to the main car park, where they intended to hold a rally before dispersing.

This all seemed fairly straightforward; especially as diversions and road closures had been arranged and would be in place for the duration of the march. However, the inspector did have one word of warning for us regarding some intelligence that had come to light. Apparently, there was a possibility that anarchists were planning to stir up trouble, by infiltrating some of the marches and orchestrating unscheduled sit-down protests to block main thoroughfares. We were advised that the sole purpose of this form of sedition would be to maximise disruption and trigger additional social unrest amongst the crowd; in other words, it would be used by those people present who harboured anti-authoritarian views as a surreptitious means of furthering their own anarchic agenda. Our inspector therefore emphasised the need to remain vigilant throughout the course of the protest march, and to be on the look out for any odd or unreasonable behaviour intended to cause trouble. Most importantly, he stressed we must not overreact in the event we faced any form of provocation, such as an unplanned sit-down protest – as those seeking to exploit the situation by causing problems would be banking on us doing just that, in the expectation it would act as the catalyst for drawing officers into a confrontation. He also stated that the type of infiltration described was unlikely to occur in smaller towns, and the warning they'd received chiefly applied to protests taking place in larger conurbations; however, this logical prediction subsequently proved to be incorrect.

Along with three colleagues, I duly arrived at the northern assembly point around 1030hrs on the morning of the march, by which time about 50 protesters had already congregated. By the time the march was due to set off this number had swelled, so in total we had around 150 protesters to escort from our end of town. It struck me that the bulk of the crowd consisted of local families, including young children – not perhaps archetypal protesters that one might normally associate with large-scale demonstrations.

As we embarked from the assembly point there was a pleasant atmosphere, with those present generally being friendly towards the police, even though they were in high spirits. The march proceeded without us encountering any real problems and, as we reached the town centre, everything seemed to be going well and according to plan. At this stage it would therefore have been easy to become complacent and wonder what all the fuss was about – but any thoughts this duty was going to be plain sailing were soon dashed.

Within a couple of minutes of reaching the town centre, we could hear the protesters approaching from the southern end as they came down the hill towards the point of their rendezvous. From the cacophony of noise emanating from this direction, which was growing louder by the minute, you could not only tell there was a much larger mass of people in this second group, but also that they were considerably more vociferous – and, by the deafening sound of their discordant chanting, potentially more raucous. Once they'd come into view, after emerging from around the bend, it soon became apparent the second group consisted of somewhere in the region of 600 demonstrators, far more in total than we'd anticipated would be taking part in the march and subsequent rally.

Just prior to them reaching the juncture where they would merge with our group, I became conscious that at the front of this contingent were a number of unfamiliar faces – people who I didn't recognise as locals from our town. With protests occurring nationwide, and there seemingly being no reason for people to travel outside of their local area if they wished to participate, this struck me as being a little peculiar and made me a bit suspicious of their motives – which rapidly became clear.

As soon as the two groups had merged, and taken up the whole of the town's market place, several of these strangers confirmed my fear that they could have ulterior motives when, as suggested, they decided to stage a sit-down protest in the middle of the town centre; an act that was no doubt intended to provoke trouble. To the crowd at large this underhand action was designed to look like it was an impromptu, yet innocent, part of the protest, but we of course knew different. We had good reason to believe this act was a deliberate attempt to sabotage a peaceful protest, and cause public disorder by exploiting the backdrop of underlying anger that existed amongst the demonstrators. The initial sit-down involved about half-a-dozen agitators, and I think they believed that once they'd done so, other members of the crowd would soon join them, especially if we intervened by trying to move them out of the way. Hence why it was vital we remained calm and didn't play into the hands of our adversaries by do something to rile the crowd or exacerbate the situation.

Although the vast majority of people in attendance were legitimate protesters, who were genuinely there to solely demonstrate against the Poll Tax, those seeking to hijack and wreck the event were aware participants were feeling aggrieved, so it wouldn't take much to incite them. In such situations even decent, law-abiding citizens can be manipulated into perceiving that injustice has occurred – which can lead to them acting out of character and behaving in a manner they would normally consider unacceptable. The aim of getting them to do so would be to convert a peaceful demonstration into civil unrest.

For the subversive element's devious ploy to work, we knew they would be banking on other members of the crowd joining them on the floor, and then reliant on us trying to remove anyone engaged in the sit-down protest – as this could unintentionally make it look like the police were being unjust and heavy-handed. To avoid this happening we had to box clever – as the last thing we wanted was for this event to turn ugly. Besides, having completely under-estimated the likely size of the protest planned for our town, we were woefully under-resourced for policing a demonstration of such magnitude if trouble flared up and we had to withstand a violent backlash.

Having been caught on the hop, we couldn't risk doing anything that may further arouse emotions, or inflame an already tense situation – especially as we could sense the unease and didn't want to expose innocent parties to any form of unpleasant experience, or put them at risk if the situation got out of hand. Normal rules of engagement therefore didn't apply, and our response to the sit-down protest had to be measured to minimise the chances of us making matters worse, and inadvertently triggering some sort of riot. Crucially, as a result of the intelligence we'd received and some sensible forward planning, we had our simple strategy to help us cope with exactly this type of scenario – and hopefully maintain order.

The fact we'd been tipped off that those seeking to bring about discord, by instigating a surprise sit-down protest, would be expecting us to start dragging them out of the road, meant we knew this was something we had to resist if at all possible. So desist we did – well, all of us bar one, the exception being the Special Constabulary's sub-divisional officer (SDO) for our borough. She took it upon herself to immediately attempt pulling a protester out of the road, and encouraged the rest of us to do the same until we rapidly explained it was our intention to let them be – and discreetly outlined the rationale for doing so. Her action could easily have sparked fury amongst the crowd, but fortunately we were able to prevent this by getting to her quickly.

Stopping her in her tracks ensured our colleague's brief attempt to intervene was over in a flash, before any other protesters even realised what was going on, so luckily no damage was done. In fairness, it wasn't really her fault that she acted the way she did because our 'glorious' leader had missed the morning's briefing and been blissfully unaware of the ploy the anarchists likely had in mind – and the passive tactics we would be deploying to counter an unexpected sit-down protest, to hopefully stop it developing into a large-scale revolt. Anyway, our simple plan to combat any shenanigans by initially ignoring anyone who took part in the sit-down protest fortuitously worked. We'd done so in the belief they would quickly get bored and get back up if we didn't react in the way they wanted – and that's exactly what happened after just a few minutes.

Achieving this objective wasn't solely down to our approach, even though showing constraint probably helped. Another reason chaos was likely averted was due to the good folk from our town sensibly declining to take the 'bait' when the 'intruders' tried to orchestrate a 'rebellion'. I think it was therefore a combination of police tactics and the abstention of locals during the sit-down protest that ultimately stopped trouble from erupting, scuppered the plans of those hoping to cause mayhem and helped foil the anarchic plot; thus preventing them from running amok in our neighbourhood.

Once the sit-down protest had failed to materialise in the way the anarchists had hoped, the demonstrators moved on as one procession to the market place car park, where members of the congregation held a peaceful rally before dispersing and making their way home.

After the protest had passed off peacefully there was a collective sigh of relief as we took stock. There was no denying we'd only marginally avoided having to deal with a confrontational situation, and we knew how terribly wrong things could have gone – especially if local town dwellers hadn't refrained from taking part in the sit-down protest. In the end though, we were just grateful to have come through this episode still in one piece without having to face an uprising of the masses – which could easily have been the case when our tactics nearly backfired due to our SDO not being privy to them!

Most duties involving crowd control are fairly routine, but every once in a while you get the opportunity to be part of something that doesn't fit into this category or classify as being the norm. That was so when I heard that our town was expecting a Royal visitation by Prince Charles. Naturally, a sizeable crowd was expected to greet him and give him a warm welcome, so a large contingent of police officers would be needed to oversee this event and make sure his Royal Highness was kept safe and secure. Members of the Special Constabulary were therefore requested to support regular colleagues on the day he was going to bless us with his presence, and I duly volunteered for this prestigious duty.

The visit was scheduled to take place on a weekday around mid-morning, so it was difficult to estimate exactly how many people would attend, but it was anticipated it could be a substantial number bearing in mind the profile and popularity of this estimable VIP. At our briefing we were informed that our primary function would entail us lining the main street to ensure public order was maintained, and that nobody got too close to the town's eminent visitor. Furthermore, we were reminded that we must remain vigilant and face the public as the Prince walked from his vehicle to a restored 18th century chapel, which would be the key focus of his visit, and then back to his waiting car. We were also made aware that before departing he would be going on a short stroll of the local area, mainly to engage with the public and give them a chance to interact – albeit from a safe distance. Our inspector therefore emphasised the importance of being especially alert during this stage of the Prince's engagement, and to be on the look out for anyone trying to get a little too close for comfort.

The first part of this event ran smoothly and there was much cheering and waving of flags as the Prince of Wales exited the royal car, acknowledged the crowd with a wave, and then made his way to the chapel – followed by an entourage of dignitaries. Some 30 minutes later he emerged from the chapel and, as expected, went for a brief tour of the vicinity before returning to the Royal car.

It was during this tour, just before the Prince reached the point where I was stationed, I was suddenly approached by an undercover detective, who showed me his warrant card and announced himself as a member of Special Branch (SB). The officer rapidly pointed out an elderly gentleman dressed in a distinct overcoat and flat cap who was hovering in the background, and told me this individual had a gripe with the Royal Family and planned to hand the Prince a protest letter – so he would therefore attempt to make a beeline for him as he passed by. He also informed me that as I happened to be the nearest 'uniform', it was imperative I block this man's path at this juncture to prevent him from approaching the future 'King of our Land' – and that he would assist me in this process.

And sure enough, within only a few seconds of receiving this news, the old chap attempted to squeeze through the crowd and make his way towards Prince Charles; except, between us, we were able to stop him in his tracks marginally before he'd entered what was deemed a restricted zone. We then held onto him until our high-ranking Royal visitor had moved on and reached his waiting transport. My colleague from Special Branch was not only delighted that any distraction to the Prince's visit had been avoided, but also that we'd managed to discreetly take control of the gentleman and usher him away without making it too obvious what we were doing. Achieving this ensured no undue alarm had been caused amongst nearby members of the crowd. Once the risk of the elderly protester accosting our country's next in line to the throne had passed, we were able to let him go on his way, knowing we'd averted any possible interference during this particular public engagement.

As soon as we'd done so, the undercover officer then explained the elderly gent was well-known to Special Branch, and was on their watch list because he regularly pursued senior members of the Royal Family whenever they had public engagements. He said this chap had some sort of grievance regarding land owned by the Crown, and frequently made attempts to accost those representing the Royal household, in order to handover his protest letter. Although this eccentric gentleman was kept under observation, he apparently wasn't perceived to be a serious threat, and was viewed more as a nuisance – but, nevertheless, a person of interest they couldn't just dismiss as a harmless crackpot. According to this SB officer, this would have been an easy conclusion to reach based on the irrational, yet well articulated ramblings contained within protest letters they'd previously intercepted. Despite reading and evaluating the content of these disparaging diatribes, which denounced the Monarch's right to reign over her kingdom and questioned the validity of the Royal Family – as well their entitlement to own certain parts of her Majesty's realm – Special Branch's hierarchy still hadn't worked out why he had these obsessions. However, since his protests had been going on persistently for some years, the security services always had to be mindful of his likely presence at any Royal engagements, and pay particular attention to him at such events.

Technically of course, our protester wasn't committing a crime by his actions. Hence why we couldn't arrest him and were only able to briefly detain him so he couldn't encroach on the Prince's personal space and possibly pose a risk to his welfare. Whether his behaviour would nowadays constitute stalking I'm not sure but, as his targets weren't specific individuals, and it was the Royal Family at large he pursued, I doubt even this modern-day harassment legislation would entirely fit the bill in this type of situation. Anyway, regarding what happened on this occasion, I believe the Prince was none the wise, and at the time should have been oblivious to the kafuffle that occurred behind the scenes; so I guess you could say we effectively did our duty.

Encountering an issue like this one, which suddenly cropped up without warning, makes you realise how you always have to be on your guard and ready for anything where policing is concerned. It also reminds you that you need to be astute and able to deal with the unexpected – or, sometimes, think on your feet and improvise when needs must. That indeed was so when I was on foot patrol with Sasha, a newly appointed fellow special constable.

We were undertaking a routine foot patrol on the northern side of town when requested to assist PJ, who was working solo covering response. He had been sent to deal with an altercation between a taxi owner and one of his patrons, and required assistance after things had become confrontational. The situation had rapidly deteriorated and resulted in PJ having to arrest the customer, who had decided he wasn't going to come quietly. At the time we received the call, Sasha and I were at the opposite end of town to where the incident had occurred, about a mile away – and, being laden down with all our gear, I soon realised it was going to take us at least 10 minutes to reach the taxi office where things had kicked off, even if we ran all the way. And, since we were the nearest uncommitted officers available to immediately attend as backup, it was necessary for us to take drastic action.

In these pressing circumstances, it didn't take much ingenuity for me to work out that I needed to flag down a vehicle, and persuade the driver to give us a lift to the location of the incident. Although surprised, the first driver we stopped with this in mind didn't take much persuading. He was glad to oblige and his face lit up when we commandeered him for this public service. However, I don't think I could have chosen a less suitable vehicle or driver for the task in hand; an old beaten-up Citroen 2CV, driven by your typical Sunday afternoon 70-year-old sightseer. So it was full speed ahead at all of 15mph for the duration of our journey! Being a cautious driver myself, I didn't have the audacity to tell him to put his trotter down despite the snail's pace. Besides, it was still quicker than it would've been walking, and we were just grateful for the lift.

Upon our arrival at the taxi office we discovered that PJ was just about managing to restrain the irate customer on the floor, but was having difficulty maintaining control because the chap's wife had become hysterical and was trying to pull him off her hubby. Sasha therefore focused on dealing with the wife and calming her down, whilst I assisted PJ. Between the two of us we soon got the prisoner handcuffed and into the back of the police vehicle, by which time Sasha had placated the wife to some extent and got her to see sense.

Once we had the situation under control, it became possible to establish exactly what had happened. We discovered that the taxi owner's reasonable refusal to provide a lift for the couple, due to their drunken state, had been the initial cause of the dispute. The prospective male customer had reacted badly to this service being declined, and become verbally abusive and threatening in his manner – which had then led to the police being summoned and PJ having to arrest the offending party for breach of the peace. Once the incident was over, and while our prisoner was being shipped off to gaol (without passing go!) by PJ and Sasha, I stayed behind to ensure the chap's wife got home safely now that she'd lost her escort for the night – so at least nobody could say the police don't take their duty of care seriously.

A couple of days after the taxi office incident, I volunteered for another late shift and found myself working for the first time with Dom, a probationary PC fresh out of his tutorship. It was a Friday evening, and we were on foot patrol together covering the town centre beat, when we got sent to a disturbance outside the local kebab house just after 2300hrs. As we approached the location we could see there was a fight going on between two lads, with several other young men stood back watching. We immediately recognised one of the lads engaged in the fight because he was a 'regular customer', and this guy did a runner as soon as he saw us nearing the scene. Since he was known to us, and would already have had a healthy lead if we'd set off in pursuit, we chose not to give chase – and instead pick him up later if it proved necessary. For now we focused on trying to find out what had caused the fight and dispersing a lively crowd that had gathered in the vicinity. Dom approached the other party we'd seen fighting and immediately arrested him for his part in the fisticuffs. Presumably he'd formed the opinion it was best to take him into custody on suspicion of committing a breach of the peace, and then find out precisely what had happened once we got him back to the police station. This is often a reasonable tactic in such circumstances, when you need to ensure calm is rapidly restored, and don't have the luxury of trying to get to the bottom of things in the middle of a hostile environment with lots of drunken people milling around.

By the time Dom had effected the arrest, the response car had also arrived on scene, so he immediately went to place his prisoner in the back of it, whilst I tried to coax the arrested chap's friends away from the area. Several of them were complaining bitterly that the lad Dom had arrested was an innocent party who'd not provoked the fight, and had simply been defending himself after being set upon by the thug who'd run away. This sounded quite plausible, but I explained now was not the time or place to sort this out, and we would explore and resolve the situation back at the police station. However, one of the friends didn't heed my words of advice. He ran over to the police car and tried to stop my colleague from putting his mate in the vehicle, which resulted in Dom also placing him under arrest for obstruction. This lad, who patently felt aggrieved, had clearly been drinking and most likely wasn't thinking straight, but that was no excuse for his behaviour.

Once we'd arrived back at base we were able to review matters in the calm light of day. Whilst I was guarding the young man who'd obstructed Dom, as he awaited his turn to be booked in at custody, I had a word with him about his behaviour (after reminding him he was still under caution). In response, he was very apologetic and remorseful. I explained from a police perspective why it is sometimes necessary for us to act in the way we did when confronted by this type of fracas – primarily to take the sting out of a heated situation and rapidly restore order. Once I'd enlightened him about our predicament he better understood the reasons for our response, and why Dom had arrested his friend before we knew all the facts, or who exactly was culpable for the fight that had occurred. By the time we'd had our 'tête-à-tête', any charges against his friend had rightly been refused because it had now become clear he was innocent of any wrongdoing.

As soon as all the information about the incident had come to light, it had become apparent that this suspect had simply been defending himself after being picked on, and he was in no way to blame for the fight, which had clearly been started by the other lad who'd run off when we arrived. This other party was known to be a pugnacious character who was prone to starting fights, and he would now need to be tracked down and held to account for his actions. In itself however, this outcome didn't mean the young man who'd overreacted to the arrest of his friend, by obstructing Dom in the course of him performing his duty, would automatically be exonerated as well, and there was a distinct possibility he could still be charged with this offence. This didn't sit comfortably with me, not least because I could see that his intervention had solely come about as a consequence of him honestly believing his friend's arrest had been unfair – which had ultimately proved to be the case. Checks revealed this defendant had never been in trouble before, so I had a quiet word with Dom to air my concerns, and to ascertain how he wanted to proceed.

In fairness to Dom, he was also feeling uneasy about progressing with a charge of obstruction – as he realised the young man who'd committed this offence had made a genuine mistake when he'd tried to stop him from apprehending his friend. Like me, he appreciated this lad's action didn't warrant him gaining a criminal record that may adversely impact the rest of his life. Equally, Dom was man enough to admit that with hindsight he'd perhaps acted a little prematurely in his arrest of the young man involved in the fight, before he'd obtained any information about how the altercation had started. Bearing these factors in mind, he agreed an obstruction charge should not be pursued, and we would just give the offender suitable words of advice before sending him on his way as a free man, without a stain on his character. All credit to Dom for putting his hands up and admitting he was wrong and had acted too hastily – and then making the right decision.

After coming to this fair conclusion we duly spoke to the young man and explained the rationale for our decision. He was very relieved because he recognised the implications of having a criminal record, and how such a blemish could undermine his whole future – especially as he was currently studying at university and had aspirations to pursue a career in a legal profession! After absorbing all the facts, and acknowledging he had technically committed the offence of obstruction, despite the mitigating factors, he was hopefully able to use this experience as a learning curve, which would aid him in his future career.

Following reflection, I'm sure he also appreciated how close he'd come to blotting his own copy book, simply because he'd been too intoxicated and outraged to think and act rationally at the time of the incident. It would have been a tragedy, and quite possibly a travesty, if this combination of drink and outrage had cost him dear, so I was delighted with the outcome. If nothing else this whole affair was a valuable lesson, which certainly gave all three of us reason for contemplation, and influenced how we'd in future deal with any similar situations. It also demonstrated that justice generally prevails once all the facts are known.

It wasn't long before I was back helping out on another late shift and once more on patrol with Sasha. On this occasion we again experienced just how thin the blue line can rapidly become when you only have a small number of bobbies on duty, and the demands stretch everyone available to the limit. At the start of the shift there were just five of us reporting for duty, with Sasha and me joining three regulars – Sian, Woody and our section sergeant – to cover our borough until the team on nights took over at 2200hrs. Sian and Woody were mobile covering response, whilst Sasha and I were on foot patrol in the town centre. Around 2000hrs, all of us – bar the sergeant – were directed to attend an incident outside a public house close to the town's Market Place, which resulted in a wanted man being arrested.

This man had been ejected from several licensed premises, from which he was barred, but was refusing to leave the area and kept attempting to enter other pubs in the locality, despite having been issued with a blanket ban. Woody and Sian, who'd arrived on the scene just prior to Sasha and I, had already identified this guy was wanted on warrant and had therefore detained him by the time we joined them. They had him handcuffed and under control but, as he was struggling to break free, they appreciated some extra hands to physically manoeuvre him into the police car. Between us we were able to achieve this, so Woody and Sian could then transport him to custody.

As the cells at our local nick were not in operation that evening the prisoner had to be taken 15 miles to the next nearest custody suite. Effectively, this meant Woody and Sian would now be out of commission for the next couple of hours, whilst they were delivering their prisoner to this alternative venue and booking him in – thus leaving our sergeant, Sasha and me as the only officers patrolling our town for the duration they were away. This wasn't ideal, but we knew that having to operate on depleted resources is something that happens regularly where policing is concerned, so it was a case of 'c'est la vie'.

Not long after Woody and Sian had departed, there was a radio message for any available unit to attend a domestic within our area, and I initially assumed the sergeant would take the call but, hey-ho, this expectation proved to be wrong. Sarge was apparently on an enquiry in a village and out of radio contact, so the only resources immediately available to respond were Sasha and I. Consequently, we were asked to start making our way towards the location of the domestic, some half a mile away, but to proceed with caution when we arrived. We were of course on foot and, with the most direct route involving us going up a steep hill, it was a challenging slog to get there rapidly. Trudging around town on two feet rather than in a police car isn't always the most efficient way of getting from A to B, but foot patrol was an aspect of police work I always enjoyed – and, from personal experience, I can vouch for the fact that it certainly keeps you fit!

Within 10 minutes we'd arrived at the block of flats where the disturbance had reportedly occurred but, before entering, I called up on the radio to update control that we'd arrived, and to check if there was any further information about the nature of the incident and how many people it involved. I also wanted to know how soon backup would be available in the event we needed assistance. Control came back to say the 999 call they'd received about the domestic had been brief, and had come from someone in a neighbouring flat who had declined to give their details because they didn't want to get involved. As a result, nothing much was known about the type of commotion going on at the flat we were about to attend. However, the radio controller was able to tell me that there was a precautionary warning marker for the address in question, which was occupied by a mother and her adult son. The marker indicated the son had been diagnosed with paranoid schizophrenia and had bouts of aggression when he was not taking his meds. Fortunately though, it was also noted that the target of any such fury tended to be inanimate objects like walls and doors, which he would sometimes punch when he got angry and lost control. That was at least heartening to know as our sergeant was evidently still out of radio contact, and our nearest backup was therefore at least 15 to 20 minutes away.

Typically, the flat we were seeking was on the top floor of the four-storey building and, since there was no lift in operation, we had to use the stairs – which was all we needed after a brisk walk up a steep hill. When we arrived at the front door of the abode, where the suspected domestic was in progress, we couldn't hear any noise coming from inside the flat, which was hopefully a good sign. Not knowing what to expect made me feel a little uneasy, but I duly rang the bell. Eventually, a guy aged 30ish – presumably the son – answered the door and, when he didn't appear too distressed, I felt more comfortable about the situation. I explained we'd received a call about a disturbance at this address from a concerned citizen, and we therefore wanted to check if everything was ok. Although a little incoherent, the young man confirmed there had been a problem, but he insisted everything was now calm and he didn't need our assistance. I asked if he could elaborate on the problem he'd mentioned, and he hesitantly informed us that he'd had a trivial disagreement with his mother after getting into a state and becoming annoyed. This had then culminated in him shouting at her and throwing a china ornament at his bedroom door; doubtless the commotion the neighbour had overheard. I pointed out we were pleased to learn the situation had calmed down, and that any disagreements had been resolved, but we would need to come in so we could check on his mum's welfare and ensure she hadn't suffered any harm. At this stage he became quite agitated, although he still agreed we could enter the property to have a word with his mum.

As we entered the living room we spotted the chap's mother sitting in an armchair looking somewhat forlorn. It didn't look like she'd come to any physical harm, but the grimace on her face gave the appearance of someone mentally exhausted who was resigned to their fate – which almost certainly included caring for her adult son for as long as she was capable of doing so, or perhaps until she reached the end of her tether. Whilst we assumed she was probably middle-aged, the abject misery etched on her face did make her look considerably older, and it seemed that life had clearly taken its toll. She admitted to us that her son's condition put a big strain on their relationship and the atmosphere at home could become very tense; especially when he failed or refused to take his medication, and his resultant behaviour became increasingly unpredictable and irrational. After hesitating about how much to reveal, the mother also tentatively told us the severity of his paranoia had been getting worse, and that recently he'd been freaking out or getting delirious more often, with episodes occurring most days.

Despite this, she was still reluctant for me to call for medical help, or refer the matter to the Mental Health team, possibly because she was fearful her son would then be sectioned, which was something she was keen to avoid. You had to admire her dogged determination, although I suspected that if the situation worsened her resistance would diminish, and she may ultimately be compelled to accept such help. This seemed even more likely when I discovered her son's schizophrenia, likely exacerbated by excessive substance abuse, was also becoming a serious cause for concern and the police had been called to this address no less than six times in the last few weeks – hence why the address was flagged with a precautionary marker. It therefore seemed it may only be a matter of time before further action would be required, and intervention became inevitable. For now however, we were able to report that both occupants of this household appeared to be ok following their fall out and things had calmed down – so Sasha and I would be resuming our patrol.

In regard Sasha, it's worth mentioning that she turned out to be something of a dark horse when it came to a particular skill set that she brought to the special constable role. I found this out when both of us were asked to represent the

Special Constabulary in an inaugural shooting contest against members of the TA – something that became an annual event. Both Sasha and I were effectively 'virgins' when it came to taking part in a shooting competition, and neither of us had ever fired a real gun up to that point. I think the closest either of us had come to discharging a weapon was firing an air rifle, so we really were complete novices. The only special in our team who was something of an expert was Spud, as he was a member of a shooting club and had a reputation for being a marksman. However, it transpired Sasha was a natural when it came to shooting and proved to be a real crack shot. Although I say it myself, I also turned out to be something of a sharpshooter, but not quite as good as my eminent colleague who confounded participants by getting the maximum score and beating everyone else with the exception of Spud, who also equalled this feat. We therefore unexpectedly won this initial contest, and were deemed to be opponents worthy of being invited back to compete on an annual basis.

Returning to the matter of dealing with public order, there were always plenty of things happening to keep us busy on this front. Some of the challenging situations that arose, for example events where there would be large public gatherings, such as protests or football matches, predictably involved the likelihood of disorder arising; whereas there were also many other occasions when things could flare up without any warning. For many officers, I guess that's what makes undertaking police work so appealing and exciting, even if things could sometimes be quite hair-raising.

During the course of my service, it also never ceased to amaze me how frequently I would witness things that were out of the ordinary, which I really hadn't anticipated would happen. The night we got called to a mass brawl – involving visiting fairground staff and a group of locals out looking for trouble – was one of those instances. Not that being called to a large fight was especially unusual in itself, even though they thankfully didn't arise too often during my time on the force. What was really surprising about this particular incident was the way Frankie, my veteran colleague within the Special Constabulary, was singularly trying to put a stop to the fight, even though it involved more than a dozen people!

Frankie was barely 5ft 5inches tall – way below the required height to join the regulars back in those days – in his late fifties and coming very close to the end of his service, but this hadn't deterred him from wading straight into the fray. He'd been the first officer to reach the scene and, when the rest of us arrived mob handed to deal with the situation, we just couldn't believe our eyes when we spotted Frankie in the midst of the heated battle trying to separate the two factions – and not without some degree of success.

This wasn't just your typical brawl that involved purely fists flying, but a full-on fight where both sides had armed themselves with anything from baseball bats to iron bars, making Frankie's fearless action even more incredulous. I think those engaged in the fight had been as amazed as us by Frankie's tenacious response and bravery, and this had actually caused some of them to cease scrapping. His actions that night also brought plaudits from some members of the public, who were expecting to enjoy the fun of the fair rather than witness a very unpleasant mass brawl. Although shocked by what they saw, they were clearly impressed by Frankie's laudable conduct, and the way he appeared to have single-handedly calmed things down before the rest of the troops had arrived.

Once we'd joined Frankie among the warring parties, and done our bit to help restore complete order, our main task entailed helping those that had been injured. As you can imagine, some of those involved had suffered nasty wounds, bearing in mind the type of weapons that had been used, and it was clear that it was the locals that had come off worst. Subsequently, further enquiries were needed to identify and arrest the main instigators of the fight; with the emphasis being on hunting down those that had committed serious assaults – which was easier said than done. Ultimately though, I'm told a number of offenders were tracked down and charged accordingly, with several cases of GBH being pursued. However, my abiding memory of that incident wasn't the final outcome, but the valiant and resolute part Frankie had played in helping to bring the situation back under control.

Another brawl ensued the following weekend when Jaffa, Nev and I were crewed together on a late turn and had been delegated to attend an international stage of a motocross event, which had been taking place throughout the day a few miles out of town. We were tasked with overseeing the safe transfer of the day's takings to the waiting security van. Due to the sizeable number of spectators there was a significant amount of money involved and, as a result of a tip off, albeit from an unreliable source, the organisers were concerned they could be the target of a robbery and had requested a police presence. As a safeguard, we'd therefore been despatched at 2100hrs to be on hand during the critical cashing-up period and, likewise, when the money was handed over to the security firm. However, we never actually made it to the event because, whilst en route, we got diverted back to town following a request for urgent assistance.

A large fight had erupted in the town centre, and the only officer on hand to immediately respond was a WPC who was working solo, which meant we needed to back her up as a matter of priority. We were several miles away when we got the call, so it was a mad dash on blue lights back to town in order to support our lone colleague. The skirmish involved a group of lads visiting from up north and some local 'toe-rags' and, by the time we arrived on scene, most of the fighting had ceased. However, the fracas had culminated in one of the local lads sustaining a nasty wound after being hit over the head with a hammer. Our female colleague had been able to get a really detailed description of the culprit responsible, which would hopefully make him easily identifiable, so we split up to look for him.

After a quick search of the area, Jaffa managed to track down the alleged offender and had the honour of placing him under arrest. Once apprehended, he was transported to the police station; whilst the victim of the assault was taken to the local A&E department for a check-up and to have his wound stitched. By the time the prisoner had been booked in and locked up, so he could subsequently be formally interviewed about the alleged assault, the victim had been discharged from hospital following his treatment and had arrived at the station to give a full written statement. This was taken by Jaffa, who'd assumed responsibility for dealing with the case and conducting the investigation.

He also did the suspect's interview once the victim had given his account of what had happened, and it was during this process the alleged assailant gave a totally conflicting version of events. The suspect claimed the victim's injury had been inflicted accidentally when his head collided with the hammer! He stated it occurred when the victim attempted to headbutt him and he'd held up the hammer to protect himself; so it was in effect an act of self-defence. Unbelievably, he had the audacity to even put forward this ludicrous defence when the case went to court, although it didn't wash with the jury or the judge. However, for some reason, he was ultimately only convicted of ABH as opposed to GBH, which was surprising considering the victim still bears the scar to this day in the form of a dent to his skull.

22　Danger Zone

DEALING WITH INCIDENTS OF PUBLIC DISORDER or unruly behaviour involving a large mass of people or dominant force, such as the ones outlined, could understandably be quite overwhelming and put you in a perilous situation; sometimes though, contending with small groups or individuals in threatening circumstances could also be very testing and place you in an equally precarious position. That was so when I was on duty with Angus, a probationary PC who was beginning to experience self-doubt in his ability to succeed as a police officer.

Angus had joined up the same time as Simmo, and back when they'd begun their service they'd both been posted to my station and allocated to group 3. As the two newbies at that time there'd been an element of rivalry between them, which had started out as a form of healthy competitiveness. However, during their first year in the job Simmo had excelled, and become the star pupil on the group. He'd made a number of high-profile arrests – some of which had been down to excellent investigative work, whilst others had been down to being in the right place at the right time. Similar breakthroughs had eluded Angus as he'd tried to establish himself, and he'd been left languishing in spite of all his efforts. This had led to a crisis of confidence.

On the evening in question, before we ended up attending the volatile incident that placed us in jeopardy, Angus and I had been patrolling the streets together and he'd confided in me that he felt he'd been floundering over the last few months, and was thinking of leaving the job. He was feeling despondent and expressed concerns about whether he was capable of making the grade. I'm sure much of this self-doubt had come about because he lacked self-efficacy and was comparing himself to Simmo, whose career had been blossoming. At no point did Angus imply he begrudged Simmo his success, or his growing reputation as an astute bobby but, at the same time, it was clear he believed he'd been playing second fiddle, and couldn't match the high standard his colleague had attained. I was aware that Simmo, a born optimist with an effervescent personality and a positive approach to both policing and life in general, had been setting the bar quite high, so I tried hard to convince Angus that he didn't need to compete. As he tended to be a pessimist, I also did my best to re-assure him he'd ultimately get plenty of chances to prove himself as a worthy copper – and, as things turned out, he certainly didn't have to wait long for an opportunity to come along.

Whilst we were in the middle of having this profound conversation, a call came over the radio requesting that all available units attend a disturbance at a wine bar and, as we were close by, we were first to respond. Upon arriving, the bar staff explained they were having trouble getting a drunken customer to leave, and asked us to escort him off the premises. We tried persuading the intoxicated man to leave of his own accord, but he rejected that idea and instantly became really stroppy. It was therefore apparent we'd have to physically eject him, which we knew was going to be a challenge since this guy was of a thickset, muscular build and clearly worked out.

As soon as Angus took hold of his arm to lead him outside a red mist came down and the chap went ballistic. His aggression level had rocketed in a split second and he started throwing wild punches, a few of which connected. With him aggressively laying into us, it was a real struggle trying to get him under control, let alone remove him from the premises. Between the two of us the best we could do was try to restrain this monster of a bloke until backup arrived; so it was comforting to know other officers should soon be joining us at the scene. Angus informed his assailant he was under arrest for assault on police, and with both of us using every ounce of our combined strength we just about managed to hold him down whilst we waited for assistance. Help probably arrived in a matter of seconds, even though it felt more like several minutes – and first to join us at the scene was none other than Simmo, who was rapidly followed by our sergeant. The four of us were finally able to get our prisoner secured in handcuffs and under some sort of control, although he continued to struggle and refused to walk to the waiting police vehicle. Therefore, we literally had to carry him to where the police Land-Rover was parked, and then manhandle him into the back of it; whilst all the time he did his utmost to break free.

All in all it was a great collar for Angus, especially when it transpired our violent drunk was also wanted on warrant for a whole string of other offences. Simmo was the first to congratulate Angus on his arrest, which made the outcome even more gratifying for him. Physically Angus had ended up somewhat battered following the prisoner's onslaught, and he was nursing some minor cuts and bruises, but that didn't seem to bother him. Clearly he was just cock-a-hoop that he'd finally had the chance to emulate the type of success normally associated with his illustrious colleague, and at last enjoy some glory of his own as he experienced something of a champagne moment. In stark contrast to the way things had been panning out up to that point in his police career, I think he probably viewed this outcome as his personal 'piece de resistance'. Knowing he'd dealt effectively with that incident in the eyes of his colleagues did wonders for his ego, and enabled him to overcome his inferiority complex – and, with his self-esteem restored, he soon re-discovered his mojo.

I'm sure what happened that fateful evening not only left him feeling rejuvenated, but also convinced him he could live up to the expectations he'd set himself, as well as those of the service. It certainly led to a marked change in his fortunes and became the launch-pad for his long and distinguished career in the police. I, for my part, also found it gratifying that I'd been involved in an event that probably acted as a turning point for him and helped towards kick-starting his career; although being caught up in the violent incident itself was anything but an enjoyable experience, and something I would happily have avoided. It was also satisfying to know that in some small way my efforts in trying to talk him out of resigning had maybe contributed to him remaining in the job.

As soon as I became involved in policing, I learned that when you're out patrolling danger can potentially lurk around every corner, so you constantly need to have your wits about you. Whilst accompanying Ivan one evening on his town centre beat, I also came to realise how your instincts, combined with the way you handle treacherous situations, can help to keep you safe. Working with Ivan was always a really informative and enlightening experience because he possessed what is described in the police community as a 'copper's nose'; a form of sixth sense, which could arouse his suspicions, and enable him to instinctively recognise an imminent threat, or when something or someone just didn't seem quite right – based on nothing but a hunch. That was the case during this particular patrol when we encountered a guy loitering down a back street.

The chap wasn't acting suspiciously as such, but there was something about him that just didn't stack up and made him look out of place. Ivan sensed it straight away, and I must admit I also felt the same, even though neither of us could explain this gut feeling – or why he made the hairs on the back of our necks stand up. Intuitively, we therefore thought he might be up to no good and decided to approach this dodgy looking character and strike up a conversation with him – to suss out if there was a reason why he'd had this affect on us.

When we approached him he didn't seem unduly bothered and, upon speaking to him, he came across as reasonably affable. We learned he came from up north and he seemed pleasant enough as he explained his reasons for visiting this part of the country. He even seemed happy to tell us he'd been in trouble in the past, had served time and was on probation, and also to give us his details without much persuasion. This was after Ivan had told him we'd had a number of burglaries in the area, so needed to eliminate him from our enquiries by doing a routine person check to ensure he didn't fit the profile of this type of offender.

Having obtained his details, Ivan then moved slightly away from our person of interest to do the criminal record check via PNC, leaving me to carry on chatting with him – and effectively trying to keep him occupied whilst it was determined if there was a reason to take him into custody. Shortly after Ivan had transmitted this chap's details, we got a coded call sign informing us we were about to receive information that is for police ears only; meaning it's necessary to turn down your radio or move out of earshot of the individual in your company. Upon hearing this, I put my radio on mute as I was still in close proximity of the guy we were questioning and didn't have a radio equipped with an earpiece; however, this was not before I'd briefly heard a further coded call sign. It was the call sign that you have every reason to dread, and don't want to hear because it indicates you're dealing with someone with a warning marker – a person who could pose a serious threat, is known to be violent, is likely in possession of a weapon, and has a history of committing assaults on police!

The feedback Ivan then received from PNC advised there were no outstanding warrants for our suspect, currently he wasn't wanted by any other force and his past convictions didn't include acts of burglary – making it unlikely he would have been responsible for such crimes in our area. This information also meant there was no reason to apprehend him. I'm sure he'd been well aware this would be the case when he'd so willingly provided his details following our request.

Although he hadn't overheard the feedback being transmitted, which Ivan had discreetly passed on to me, he would have known it would contain a detailed account of his past violent conduct, and how such violence had often been directed at police officers – and, consequently, that we'd now be aware of the threat he would pose if we needed to arrest him. Based on the way this dangerous individual observed us once we'd learned of his menacing background, I suspect he was trying to gauge our reaction and hoping it would make us squirm. Knowing this was likely, there was no way Ivan or I were going to outwardly show we were bothered, or give him the satisfaction of thinking we were fearful. Nevertheless, I freely admit I was feeling a degree of trepidation at coming face to face with someone who had this type of offending pattern, and was constantly wary of how he may react.

In spite of the unease we felt about this guy, we both realised that once we'd taken into account the info we'd received we clearly had no justifiable reason to arrest him. That was probably just as well as I don't think he would have submitted passively, and would undoubtedly have been physically aggressive towards us. Being spared from going through such an ordeal with him was a relief, not least because we knew that had there been evidence to warrant us taking him into custody we would have done so – despite the fact he was known to be a formidable foe who would have presented a significant threat to our wellbeing.

Other than doing a quick search to ensure he wasn't concealing any weapons about his person, which he actually allowed us to do without any objection – no doubt because he knew he wasn't in possession of anything incriminating – that was the end of the matter. However, this event does once again highlight how easily police officers can sometimes stumble into threatening situations, where they may find themselves having to confront or deal with imminent danger – as further epitomised by my next brief tale.

Within the world of policing, you know you'll occasionally have to deal with challenging incidents that arise out of nowhere, and that was certainly so when I was once more accompanying Ivan during a late shift. We were covering response, when a member of the public informed us he'd just seen a group of around a dozen feral young people behaving in an anti-social manner down a backstreet. He told us he'd felt intimidated when they'd made some derogatory remarks about his appearance, so we went to investigate.

Upon arriving in the backstreet, the group the complainant had described were still there milling around, so we pulled up alongside to have a word with them about their behaviour. Ivan's side of the car was nearest to the group, and as he got out of the vehicle to confront them he was instantaneously engulfed by the youths. As this happened so quickly, and he'd immediately disappeared from my view into what looked like a mass of writhing bodies, it felt like he'd been ambushed. It also seemed as though there must have been some sort of skirmish, resulting in him being wrestled to the ground. Fearing the worst, and being concerned for his welfare, I therefore decided to raise the alarm by radioing for urgent assistance before joining in the fray.

By the time I got around to the other side of the car Ivan had re-emerged from the mêlée, fortunately none the worse for wear, and I discovered things weren't quite as bad as I'd first feared. When he'd been set upon by members of this unruly group, I honestly believed it was more than a scuffle and they'd started laying into him, so it was a relief to find out he'd only been jostled and not struck to the ground after all.

Even so, I knew we still faced a hostile situation, not least from the ringleader of the group – an invidious crackhead who was regularly involved in bouts of anti-social behaviour. He was not only a prolific offender well-known to police, but also a nasty piece of work who could be exceptionally aggressive and obnoxious, especially if he was high on heroine. I was aware from previous encounters, that even when he appeared calm at the outset, such a situation could change in a flash because he was prone to sudden and unaccountable changes of mood, which could result in violent outbursts. I also knew this individual was currently wanted on suspicion of committing several offences, and that taking him into custody would be a major challenge – irrespective of whether he was initially compliant, and despite it now appearing that his band of followers could be less of a threat to us than I'd originally envisaged. Therefore, having requested urgent assistance, and knowing that as a result all available resources would have dropped everything and be en route, was actually no bad thing – even though I might have been a little premature in doing so!

The extra help I'd summoned definitely proved to be invaluable because as soon as Ivan and I tried to arrest the wanted man he made a break for it. However, his planned escape route was effectively blocked by Ron, the first officer that happened to be coming to our aid. Ron's timing was impeccable because he'd come running around the corner towards us just as the defendant had escaped our clutches, and made his bolt for freedom. As the escapee tried to evade him, our colleague managed to put in a textbook rugby tackle on the fleeing yob, which brought him tumbling headlong to the ground. By chance, the pair of them went hurtling into a grass verge and had a reasonably soft landing as they crashed to the floor, so neither of them came to any harm as a result of Ron's crunching tackle; although I think the force of being taken down in this fashion winded our fleeing prisoner, as he didn't resist after that, which was rare for him. Doubtless, having another three colleagues arriving on scene also helped as well - so, it was then game over for this reprobate.

These detailed accounts of disorderly conduct further demonstrate how you can be putting yourself in the firing line every time you don the uniform, and sometimes face aggression and violence when it's least expected – without experiencing any obvious warning signs. Hostility towards police officers is of course not just confined to when they are patrolling the streets, and can occur anytime, whether in uniform or not, and even when off-duty. Several of my colleagues were subjected to intimidation or attacks in isolated or obscure situations. That was the case in respect of one officer from my station who was viciously assaulted by two thugs whilst off-duty, when he happened to encounter them as he was walking home after a night out.

In this type of situation being recognised as a police officer by certain undesirable characters can make you susceptible to reprisals, and that was so when these hooligans launched a ferocious attack on this colleague, which left him with multiple injuries. Ultimately, these contemptible yobs were apprehended, and got lengthy custodial sentences for carrying out this abominable act – rightly so, considering this unprovoked beating resulted in this officer being off work for several months.

As a rule, violence towards those upholding the law is mostly aimed at the 'police service' and what it stands for in its broadest sense, rather than individuals, even though it is of course the officers themselves that are subjected to such behaviour. However, there can be occasions when it becomes personal, and a particular officer is specifically targeted – because, in their warped view, some violent criminals can see officers as legitimate targets for recrimination. That was almost certainly the case in regard to the appalling attack on the off-duty officer, where it was likely some form of cowardly retaliation connected to a previous run in he'd had with the thugs, rather than a random assault that occurred because they recognised him as a copper – which, in itself, can also sometimes be a motive.

I hasten to add that thankfully serious assaults on off-duty officers, such as this deplorable attack, are still relatively rare. As mentioned before, I wonder if this is because the uniform offers those working in law enforcement a degree of anonymity – meaning they are not routinely recognised by criminals when in civvies. Even so, this example does serve as a reminder of the vulnerabilities you can all too easily face as a police officer in the event you become well-known within your local area, or too easily identifiable by certain elements of the criminal world, and are no longer able to go about your daily life outside of policing incognito.

That said, and to ensure I present a balanced view, there are also odd occasions when being a familiar face can be an advantage, and I recollect one such instance when that proved to be so. At the time I was out on patrol with my sergeant during a Saturday afternoon and we were asked to attend an incident at a flat, where the occupant was having difficulty evicting a visitor who'd outstayed his welcome. According to the information we received, the female tenant had been involved in a disagreement with a boozed-up male associate, who had refused to leave her abode on request and had instead put himself to bed.

Upon our arrival the tenant explained she only vaguely new the inebriated man, who had come to a party in her flat the previous evening along with a group of her friends. Now, despite politely requesting him to leave, he'd declined to go. Not only had he repeatedly ignored her perfectly reasonable requests, but he'd also had the cheek to tuck himself up in her bed!

When we entered her bedroom we discovered the unwelcome guest was out for the count. Initially, we attempted to wake him from his drunken stupor by speaking to him loudly but, when this failed, sarge tried to rouse him by giving him a firm shake. Doing so not only brought him around, it also caused him to jump out of bed and take up an aggressive stance – making it appear as though he was going to cause us some serious bother and we could be in for a bit of rough and tumble.

Through good fortune however, it was at this point we both recognised each other and he suddenly seemed to see things in a different light because his stroppy attitude towards us changed dramatically. I knew his family quite well and, in a split second, it felt like he'd gone from viewing us as his enemy to being his long-lost friends. Consequently, we then had no trouble convincing him it was time to apologise to his host and make his way home.

My sergeant appreciated the positive impact I'd had on this young man, due to my links with his family. He felt my familiarity had played a useful part in defusing a likely volatile situation, and probably prevented the problem from escalating. As he put it, my very presence could even have stopped us getting a pasting, as this lad was actually a renowned local boxer who could be a bit fiery. From my perspective, I was just pleased that being known to someone had turned out to be beneficial for once because frequently it can have the opposite affect, and lead to those in a similarly drunken state becoming more verbally abusive, obstinate or threatening than normal.

Further to my tale about the off-duty officer being intentionally targeted, I'm glad to say this was an isolated incident during my time as a serving special. Statistically, the probability of you coming to harm whilst actually on duty has, understandably, always has been much more likely – sometimes when you're caught completely off guard. Nev and his sergeant found this out through painful experience when they became the victims of totally unprovoked assaults whilst undertaking routine duties – Nev whilst on foot patrol one evening (as alluded to in Chapter 12) and sarge when he came to his assistance.

The assault on Nev occurred when he was walking his town centre beat, and happened to pass by an ex-squaddie who had a drink problem. This former paratrooper was known to police as he'd developed into a violent alcoholic after leaving the army, so Nev knew he was unpredictable and someone to be wary of. However, as they neared each other, it wasn't apparent this chap was about lash out, and it came as a complete surprise when he suddenly threw and landed a powerful punch to the side of Nev's chin, causing him to almost tumble to the ground. Although the force of the punch stunned Nev, he somehow rapidly overcame the impact of this vicious assault and then attempted to apprehend his assailant. Being well-built and tall this army veteran could be a real handful, but Nev is even bigger and very strong so he soon got the upper hand, despite suffering the after effects of the punch he'd received.

Having managed to restrain this guy by placing him in a headlock with one arm, he was able to use his free hand to call up for assistance – and, in response, his sergeant was the first to arrive on scene. Between them they successfully got their prisoner in the back of the police car, so they could transport him to the station. It was while they were en-route that this aggressive alcoholic committed his second assault on police that evening, this time on the sergeant.

During the short journey sarge drove the police car and Nev went in the back to keep the guy in check, but doing so proved to be easier said than done as he was determined to put up a fight. This meant Nev had to constantly grapple with him in order to keep him restrained. While he was doing so, the prisoner ended up on his back and somehow managed to raise his leg in order to kick the sergeant forcefully on the rear of his head, causing him to almost pass out and lose control of the car.

Like Nev after he'd taken the punch to his chin, he recovered his senses quickly enough in the short-term to regain control of the car, and then continue driving to the 'nick'. However, that was his lot for this particular shift because the almighty blow had left him with a large contusion and a thumping headache. It had also made him feel very groggy, so he had to go to hospital to be checked out for possible concussion. Indeed, following a medical examination, he was diagnosed as suffering with this condition and was signed-off for more than a week. Subsequently, he also suffered with recurring migraines throughout the rest of his life – a chronic medical condition he'd not experienced before enduring the fearsome kick to the back of his head.

Considering the seriousness of these assaults, it was perhaps questionable whether the defendant was treated with undue leniency when he was put before the court because he didn't receive a custodial sentence. Instead he was bound over to keep the peace – on the proviso that he also sought help to address his alcoholism. He duly did so, and this did lead to him undergoing a brief spell of sobriety whilst in rehab. However, within a matter of weeks of leaving the rehab facility, the offender did his best to demonstrate that neither the justice system, nor the rehab programme were working effectively – well, not in his case, because he repeated the offence in very similar circumstances. On this occasion it was Royston that he punched whilst he was out on foot patrol one evening, leaving him with a nasty black eye. As before, the guy gave no inkling he was about to strike this colleague.

Once more he was arrested for launching an unprovoked attack and put in front of the magistrates – and again he was convicted of the offence. This time he did get a short custodial sentence; although you knew this wasn't going to solve the problem and he would forever be stuck in the same vicious circle, unless he got ongoing help to overcome his alcohol dependency. Worryingly as well, you anticipated that without an appropriate intervention to address his drinking compulsion, there was every chance this former soldier's condition would deteriorate and his behaviour worsen; perhaps to the point where he could easily maim somebody or, perish the thought, end up killing someone – quite possibly a police officer, since members of the Constabulary were often the target of his aggression. Fortunately, it never came to that as his health declined to the point where he no longer posed a serious threat, and within a matter of months he sadly took his own life – which was such a shame considering he'd served Queen and country. It was also a shocking indictment of society at that time, when you factor in that a lack of appropriate support systems meant he was unable to access the prolonged treatment he so desperately needed, in order to help him combat and overcome his addiction, which might well have been caused by PTSD.

23 Hellbent on Criminal Intent

Thankfully occurrences of street robberies and muggings are few and far between in market towns compared to inner cities, but every so often we would experience this category of crime, and I remember being involved in dealing with one particularly callous incident of this nature. It occurred on a Saturday afternoon on the day the town's junior carnival was taking place, and at the time I was working with my full-time colleague Nathan, who was acting as our sergeant for this shift. We got a call informing us that a cub had been attacked and robbed of his charity collection box, so we rapidly made our way to the scene of the mugging. Upon our arrival we found the young lad in a distressed state, but luckily not too badly hurt. A member of the public had come to our victim's aid and called 999 to alert the police to the emergency.

Although still in state of shock, the young cub (who was only 10-years-old!) was able to give us a good account of what had happened, and a surprisingly detailed description of his attackers. He told us there had been four of them aged between about 12 and 16 and that they were all really scruffy. Helpfully, and somewhat amazingly considering what he'd been through, he was also able to tell us that three of them looked very similar and he thought they were possibly brothers. This was really useful information as it gave us a good idea regarding the likely perpetrators.

As luck would have it, Nathan and I had been on mobile patrol in the vicinity close to where the mugging occurred shortly before it had taken place, and we'd 'clocked' a gang of young lads hanging around in the area who were known to us. These lads not only had a history of thieving, but also fitted the victim's description of his assailants to a 'T' – as they were really scruffy and just happened to all come from the same family! Three of them were blood brothers, who uncannily did look very much alike, whilst the fourth and oldest member of the gang was an adopted sibling – and hence why he didn't resemble the other members of his family.

The plucky young cub relayed exactly what had happened at the point the muggers had menacingly confronted him. He explained that he'd been out selling programmes for the carnival, and was just making his way home with his collection box when he'd been set upon by the four lads. In his explanation he said that while he'd been walking down a quiet lane they'd approached him from behind and immediately surrounded him; then in a threatening manner had demanded he hand over the collection box. Before he'd had a chance to do so, one of them had then cruelly pushed him to the ground and grabbed the collection box from his grasp. Next, all four of them had run off in the direction of the railway station, leaving him lying on the floor. Thank goodness, other than some grazes to his knees, the poor lad hadn't suffered any serious physical injuries; however, Nathan and I wondered how this trauma would impact on his confidence in the longer-term – even though he'd been remarkably courageous during the ordeal, and put on a brave face when he was handed over to the care of his parents.

Having obtained enough information to form a good picture of the lad's alleged attackers, Nathan and I set about tracking down the culprits responsible for this disgraceful crime. After reaching the conclusion this 'joint enterprise' had likely been down to the four lads we had in mind, we decided to re-trace the steps we thought these young criminals could have taken if they'd headed straight home with their bootie after committing this heinous act. The fact they'd run off towards the railway station lent itself to our theory because they lived close to this amenity. And our hunch soon paid dividends when we stumbled upon a discarded charity collection box; presumably the one that had been stolen during the mugging. It was in a garden hedge nearby to where these lads resided – no doubt it had been lobbed into the bushes soon after the thieves had managed to break it open and remove all the cash. Naturally, we bagged this item in the hope it could provide some irrefutable forensic evidence, such as fingerprints, linking it to the felons.

Our good fortune didn't end there, as we then came upon two of the young tearaways we were seeking in connection with the street crime. They were nearly at their home, and appeared to be just returning from a trip to the local grocery store as they were carrying a hoard of sweets and cigarettes – which, in all probability, had been purchased with some of their ill-gotten gains. Since we had good reason to believe they had committed the mugging we detained them, escorted them the rest of the way to their abode, where we next carried out an initial search of the two lads in the presence of their parents. In spite of the spending spree they'd just been on, this revealed they still had a significant amount of money on them, which they couldn't reasonably account for, so they were both placed under arrest.

Whilst we were still at the house the gods must have continued smiling on us because the two other siblings, who we suspected of being involved in the crime, also happened to return home. I think they got the shock of their lives when they walked in and effectively found Nathan and I waiting for them. We hadn't actually been waiting for them as such, and it was just another stroke of luck that they'd come back home while we were still there dealing with their brothers. They were also carrying a bag containing a stash of sweets and ciggies, and in possession of quite a bit of cash, mostly in the form of loose change, so they were similarly apprehended on suspicion of theft.

As we now had all of them in custody, we needed to summon another police vehicle so we could ship them back to our nick, along with their mum – because she would need to be present to act as a responsible adult when we conducted interviews with our suspects. In this instance though, it was more a case of an irresponsible adult taking on this role as their mother (and also their father) already had a string of convictions for carrying out a range of petty crimes. Neither parent had been keen to act in this capacity, since they were anti-police but, ultimately, the mum begrudgingly agreed because the alternative would mean getting the family social worker involved – which was something both parents wanted to avoid.

Having to await the arrival of another police vehicle, meant we had to stay much longer in this obnoxious family's household than we really would have liked, especially as it wasn't the most welcoming environment and anything but a pleasant experience. Quite apart from the inhospitable atmosphere, we also had to endure the awful stench you encounter when a property is in a squalid and disgusting state, and clearly hasn't been cleaned for some considerable time – if ever! A lack of hygiene meant the place was really filthy, and the lingering putrid smell made it obvious that at least one of the family's pets must have recently messed inside somewhere – and that its deposit hadn't yet been cleared up. In the circumstances, Nathan and I rapidly came to the conclusion this was definitely one of those homes where you would certainly decline a cup of tea – not that we were ever likely to be offered one – and need to wipe your feet on the way out!

If you can picture the living conditions of this family, you will I'm sure appreciate why the pair of us didn't want to remain a minute longer in this abode than was absolutely necessary – and also why I started to have some sympathy for the four lads that had to live in that squalor, in spite of the despicable and cowardly crime they had committed. The level of deprivation they'd no doubt faced throughout their brief lives was almost unbearable to stomach for even a brief period, and it struck me these lads had got a pretty raw deal when it came to their upbringing to date. Not only did they live in such unpalatable and impoverished conditions, but the very people who should have been their role models had also set them a bad example. Coming from a notorious family of petty criminals they probably had no chance, and were always likely to follow in the footsteps of their villainous parents. The term vicious circle springs to mind and, if my experiences of police work taught me one thing, it's how vital it is to find ways to break that cycle; especially when you bear in mind it's principally the experiences we endure when growing up that largely shape, define and influence us – and, in this type of circumstance, probably set people on a wayward path where they will frequently make the wrong choices and get into bad habits.

None of this of course justified them carrying out the abhorrent attack on the young cub, but it does help you to understand why such appalling crimes occur, and are sometimes committed by those of such a tender age, often because their minds have already been contaminated and corrupted. In this instance, with the evidence stacked against them, all four of the accused came clean about the part they'd played in the mugging, and they were duly dealt with through the Juvenile court system. The sentences they received befitted the crime, but I was at least heartened by the fact that one of them – the adopted member of the family – did show genuine remorse for his behaviour and involvement. He also went on to amend his criminal ways and turn his fortunes around, despite the fact he'd grown up in an environment where there was a lack of any form of moral compass.

Some years after this incident, I was therefore delighted to discover he'd made something of his life, and had secured a good job. Even though he ultimately became estranged from his adoptive parents, after being vilified and ostracised by them for choosing to go straight, you would hope his success could have demonstrated to his siblings that crime doesn't pay, and that an alternative lifestyle can prove to be more rewarding. Sadly, however, this wasn't so as they also shunned him and stayed blind to that option, and went from being little brats to big brats when they grew up – with long-term prison sentences beckoning.

On another occasion when I assisted in dealing with a street crime, we were regrettably unable to crack the case and track down the person responsible. In this instance, the offence involved a thief grabbing a middle-aged woman's handbag, and running off with it before she'd even had time to fully realise what was happening. She was understandably still in shock by the time I arrived at the scene of the mugging along with other police colleagues, and in her anxious state she was unable to provide any detailed information about exactly what had happened, let alone tell us much about her attacker. However, two other members of the public, a man and a woman – who'd observed her having her bag snatched – were more than willing to give statements. At first, it therefore looked promising that we'd get a good description of the culprit, which would substantially increase our chances of identifying the offender – or that seemed to be the case until each of them independently described what the mugger looked like. About all they were able to agree upon, and corroborate within their conflicting accounts, was that the assailant was male. The female witness described his appearance as Caucasian, short, blond and stocky; whilst the guy insisted the subject was tall, dark and skinny with an olive complexion. Not a lot of help really when you're trying to establish a clear image of what someone looks like – although, perhaps based on what they told us, we should have assumed the mugger was most likely of medium build and average height, with brown hair!

If these eyewitnesses did possess any powers of observation, then clearly they had deserted at least one of them on this occasion because they also gave conflicting accounts in regard to the perpetrator's approximate age and what he had been wearing – so, all in all, we had little to go on that would help us make a breakthrough in our enquiries. Normally, having independent witnesses to any crime would be a real advantage; however, in this instance, it proved to be anything but. In fact, bearing in mind the disparities between the two descriptions, the info they'd given us was about as useful as a holed bucket, and we were all left scratching our heads. Other than discovering the victim's discarded handbag, minus her purse and a couple of other valuables, little headway was ever made during the ensuing investigation into this crime – especially as the handbag unfortunately didn't provide any forensic leads – and, to the best of my knowledge, this particular assailant was never identified.

One of the last times I worked with Ivan before he was seconded to the Regional Crime Squad (RCS), and subsequently the National Crime Squad (NCS), was on a Saturday late turn. From recollection the initial part of our shift had been uneventful, and the first incident we were requested to attend occurred during the early evening.

A report came through advising us a group of lads had been seen climbing into a scrap yard and, believing they'd be up to no good, we went to investigate. Another unit also responded; so, between us, we were confident we could close off any means of escape and catch them red-handed. However, there was a lookout who spotted us approaching before we'd had a chance to get into position and they all scattered. One of them came in the direction of Ivan and I, but was about 50 metres ahead of us as he made his dash for freedom along a pathway. We gave chase but briefly lost sight of him as he rounded a bend. It was probably only a matter of seconds until we reached the bend from whence he'd disappeared from our line of sight but, much to our surprise, we couldn't see him anywhere.

However, we did spot a group of lads out for a run coming towards us, and it turned out they were members of the local football team who were out training.

As they jogged by we couldn't help but notice that the lad bringing up the rear looked somewhat out of place. In fact, he stood out like a sore thumb because he was overweight, puffed-out and not exactly fleet of foot. Also, unlike the others, who were dressed in sports gear, he was wearing a hoodie, jeans and Doc Marten boots – perhaps not the ideal disguise if you're attempting to pass yourself off as a budding athlete! With our suspicions therefore aroused, Ivan and I started running after the group or, more to the point, the lad who was tagging along at the back of the pack. It probably looked like a scene from one of those Benny Hill episodes as we joined in the chase, and I can recall one member of the public rather rudely enquiring why we were chasing after these lads, to which Ivan sarcastically responded:

'Why do you think? Because we're playing kiss-chase of course!'

In the circumstances it didn't take us long to catch up with the lad we were after and, when we collared him, he actually seemed relieved as he was so unfit he needed a breather. It had been a good effort on his part to try to evade capture, but I think deep down he realised that he was never really going to blend in with a group of fit footballers, especially as his particular attire wasn't the ideal camouflage and was going to draw attention to him rather than deflect it. Although he hadn't exactly been caught bang to rights, he opted to admit he'd been one of the crew that had broken into the scrap yard. However, in his words, 'he wasn't prepared to 'grass-up' his accomplices', so they weren't identified and it was only him that carried the can. For him, this breach of the law resulted in a return to a youth offender institute – as he was currently out on licence after serving part of a previous sentence for burglary.

Criminals come in all sorts of forms, and a crime-lord nicknamed 'Mr B', who was allegedly heavily involved in the world of vice and extortion and owned a business empire that had been built on porn, chiefly through the exploitation of vulnerable young women, didn't classically look or behave like your stereotypical villain. He lived in a grandiose house in an affluent local village, a place that he seemed to treat like his own personal enclave and, ironically, he had a reputation amongst his fellow parishioners for being a pillar of the community. This was no doubt how he liked to portray himself to the locals, but he was far from being an upstanding citizen, and anyone who mistakenly looked upon him in that light was way off the mark. The air of respectability he appeared to convey belied the truth, and we had good reason to suspect that underneath this façade he was ostensibly the complete opposite of a model member of society. However, to prove beyond doubt that was the case – and ultimately deflate his over-inflated ego – we needed to find incontrovertible evidence.

I first had the misfortune to cross his path when I was commandeered to assist in a search for illegal pornographic materials during a raid on his premises, and on this occasion I have to admit he did initially come across as quite charming. Therefore, I could see why he was perhaps viewed more fondly than he should have been by those who didn't know the real 'Mr B', or have an inkling about his suspected links to organised crime. However, in spite of his charm, I took an instant dislike to him, which is rare for me when I first meet someone. I don't know whether it was some form of sixth sense, but there was just something about this prominent villager that I immediately detested and, although I couldn't instantly put my finger on why, the reasons rapidly became all too apparent once he revealed his true colours.

The reason I became involved in a raid of this nature, which was carried out by a task force of bobbies from our station and led by one of our section sergeants, was purely down to the fact that I just happened to be on duty the day it took place. I was therefore asked to tag along in support of my full-time colleagues – as they apparently needed as many officers as they could muster for this mission. Normally this type of investigation would have been conducted by members of the force's Vice Squad, with the search warrant being carried out by their own personnel, but they had asked for local officers to mount a raid because their resources were already committed on another large-scale operation.

By the sound of it, the Vice Squad had received a tip-off from a disgruntled ex-employee who'd recently been sacked by 'Mr B', informing them that his company was involved in the making and distribution of illegal videos, depicting obscene acts of depravity, which could include some scenes involving under-age girls. Hence why it was vital this matter was looked into expediently.

It was conceivable the unhappy former employee simply had an axe to grind and was looking for retribution, and her information had therefore been exaggerated or embellished to cause some inconvenience to her old boss and his servile foot soldiers; naturally though, the police couldn't take any chances in view of the seriousness of the allegation. Besides, since those involved in orchestrating organised crime rarely get their hands dirty and normally distance themselves from any direct criminal activity, this was an opportunity to have a shot at bringing down someone at the top, rather than one of the underlings. It was too good a chance to miss, so our station boss was delighted when a local magistrate sanctioned the raid on 'Mr B's' premises by issuing a search warrant.

When we first arrived at our suspect's home address to serve the warrant, we received a surprisingly polite and warm welcome from 'Mr B' and, as already indicated, he was charm personified. Based on his reaction, you would have thought he had nothing to hide, so I think we all started to wonder whether we'd been sent on a wild goose chase. And even when we uncovered numerous porn videos stored about his home and in various outbuildings – so many it was obvious they were for distribution rather than personal use – he still remained cool as he displayed a degree of indifference, protested his innocence and kept up the pretence that he'd done nothing wrong; stating he was simply a hard-working, successful and legitimate businessman.

The fact that he'd amassed a fortune through his so-called business ventures was evident from the signs of his obvious opulence, which were displayed all around his house, but his claim that his practices had been legitimate was, in our view, open to question. Anyway, from the onset of our search, it was clear he must have worked out that we'd received a tip-off because he did suggest he'd perhaps been wronged by someone out for revenge, or jealous of his success and lifestyle. He maintained his composure right up to the point where our sergeant informed him that his computer and trading records were going be seized – along with all of the videos, so we could check if they contained anyone performing an illegal act, including minors engaged in sexual activities.

Once our leader had made this announcement, his whole demeanour and attitude towards us certainly changed, as a more latent aspect of his personality began to emerge. Gone was the cordiality he'd displayed up till then and, as he became increasingly indignant, we instead got a glimpse of the ruthless, gangster-like character the informant had described. In fact, this source had apparently referred to him as a brazen scumbag, who was a sanctimonious twat, and inferred that he showed utter contempt for his fellow beings – and this was a side to his personality that had now come to the fore. He let rip with a broadside of choice obscenities and, within his vitriolic condemnation of us, there was a tirade of abuse, which ranged from questioning our parenthood to veiled threats regarding our future wellbeing. His defamatory declamation, combined with his show of malevolence, served to convince me that my initial perceptions about him hadn't let me down.

Having discovered and seized this stockpile of porn movies, we now had the unenviable task of going through them to identify any illegal acts that would incriminate 'Mr B' and, most importantly, warrant them being permanently confiscated. In turn, finding anything of this nature would subsequently justify arresting, charging and pursuing a prosecution against him under the appropriate legislation pertaining to the illegal publication, filming and distribution of obscene materials – which would be most satisfying in view of his pretentious display of omnipotence, and the totally unacceptable attitude he had towards the victims of his exploits. Being able to build such a case against him, and his band of sycophants, would rely on us having the evidence to do so, and it was at this point I realised why my services had really been needed for this operation – because watching all these videos was clearly going to be a huge job that would require all available hands on deck!

Before we started the laborious task of viewing the videos, which wasn't something I relished, our sarge explained that a lot would be hinging on us finding something incriminating. Primarily this entailed scrutinising the videos to check if they included any sex acts involving a minor – the thought of which filled me with revulsion. Equally, as part of his briefing, he reminded us that it was illegal to record pornographic material for distribution and public consumption that contained certain gross sex acts, which are best left to the imagination. These also included one particular sex act (that again I won't elaborate on) deemed legal when practiced by consenting adults in private, but considered illicit under relevant obscenity legislation if filmed for the purpose of wider circulation – and to log anything we came across in these porn movies that crossed that particular line. In addition, he then pointed out that we would need to be meticulous whilst viewing the videos – as it wouldn't necessarily be blatantly obvious whether some of the sexual activities performed within these porn movies, actually fitted into one of the categories he'd highlighted.

As we ploughed through the videos, fast forwarding whenever possible, there were occasional exchanges of banter – and, surprisingly, it was the two female officers in the team that came out with the wittiest remarks, more so than their male counterparts. However, everyone remained suitably respectful, and there weren't any comments made that were inappropriate, in terms of them being insensitive or offensive. I think for several colleagues, trying to make light of the hideous sights we came upon was the only way they could stay sane because much of what we witnessed was pretty sickening. And quite how anyone can find porn sexy and entertaining, or would want to be constantly watching this sort of material, is beyond my comprehension. This wasn't the type of soft porn you might find on the TV, or even on the top shelf at the local video shop, but your full-on hardcore stuff, which to my knowledge was only ever available from what was known as 'under-the-counter'.

Ultimately, during this gruelling shift when I was involved in helping to go through the videos, what we observed appeared to be solely sex acts between consenting adults, and we didn't identify anything where we could conclusively demonstrate a line had been crossed in terms of the law being broken. There were a few scenes whereby it initially appeared as though one of the particular acts we'd been briefed to look out for had taken place; however, on closer inspection, we'd found it impossible to categorically state this had been the case because it could simply have been an optical illusion created by the position that the copulating couples had adopted. There was also a distinct possibility that such an act was just being simulated or mimicked, with those participating deliberately trying to portray the impression they'd taken things further; so, in essence, there was no way to prove beyond doubt that this particular screening offence had occurred. And, with it being inconclusive, there was no prospect of pursuing a prosecution in respect of this element of dubious material.

On the plus side, and to my relief, we didn't spot anyone engaged in sexual activity who appeared to be underage – well, at least not whilst I was assisting with the viewing of the pornographic videos. However, that didn't mean there weren't going to be examples of such appalling abuse or prohibited material in the remaining batch of films that still needed to be checked, especially as we'd barely scratched the surface during my shift. What I'd seen was just a small sample because it evidently took several days to get through all the videos, and I never did get to hear whether any of the material included minors engaged in sexual activities, or if any of the other ghastly or gross acts we'd been briefed to look out for were ever discovered in any of the remaining films – and, to be quite honest, I'm not sure I really wanted to know.

In the short-term, I don't believe our enquiries into 'Mr B's' suspected criminal lifestyle led to him being charged, but I'd like to think our raid and the ensuing lengthy investigation did at least curb his activities. Hopefully, it also made him think again about exploiting the fallibilities of vulnerable young women – even though I know that having such an outlook was most likely wishful thinking on my part.

Several months after I'd been involved in this raid, and the preliminary stages of our investigation into the business empire run by 'Mr B', I had the misfortune to bump into him again – this time at a social event. Luckily he didn't recognise me out of uniform, which was something of a blessing because, had he done so, I'm sure I would have felt pretty uncomfortable. During the evening I kept well away from him, as I had no desire to share the company of an arrogant and delusional narcissist at an event attended by a lot of decent people. However, it was interesting to observe his behaviour from a distance, knowing as much as I did about his true character, the contempt he had for the law and the seedy side of his business operations. It once more turned my stomach to see this pretentious charlatan masquerading as a law-abiding citizen, and playing to his crowd as though he genuinely held some esteemed role within his community.

Despite his arrogance and obvious self-indulgence, you couldn't deny he came across as plausible and, for someone with a villainous background, whose ostentatious lifestyle was likely funded by the proceeds of crime, he had an amazing knack for hiding in plain sight. I therefore have to admit that as I watched him fraternise from afar, he gave an exceptionally believable performance of being the very epitome of a true gentleman. In the circumstances, I wondered what the vast majority of his admirers, associates and 'so-called friends' would really think of him if they knew that hiding behind the mask of respectability, which he convincingly wore, there was actually a sleazy and manipulative racketeer; in fact, a thoroughly vile and creepy man, who'd almost certainly acquired his position and wealth by taking advantage of those less fortunate than himself, and exploiting them to make money.

As galling as it was to see him conning many of the people around him by acting like a pompous member of the local gentry, I knew there was nothing I could do about it, except suppress my feelings of disdain and hope that some day my colleagues would make a breakthrough, which would lead to them finding enough evidence to get him convicted. And, some years later, I did learn that my hopes he would one day get his come-uppance had partially come to fruition, when I discovered he had at least faced some lesser charges relating to the publication and distribution of obscene materials. If nothing else, I thought this might finally help to curtail his criminal activities, bring about his downfall and tarnish his reputation within his local community. I also found out that he was likely to be appearing in court after being implicated in running a prostitution racket. Hearing such news was especially pleasing because it always seemed like he considered himself to be untouchable, above the law and immune from prosecution. So, maybe he wasn't as invincible as he thought and he did ultimately fall from grace – and, who knows, perhaps crime doesn't pay in the long run, justice generally prevails, and he did lose his status as a kingpin within the criminal fraternity and a big-wig in his village – we can but hope!

As I neared the end of my time as a special, we faced an upsurge in the number of sex related crimes being committed in our local area – or, at least a big increase in the amount of such crimes being reported. Of particular note was the high level of flashing offences that were occurring, and witness testimony indicated that in the vast majority of cases this could be the work of one young male, and that we most likely had a serial flasher on our hands. This matter had become the talk of the town and, in a short space of time, such offending had reached an epidemic scale, with reports of this lewd activity coming in on a daily basis; so naturally it was imperative this perpetrator was caught as soon as possible in order that he could be brought to justice.

Understandably his lurid behaviour was giving cause for concern, not only because his offending had been engendering fear and alarm for his female victims – in the main aged between 15 and 30 – but also because it needed to be nipped in the bud before it escalated and led to more serious acts of sexual deviancy being committed. In fact, there had already been worrying signs this brazen flasher was getting out of control, as his more recent offences had involved him jumping out in front of vehicles being driven by young women – and, in one instance, he'd actually climbed onto a car bonnet to expose himself.

It was good to see that the alarming actions of this offender were being taken very seriously because, in some ways, that was a million miles away from how indecent exposure was looked upon when I first started as a cadet. In those days, I got the impression that anyone doing so was generally seen as being a bit of a nuisance and, to some extent, dismissed as being a harmless exhibitionist – perhaps because the link between such insidious behaviour possibly manifesting into a more disturbing and sinister form of sexually motivated offending wasn't fully appreciated. I don't think this outlook was in any way due to a blasé attitude back then; I suspect it was more likely down to there being a lack of detailed and widely shared scientific data about the likelihood of there being an obvious connection.

In an effort to catch this particular offender, a local beat officer had been assigned the case and tasked with co-ordinating enquiries, and when he asked for volunteers to assist him with his investigation, a fellow special and I were quick to respond to his request. I had a vested interest in willingly doing so, as it was my neighbourhood that was predominantly being plagued by this shameless serial offender, with many of his flashing offences having taken place in close proximity of my home address. Being the father of two young daughters, I naturally wanted this deviant man apprehended and off our streets as a matter of priority. Working under the direction of the investigating officer, my Special Constabulary colleague and I therefore spent many hours patrolling those parts of town our flasher seemed to favour in the hope we'd spot him loitering – or even catch him in the act. Mostly we operated covertly and went out in civvies so we would remain inconspicuous but, occasionally, we would also patrol in uniform to act as a deterrent and give members of the public some reassurance. As an integral part of our proactive duties, we also made a number of relevant enquiries, which included re-interviewing victims to see if they could recall any further details about the offender that would aid the investigation. More in hope than expectation, we additionally did some routine house-to-house enquiries in locations where the offender had exposed himself, on the off chance we might come across other witnesses to his deviant acts, who hadn't yet come forward after enduring such an ordeal.

All of our efforts to track down the flasher regrettably came to no avail, even though there was one brief occasion when we thought we'd stumbled across our target. Whilst we were out on foot one evening, we spotted a young lad who looked the spitting image of the photofit of our suspect, which had been compiled as a result of witness descriptions and, at first, we couldn't believe our luck. When we initially saw him it was from some distance away and, as his physical appearance in terms of looks, height, build, hair colour and hairstyle all closely matched the flasher's description, we both thought there was a strong chance he could be our man; however, once we got closer to him, we soon realised he was much younger than the suspected perpetrator. Witnesses had suggested the flasher was aged between 25 and 35 years, and this lad was only about 14-years-old, and it therefore soon became apparent it wasn't him. We did have a word, but this simply re-affirmed it definitely wasn't this innocent young lad. He was in the area waiting to meet up with some pals and it was pure co-incidence – and bad luck on his part – that he happened to resemble our quarry.

The reason the serial flasher was ultimately traced was actually down to Ivan, who at the time of this guy's prolific offending was still away on attachment with the NCS. Ivan's family home was still back in my town and, as soon as he heard about the search going on for this offender, he put forward the name of a possible suspect. This was based on this particular young man's offending history when he'd dealt with him several years earlier, and it turned out to be an excellent hunch. The guy he'd put in the frame as a probable exhibitionist was placed under observation and, sure enough, it wasn't long before this person of interest was caught in the act of exposing himself; thus finally enabling him to be charged with numerous counts of outraging public decency. Consequently, this outcome demonstrated you cannot beat local knowledge and criminal intelligence, which has been acquired over many years, when it comes to investigating and solving crime. Without Ivan's timely intervention, who knows how long this unsavoury chap's campaign of terrorising young women would have continued as it seemed unlikely his thirst for doing so would have waned any time soon; bearing in mind he clearly got a thrill from actively tormenting those he subjected to his flashing.

So often the punishment doesn't befit the severity of the crime, and therefore everyone was delighted when the court viewed this defendant's lurid and intimidatory behaviour in a very serious light and handed him a custodial sentence. It was definitely warranted in this instance considering the extent of his terrifying offending, and the damaging impact his vile actions had inflicted on his victims. Sometimes, in cases of this type, the accused tries to deny it was exposure and instead claims it was down to a call of nature – but, with this warped defendant's actions being so outrageous, such a defence was never going to stand up and he couldn't use this charade as his absurd excuse. Besides, taking into account how many times he'd been witnessed flashing his genitalia, he would have needed to prove he had the weakest bladder in the world to be taking a leak in public as frequently as he did!

The longer his offending had gone on without him being caught, the more emboldened he'd become, and with his trademark flashing M.O. being designed to not only outrage public decency, but also to shock and distress his victims, it was even more essential he was taken off our streets to make them a little safer. All in all, finally catching him and the court ruling were therefore excellent results; albeit it took a lot longer than anyone would have liked and justice eventually came about as a result of one officer's comprehensive local knowledge, which had then facilitated a targeted investigation. Still, with this persistent offender now behind bars, local residents – particularly young ladies who lived in my neighbourhood and were at greatest risk of being subjected to his deviant behaviour – could at last breathe easy again.

Sometimes it's not so much a case of catching someone whilst they are in the process of carrying out a crime or after the event, but actually preventing a crime from occurring in the first place through timely intervention. In such circumstances you don't always have the evidence to take matters further, or even know for sure that anyone challenged prior to committing an offence was definitely planning to break the law. However, I'd like to think that there were a number of occasions when my actions, or those of colleagues that I was working with at the time, did help to thwart certain individuals who likely had criminal intent in mind. This might well have been so when my sergeant and I responded to a concern raised by a pub landlady after closing time one night. I'd actually taken the phone call to our police station from the landlady, and I recall that she'd expressed some alarm that three customers were still hanging around in the pub car park about an hour after chucking-out time, even though they didn't appear to have a vehicle.

The public house was located in a remote part of the countryside about four miles out of town and, as the landlady lived alone, she had clearly been unnerved by the presence of these guys lingering in the vicinity – especially as they weren't known to her as regulars at the pub. She described them as being rough and ready with an unkempt appearance, and she told me that based on their earlier behaviour she was worried they'd been casing the joint – perhaps with the intention of breaking in once she'd gone to bed. Although she appreciated they could just be waiting for a lift or a taxi, she felt this was becoming increasingly unlikely in view of the amount of time they'd been hanging around. She definitely had the impression that they'd deliberately been keeping a low profile whilst they waited for everyone to leave the pub, and feared they were up to no good, so I assured her we'd get an officer to respond as soon as possible. Once I'd relayed this information to my sergeant, he instantly decided that we would go ourselves to check out the situation, as the there was no other mobile unit within reasonable proximity available to immediately attend.

Upon our arrival, we instantly spotted three chaps loitering in the pub car park – presumably the same ones reported by the landlady since they matched her description. They were known to us, as each of them possessed a string of convictions, mainly for committing theft, including opportunistic burglaries and shop-lifting – often at the direction of someone further up the food chain within the criminal world. We were sure the landlady's concerns were well-founded but, in the absence of any evidence to show they were going equipped, we weren't in a position to arrest them, even though we knew it was likely this shower of contemptible 'toe-rags' had been conspiring to commit burglary later that night, and simply hadn't yet had the chance to follow through with their cunning plan.

When we enquired why they were hanging about in the car park, they informed us they'd been expecting a mate to give them a lift, but he'd not turned up so they'd just decided they would have to walk back to town. We knew the likelihood of this being true was improbable, but there was nothing we could do to prove otherwise, especially as this would normally be a perfectly plausible explanation. The last thing we wanted to do was leave them in the area so, in order to get them out of harms way and ensure they wouldn't pose an ongoing burglary threat to the isolated pub, my sergeant decided we would transport them back to town. After I'd briefly advised the grateful pub landlady of our intentions (to put her mind at rest), we left the scene with the three stooges in tow, knowing that hopefully our intervention had put a stop to their antics that night and potentially prevented a crime from being committed – at least at that particular establishment! Having deposited them back in town, we hoped these repugnant members of the lowlife would now opt to steer clear of trouble that night; although we feared it was just as likely they may instead find an alternative venue to burgle.

I can also remember two other occasions where my actions might have helped prevent a crime, or caused certain individuals to think twice about going through with a possible felonious act. Both of these arose when I was off-duty and happened to come upon situations where I believe certain individuals were about to commit an offence – or, quite possibly, had already embarked on doing so, but were in the preliminary stages.

The first of these came about when I was walking my fiancée home in the early hours and spotted a couple of men behaving suspiciously. They were a pair of burly chaps, well over six-feet tall, and they were wearing dark clothing and baseball caps. I saw them disappear up a pathway towards a bungalow, and I initially assumed they might live there and be returning home after a night out, but something didn't sit quite right. It appeared like they were trying to creep about unnoticed, and I got the distinct impression they ducked down as we passed by. Once I'd walked my fiancée home, I therefore retraced my steps and, during my return journey, my suspicions became increasingly aroused when I got another glimpse of them – because this time they were surreptitiously heading up a pathway towards a different property, which neighboured the bungalow where I'd first spotted them.

This convinced me they were likely casing the area, and my first thought was to challenge them; however, as I was outnumbered and had no means of immediately summoning assistance, I soon realised this was another occasion where discretion was the better part of valour. I therefore decided my best course of action was to leg it to a nearby phone box, located at the end of the street, and ring for help – hopefully without making my actions too obvious and drawing attention to myself. By chance, I was able to make the call whilst subtly keeping observations on the two suspect rogues from a discreet distance away.

Three uniformed colleagues arrived within minutes of my call and, by this time, I'd become certain the two dodgy looking men were up to something as I'd seen them check out a couple of further properties. I hung about for a while in case my assistance was needed but, once the two guys had been detained, so their reasons for being in the vicinity could be checked out, I decided I'd done my bit and headed home to bed.

I later found out the two chaps had claimed they were trying to find the house of a mate, who supposedly lived on the estate. This was almost certainly a fictitious storyline – especially as their explanation had apparently been vague and the pair of them had a history of committing thefts. Although my colleagues had therefore doubted their candour and suspected they had criminal intent, they'd evidently found nothing tangible or incriminating to disprove their claim. As a result, no further action had been taken against them; nonetheless, I'm still confident this was yet another instance where the steps we'd taken had probably averted a crime from being committed.

The second occasion when I came across a situation where I suspected someone was endeavouring to commit a crime right in front of me, again while I was off-duty, occurred whilst I was in a queue at my local newsagent. It was a Saturday morning and, whilst I was waiting my turn to pay for my paper, I became aware that the man in front of me appeared to be giving the shop assistant a hard time. Initially I was pre-occupied looking at the sports section of the paper, but my ears pricked up when I realised this chap was remonstrating with the woman behind the counter about not receiving sufficient money back after he'd paid for the item he'd purchased. He claimed he'd originally given her a £20 note, and was insisting she hadn't returned it to him once he'd realised he had enough loose change to pay for the item he was purchasing. As he argued with her, it sounded to me like he was deliberately trying to confuse her to the point where she didn't know if she was coming or going, let alone have any idea whether or not she'd given the note back. Normally I wouldn't have taken much notice as such misunderstandings can easily happen, but something about his M.O. made me ultra-suspicious.

Only a few days earlier a similar thing had happened to my former wife, who at the time was the manageress of a local shop that sold nursery goods. She'd had a chap come in to buy a relatively small item, which only cost a couple of pounds, and he'd initially proffered a £20 note. He'd then decided he had enough change to pay for the item and, according to her, had actually retained the £20 note he'd originally offered and put it back in his pocket, whilst visually and verbally doing his utmost to distract her. Next he'd claimed she hadn't given him back his £20, and an argument had ensued when my former wife had disputed this claim. This had resulted in him invading her space and becoming aggressive when she'd stood her ground and refused to give him the £20, which he maintained had not been returned.

In spite of his insistence and threatening manner, she'd still declined. She was certain he was trying to hoodwink her using trickery and deceit, and had told him that it wouldn't be possible to meet his demand until she'd completed a quick interim cashing-up process to check if the till receipts were over by that amount. He'd not been prepared to wait for her to do so; no doubt because he'd known full well the outcome would prove him wrong and establish it had been a ruse. At this point he'd therefore left the shop, cursing her as he went.

Understandably this intimidating experience had been upsetting and, although it hadn't knocked her confidence too much, it had made her feel a little uneasy and a bit more wary. Afterwards she'd reported the incident to her boss, but the police hadn't been informed because it had been assumed he was just a bolshy customer who'd taken exception to being challenged. However, she'd subsequently heard that something similar had happened in several other shops around town. It therefore appeared this artful chap had likely been trying to deceive a number of shop assistants into giving him back money – which he'd only proffered and not handed over – by using a dastardly ploy designed to cause maximum confusion. Taking this into account, it seemed to me the practices of this suspicious character were tantamount to demanding money with menaces; except he was applying a devious and protracted deception technique that involved distracting and baffling his victims, which would therefore make it difficult to prove he was intentionally committing a criminal act.

What I'd witnessed while waiting in the queue at the newsagent, made me almost certain the shop assistant had been conned into giving her cunning and argumentative customer an extra £20. Therefore, as the suspected con artist left the shop, I quickly checked with her whether she believed she'd been taken for a ride and swindled out of £20. She acknowledged this was likely – although, she seemed so bewildered by what had just happened she probably felt she was going around the bend.

I had no time to lose if I was going to challenge the suspect so I dashed out in pursuit of him, not having a clue how he'd react or quite how I was going to handle the situation, especially if he got shirty or became aggressive. All I did know at this stage was that he matched the description given by my former wife of someone short and stocky in their late twenties, with dark hair and a broad Lancastrian accent, who'd tried to trick her into giving him back £20 to which he wasn't entitled – and that this Machiavellian character could be a serial offender, who was using a practiced distraction technique to illicitly obtain money.

Luckily the chap was still hanging around in the precinct when I exited the newsagent, so I was able to approach him, announce myself as an off-duty special constable and show him my warrant card. I explained the reason I wanted a word and, in fairness, he responded amenably to my explanation and intervention. Much to my surprise, he also agreed to return to the store so we could sort out any 'misunderstanding' that had arisen. Although he denied any wrongdoing, he didn't come across as a particularly nasty or shady character; however, I suspected he had an edge and would soon show me another side to his personality if he felt cornered, so I knew I had to tread carefully. After he'd come back into the shop with me, I once more spoke to the perplexed shop assistant to see if she could be any more certain about what had happened. I asked her if she could confirm whether she'd given the chap back more than the original £20 he'd tendered, but she really couldn't be sure. She explained that the only way she would know for certain was when they cashed-up and checked the till receipts against the takings.

However, since the manager of the store had joined us by this point, and stated it wouldn't be possible to complete the cashing-up process until the end of the day, there was little else I could do to get to the bottom of what had actually gone on.

In the absence of any concrete evidence to show that a crime had definitely been committed, let alone substantiate he'd done something wrong, I knew I didn't have any grounds to justify arresting him on suspicion of obtaining money by deception. The best I could therefore do was request his personal details, which at the time he obligingly gave me without any fuss. I have no doubt he acquiesced because I wasn't on duty, and he knew full well I couldn't do a person check over the radio to find out if they were fictitious – which was highly likely. Interestingly though, the address he gave me was for a street in Bolton, so at least that was fitting for someone with his accent, even if it was false.

After this event, I completed an intelligence report with the collator at our station to ensure the matter was logged, and that local shops were alerted to this particular incident and the other suspected occurrences of subterfuge that had likely taken place – and therefore made aware that we might have a con artist operating in our force area. A check on the details the guy had given me came back as no trace, so had almost certainly been fake; much as I'd anticipated. However, on the plus side, there were no further reports from our local shops during the next few months of someone carrying out similar attempts to deceive staff using the M.O. outlined. Hopefully my intervention therefore had a positive impact and, if nothing else, did at least warn him off and perhaps briefly put a stop to his unscrupulous conniving.

24 'Mispers'

Aside from the missing person enquiries already mentioned, I was involved in others that were equally memorable. The first of these occurred during my early days as a special constable when I was working with Nev on a late tour of duty. One Saturday evening, around 2100 hours, we received a radio message asking us to attend the home of a distressed mother, who'd reported that her 15-year-old daughter hadn't returned home for tea after a day out with a friend. Our first job was to enquire into the circumstances, and ascertain whether there was a history of similar disappearances.

Upon our arrival, the distraught mother gave us her account. She explained her daughter had been expected home by 6pm, and that when she failed to return she'd contacted the friend with whom she'd spent the day. On doing so, she'd learned her daughter had left this friend's house earlier in the evening, presumably to head home. Understandably she was now incandescent with worry as several hours had elapsed since her daughter had set off to return home. This young girl's welfare was also a matter of concern for Nev and I – her safety was paramount and the circumstances warranted an immediate response – but first we needed to speak with the friend to get her take on the situation before we called up the cavalry, and set in motion a wide-scale search. So, after obtaining the friend's details, we headed straight to her home.

During our interview with the friend we sensed there was something she wasn't telling us. She stuck to the story she'd given to the mother, and denied knowing any more, but seemed coy and evasive when answering some of our questions. In spite of her reticence, we sensitively probed further in an effort to prise out some helpful information – being careful not to give the impression we thought she was lying.

Our perseverance led to a breakthrough in our investigation when she finally admitted that, unbeknown to her mother, her friend had been dating a boy and she might have gone to his house. Nev and I were relieved our hunch she likely knew more than she'd been letting on was correct, and appreciated her reluctance to initially reveal more had probably been out of blind loyalty to her friend. Importantly, we now had another line of enquiry to pursue as she gave us the name of the mystery boyfriend, and told us roughly where he lived. Armed with this new information, we delayed requesting a full-scale search until we'd had a chance to follow it up. Our decision to hold back proved to be the right one because we tracked down the missing girl at her boyfriend's house, and returned her forthwith to her anxious, yet grateful, mother.

Where missing persons are concerned, particularly when it is a child or vulnerable adult, time is always of the essence, so making the right judgement call about when to instigate a full-scale search is vital. In this instance, Nev and I were lucky that our gut feelings, and sneaking suspicions the friend was holding something back, turned out to be spot on, but nobody would have blamed us if we'd recommended an immediate response from all available resources – as it's always better to be safe than sorry. It's heartening when there's a positive outcome – you always hope for a happy ending when dealing with 'mispers' – but, regrettably that is not always the case, and feelings of euphoria are sometimes replaced by those of utter dismay.

Sadly, that was so when a middle-aged woman was reported missing and hadn't been found after several days, despite extensive enquiries and a wide-ranging search. By the time she was eventually discovered, she was no longer alive; a hiker had come upon her naked body in a field on the outskirts of town. The circumstances suggested foul play and the site was sealed off. However, once the Home Office pathologist had arrived at the scene, and conducted an initial examination of the body, a different picture evolved.

On moving the deceased woman's remains, a suicide note was discovered – and it became clear that she had taken her own life. A post-mortem established cause of death was due to the effects of an overdose combined with hyperthermia. It saddened me greatly to think this woman had passed away alone, and in such an undignified manner. Equally, it was concerning to find out – too late – that a witness had seen a naked woman running across the field a couple of days before her demise. The witness had spotted her when he'd glanced out of his hotel window, but had assumed she must be a naturist out for a jog. The chap had come forward after reading about the incident in the press, and it made me wonder if her suffering and premature death could have been averted if he'd reported the matter at the time.

Working in my own community meant that I could occasionally be involved in dealing with incidents that were a little too close to home. An example of this was an evening shift when I was paired up with Gavin. We were assigned another missing person enquiry – a married woman in her forties, who lived in a village on our patch, had left home after an argument with her husband and threatened to kill herself. It was clearly imperative she was located as soon as possible.

Gavin and I went to see the husband to sensitively obtain information about her state of mind, and find out what had happened during the argument to cause her to threaten such action. We enquired if his wife had any underlying mental health issues, which included a history of threatening to take her own life, and whether he had any idea where she might go when upset. His answers made the picture much clearer. He explained his wife had been having an affair, which her married lover had recently ended after they'd been caught in a compromising position by a work colleague. According to her husband, his wife had been devastated and had told him about her feelings for this other man. This revelation had led to an argument and she'd stormed out of the house, threatening to end it all.

The husband gave us the name of his wife's former lover and, much to my surprise, he was a relative of mine! He then told us he didn't know where she'd gone after storming out, but he knew that a nearby wood was her favourite place to go for a walk. As an afterthought, he also hinted there was a distinct possibility she had decided to confront the love of her life about his decision to end their relationship – and he might know where she was; for example the location where they had their secret liaisons.

Knowing our next port of call would need to be the former lover – who was of course my relation – I felt I shouldn't be involved in the ongoing enquiry and declared a conflict of interest. However, with only three of us on duty for this shift, and with the missing woman's welfare our main priority, Gavin decided my continued assistance was necessary. All the same, to avoid any embarrassment to my relative, we agreed it would be best if I stayed on the periphery of the investigation while Gavin went to interview him. I therefore made myself scarce by going to search the nearby wood the husband had mentioned. This proved fruitless, but at least it enabled us to eliminate this location from our enquiries.

Having finished his interview, Gavin picked me up so we could continue our search jointly and we headed to a beauty spot in the area, which my relation had mentioned was a regular haunt for them. Our arrival at this location was a 'bingo moment'. We immediately spotted the missing woman's car, with her still in the driving seat, distressed, but otherwise unharmed, so it was good to have a happy outcome. Gavin gave her a lift home in the police car as she was in no fit state to drive and had declined to go hospital to be checked out, whilst I drove her car back to her house. Her husband seemed relieved to have her back in one piece, but it was hard to judge how she felt or whether she was pleased to be home.

Some of the teenage residents from our local children's home were regularly reported as 'mispers'. They had a tendency to go missing for a pastime, and it could be a bit like a game of hide & seek because they were practiced at giving us the run-around when they chose to go AWOL; sometimes disappearing for several days before re-emerging. Many of them had family or other connections outside of our area, so you never knew if they were likely to still be in the locality when they did a vanishing act. In view of their vulnerabilities, there was always considerable concern for their welfare whenever they absconded, especially as some of them experienced complex issues and came from challenging backgrounds.

Invariably, such investigations involved liaising with other police forces, and could be resource intensive. Thankfully though, those who continually went missing were usually found before they could come to any harm. However, as there was always the potential that something awful could happen, any report of a juvenile going missing was given a high priority, with investigations being thorough and meticulous. That was so when a couple of the home's younger residents – two 10-years-old boys – failed to return after visiting the local park one Saturday afternoon.

On that particular day, I was on foot patrol with Spud in the town centre when the call came over the radio to be on the look out for the two missing boys. Shortly after that, a member of the public reported seeing a couple of lads matching their description playing on a nearby railway line, so Spud and I were despatched to search the area where they'd last been seen. We spent a couple of hours walking up and down the track to see if there was any sign of them. This line was solely used by goods trains, which were infrequent – and when we did encounter one there was plenty of time to get out of the way. Even so, we were well aware that many youngsters get maimed or killed on railway tracks each year, and knew it was imperative we made certain these two boys weren't on the line or playing nearby.

By the time the light was beginning to fade, we still hadn't come across the pair of them, but then we got a radio update – they had returned to the home. I immediately felt a sense of relief and my first thought was, 'phew – thank goodness for that', not only because the two children had turned up ok, which was great news, but also because I was exhausted from traipsing up and down the railway line!

Following this message, I didn't give the matter another thought at that stage, and resumed my patrol with Spud until it was time for us to clock off. Next morning, however, when I attempted to get out of bed, I was reminded of our previous day's exertions on that railway track because my legs refused to work. They'd seized up! My ankles and calves were so stiff I thought I must have aged about 30 years overnight. It took a moment or two before it dawned on me that the motion of going up and down over the sleepers, during my trek along the railway line, was why I now felt like an old man. I must have been stretching muscles in my legs and tendons in my ankles that simply weren't used to that level of exercise. The stiffness only lasted for a day, but running or speed walking was certainly out of the question during that period!

25 End of the Line

AFTER MORE THAN 22 YEARS of serving my community, initially as a police cadet and then as a special constable, my tenure within law enforcement came to an end, almost as abruptly as when it had started many moons before. This came about for a variety of reasons, not least because my day job had become increasingly challenging. At the time I decided to call it a day, I was trying to deal with a number of profoundly complex issues, which were not only work-related as they also impacted on my personal life. I knew resolving these matters was going to require all my attention, so it was therefore essential I once more took stock of my situation, did some soul-searching and considered my priorities in life.

A number of determining factors came into play, and it wasn't just the dilemmas surrounding my work situation and personal life that ultimately influenced my decision to call time on my role as a special constable. To be honest, it was once again one of the toughest decisions I've ever had to make, especially as I still held dear my sense of duty and thoroughly enjoyed performing most elements of police work. However, due to a number of structural and operational changes that had occurred during my latter days in the Special Constabulary, I'd increasingly found myself undertaking certain duties that had started to detract from that enjoyment, not least acting as an escort when prisoners had to be transported to custody suites.

This particular task had started to arise more frequently because a lot of the smaller nicks had been downgraded and had their custody suites closed, including our station. In turn, this had meant that any prisoner arrested in our borough, who needed to be detained, now had to be transferred to our Divisional HQ, which still had a custody facility – or, subsequently, to a centralised custody suite once it had opened. For officers based at my station this entailed making a round trip of more than 40 miles, with such journeys normally taking a minimum of two bobbies away from directly policing the streets of our town for around two hours; sometimes longer if there were delays booking in the prisoner. As resources in our borough would therefore be depleted for the duration they were absent, it wasn't unusual for special constables, including myself on a number of occasions, to be allocated the task of supporting a regular colleague when prisoners needed to be escorted. I could totally appreciate why we were utilised in this way, and I never really objected at being asked to assist with prisoner escorts, even though it was one of the more boring aspects of police work. However, when it began to happen routinely, I did begin to feel a little disillusioned, mainly because it started to diminish the contribution that volunteers based in rural stations were able to make towards policing our local communities. This was especially so when carrying out this particular duty sometimes eroded most of the time you had available to devote to a shift, and therefore impinged on your ability to 'make a difference'.

In themselves, my concerns relating to operational aspects of the role weren't huge considerations as I went through the decision-making process about whether I should continue serving as a special, but they perhaps ultimately helped to tip the balance.

Unquestionably, becoming a dad was a much bigger factor that influenced my decision to quit. Fatherhood had come a little later in life for me compared to most blokes and, as soon as I had a young stepdaughter and a baby daughter of my own, they immediately became my pride and joy. Up to the point I'd become a father, I'd never really thought too much about the dangers you could sometimes encounter when on duty, and the associated risks of confronting certain situations where you could possibly put yourself in harm's way. That's not to say it didn't bother me deep down, as I of course knew I would occasionally have to deal with violent people who could pose a threat to my physical wellbeing, but it wasn't something that had ever really played on my mind prior to me becoming a father. However, that suddenly altered as soon as I had children to consider and had acquired parental responsibilities.

There's nothing more precious than having children, and whenever I was on duty following the most meaningful events in my life, I constantly found myself thinking about how it would affect my daughters if I came a cropper in some way. Having such thoughts feature prominently in your mind is not a good place to be when you're involved in frontline policing; especially if they start to impact on the way you react in some situations, or deal with certain scenarios; for example, when you encounter a volatile incident. A person's natural instinct is to get away from danger but, as a police officer you go towards it and, although I hadn't lost my nerve, it was evident to me that I'd become more circumspect. Having such an outlook is not ideal in any circumstance where you have to think on your feet, and sometimes act swiftly in order to get the upper hand before a problem escalates. In the end, I think this therefore became the most telling reason for me coming to the conclusion that my days in the force were numbered.

Once I'd stepped down as a result of the factors I've highlighted, the time was ripe for considered reflection. In the main, I have nothing but fond memories of those days, and I like to think I did my best for the local community, although I will leave it to others to judge whether my stint as a special constable was illustrious or not. I pretty much enjoyed every minute I spent performing this role, but – as previously alluded to on several occasions – I have to say it was the community policing element that appealed to me most of all, as opposed to the more exciting aspects, such as the thrill of the occasional chase. I guess hearing that won't come as a surprise to anyone who knows me well, as they'd appreciate I'm not much of an adrenalin junkie. Being more of a philanthropic type of person, who has an easy going and phlegmatic approach to life, it was meeting people and having the chance to help them that was more my forte. That's largely what attracted me to join the specials, even though it perhaps makes me sound overly altruistic. It's also why I generally preferred being on the beat rather than stuck in a patrol vehicle. Ordinarily, when you're out and about on foot you get more opportunities to interact with the public at large – which to me was a really satisfying part of the role.

It would be easy to overlook or forget that in police work you often encounter heart-warming as well as heart-stopping moments, and I especially got a buzz from assisting more vulnerable members of society. I can recall two incidents in particular where that was so, when I went to the aid of some elderly folk.

The first of these was when a very frightened old lady had phoned in to say she'd heard some gunshots coming from her back garden. On this occasion, I was nearby the caller's house on foot patrol, so I offered to attend. I was there within minutes of her making the emergency call and could immediately see she was petrified. In this instance, I was rapidly able to put her mind at rest by explaining that the bangs she'd heard were actually caused by fireworks, which had been let off during the town's 'Extravaganza' celebration taking place that night. Her fear soon subsided on hearing this, but I still stayed with her a while to help calm her nerves. I felt this was important in order to give her some further re-assurance, especially as I knew that she was likely to have already been on edge even before hearing the bangs, due to a recent murder that had occurred in the vicinity; in fact, just three doors away from where she resided.

The second similar incident arose when I was on mobile patrol with Ant, a regular colleague who'd formerly been in the army and come to our borough after joining the police. It was late at night when we responded to the report of a prowler on a site for residential park homes located a mile out of town. The report had come from an elderly female resident, who had spotted a man looking through her bedroom window as she was about to retire for the night. By the time we arrived, there was no sign of the peeping tom in close proximity of this lady's home as this individual was probably long gone, but I nevertheless stayed with her whilst Ant carried out a thorough search of the surrounding area.

Coming across someone peering through your window late at night would be enough to spook anyone, so I expected her to be a nervous wreck; however, I soon realised she was no shrinking violet, and was actually a gutsy lady as she seemed more incensed than scared by the experience. Although we didn't trace the prowler, I've no doubt she did spot someone because Ant found footprints in the flowerbed outside the relevant window. We therefore promised the complainant we'd carry out frequent patrols of the area for the rest of that night, and then ensure that passing attention was given to the site over the next few weeks. Despite her stoic reaction to the incursion on her property, the delightfully courageous OAP was visibly relieved and really appreciated our efforts; so, even though we hadn't tracked down the voyeur, Ant and I departed the scene knowing we were leaving behind a grateful senior citizen.

These two experiences of responding to the concerns of elderly members of the community epitomised the value of neighbourhood policing in my eyes, and it was their reactions that made this element of the role feel so rewarding.

Whilst further reflecting on my time as both a police cadet and a special constable, I considered what had driven me to take this path. I wouldn't describe myself as an obvious candidate for police work. I'm not especially brave, and nor am I someone with a lot of bottle, but perversely I have always thrived on testing myself in challenging situations – and oddly, I did find some elements of police work therapeutic; perhaps because it was so different to most other things that I experienced in my day-to-day life. I've already mentioned many times that I got my kicks out of helping people, and how I wanted to do something that impacted positively on my community but, in addition to this, I think I've always had this deep-rooted, overwhelming desire to do the right thing when confronted with injustice – and, in police work, you definitely get the opportunity to defend your fellow beings by tackling maltreatment, exploitation and oppression head-on.

I suppose I've always known that I have protective instincts because they sometimes came to the fore in my younger days, whenever I needed to stand up for the defenceless or against any form of travesty, but I never really understood what made me act in this way. However, as an adult, I often wondered if subconsciously this was due to an event I witnessed in a large city when I was just six-years-old because it certainly left an indelible mark in my memory – and I'm sure that certain experiences we go through when growing up do help to define and shape us as we progress to adulthood.

Along with my younger brother, I'd been left very briefly in my dad's car whilst he had popped into an office to drop off some paperwork, when I saw three white men attacking a lone black man. Although being so young I didn't fully understand what was going on, I'm sure they must have beaten him up really badly because I recall he ended up bleeding a lot from his mouth and nose. It all happened in close proximity and, at one stage, the victim actually fell onto the bonnet of our car, at which point two of the men pinned him down whilst the other one punched him repeatedly in the face. As far as I can remember, it was all over quite quickly but, as you can imagine, witnessing something so violent was pretty scary for two young lads – and I'm convinced that somewhere deep in my psyche it left a subliminal message, which possibly accounts for my protective nature.

I've no doubt that when I joined the Special Constabulary, some local people that didn't know me that well possibly believed I only did so due to the glamorous way policing is frequently portrayed on TV shows, and also because they perhaps thought that being in uniform was something that appealed to me. However, I can honestly say that neither of these factors entered my thinking at the time – besides, there's nothing especially glamorous about the reality of police work, and the uniform in itself is far from flattering. I did though wear it with pride, and am immensely proud of the time I served. As stated before, it has left me with a host of wonderful memories to savour and, most importantly, friendships that will last a lifetime. There is something uniquely special about working with like minded people, in order to achieve a common purpose, when you are faced with constant challenges and tested to the limit. For me, it was a privilege being part of the police family and having the chance to share the experiences of those who fulfil this role as regulars.

Based on my time as a 'volunteer bobby', I would recommend the Special Constabulary to anyone who wants to play a part in policing their local community – and, let's face it, everyone should take some degree of responsibility for the security of their own neighbourhoods, and not just rely totally on the regular police force to keep us all safe. Not that I'm advocating everyone should be out on the streets doing their bit, as I do appreciate that in many cases it wouldn't be either a feasible or a desirable option, and there are many practical reasons why a considerable number of people wouldn't be able to get directly involved. I also recognise that enlisting to undertake frontline policing is primarily a vocation. However, simply by looking out for one another, perhaps by joining a 'Neighbourhood Watch' scheme, anyone can participate and help to make their community a safer place to live; so, as a society, we should be grateful for the contribution such public-spirited people make in the war against crime.

For those who do go that step further, by putting on the uniform and going out to police the streets, I have nothing but total respect because I know from personal experience just how wild it can get out there at times, and what a tough job it can be. Yes, you will get a few bad apples – and even a small number of rotten ones – who join up for the wrong reasons, and abuse the powers entrusted in them to uphold the law, but the vast majority of police officers are truly decent people who are focused on serving their communities and watching over the folk that live there. That's why I feel that those who don the uniform are my unsung heroes, especially the colleagues I worked closely with during my service, not least Ivan and Nev, with whom I will always share a mutual affinity and lifelong bond. Much of that special connection and kindred spirit undoubtedly emanates from our shared experiences, including our respective close brushes with death. Some of it is also borne out of witnessing first-hand a turbulent, toxic and sometimes quite horrific side of life, which fortunately remains hidden from many people.

I was lucky, in as much that I only caught fleeting glimpses of the most dreadful sights that you encounter on duty, unlike my intrepid full-time colleagues who were dealing with it on a daily basis. However, without pulling any punches, I can confirm that once you've opened 'Pandora's Box' you're no longer shielded from the shockingly harsh realities of life, and you will always have those haunting memories – whether it's observing the bloated and mutilated corpse that washed up on the shore, seeing limbs and body parts strewn over a railway track after a suicide, or coming face-to-face with a crushed body following an RTC, they all take their toll. It can tear you apart deep down, in spite of all the bravado that might suggest otherwise and, since you can't turn the clock back once you've seen such awful things, you just have to learn to manage the impact so it doesn't slowly but surely eat away at your inner soul, and then gradually erode your ability to continue functioning effectively. That's where being part of a fellowship and having the support of those with whom you've been through thick and thin can help you maintain your emotional stability, come to terms with the harsh realities and develop coping mechanisms. This can then enable you to deal with any fall-out in a considered and reasoned way, and keep at bay any demons that arise as a consequence of going through traumatic experiences. For that, I'm eternally grateful to my former colleagues, many of whom I'm honoured to call my friends.

Hopefully, within my accounts of policing, it should be clear that I had nothing but total admiration and the utmost respect for those regular officers I worked alongside, who constantly displayed an abundance of courage, along with a selfless attitude, in their fearless approach to performing their duty. I think on the whole that feeling was mutual, and the vast majority of them valued the contribution made by specials. Certainly it seemed like they respected us for joining them in the fray on the frontline, and appreciated our wholehearted commitment and willingness to boldly go where many people understandably fear to tread. However, I also think some of them thought we must be mad to do it for nothing – and, after serving in the Special Constabulary for all those years, I tend to agree they have a point!

At the stage I stepped down from being a special constable, I knew it was the right time to hang up my boots. Nonetheless, as already indicated, I still had mostly positive and cherished memories of all my experiences and, despite encountering some hair-raising moments and many unpleasant sights, wouldn't have changed anything. I didn't go out with a bang in a blaze of glory – just faded away really – and, not being one for the limelight, that suited me fine. I only played a small part in policing my community, but I truly hope that my minor role did help make a difference, and that my memoir reflects that might have been the case.

So that was me done and it was time to sign off…or, using the correct police call sign of my era, time to say:

'10/10 Foxtrot Romeo – over and out!'

Epilogue

It will have become apparent from my memoir that I never did return to full-time policing as a regular. Looking back, I think not returning in this way did mean there was a small part of me that was tinged with regret for a while. However, on the other hand, I soon recognised that in some ways becoming a special meant I did perhaps have the best of both worlds, simply because being a part-time voluntary bobby allowed me to experience working as a police officer without having to give up the career I'd carved out for myself in training and mentoring young people – and I believe the two roles complemented each other.

I learnt so much about life and people from my time in the specials and, if there's one thing being exposed to policing taught me during my 20+ years of service, it's the ability to keep everything very much in perspective – and I think doing so generally enabled me to stay grounded and remain calm when contending with any of life's challenges. Perhaps, for me, the biggest obstacle to overcome when I became involved in police work was getting used to the fact that you go towards danger rather than shy away from it. Up to that point, I don't think I knew if I had what it takes to confront a threatening situation. As mentioned, on doing so is when you truly discover whether you fit into the fight, flight or frozen with fear category – although I totally empathise with anyone who finds out it's either of the latter two. Generally, I discovered that when you do encounter instances where you could be at risk the adrenalin kicks in and helps you get through it – and it's usually after the event, in the cold light of day, that it hits home and you really think about the severity of the situation you faced, and fully appreciate just how much peril you were potentially in at the time.

Something else that took a fair while to get used to when I first embarked on policing was the amount of times you can be subjected to withering verbal assaults. Such attacks can initially be seen as very personal and insulting, particularly when they are casting aspersions by questioning your birthright or manhood, but you soon realise it is generally the uniform and what it stands for that they are aiming their torrent of abuse at during these monstrous outbursts. Naturally, whenever this occurs, you cannot let them have the satisfaction of thinking their derisory and inflammatory language, or their demeaning behaviour, which are intended to intimidate and provoke a reaction, are having the desired affect. After a while you do get used to hearing all the derogatory comments and slurs and, in time, this form of denigration has little impact and becomes like an everyday norm, which in some ways is sad because being maligned is something nobody should have to tolerate.

Right up to the stage in my life when I experienced policing first-hand, my default position had always been to trust people unless they had given me a reason not to and, although I appreciate that being involved in police work can change that outlook and make you more wary, I like to think I always kept an open mind and never pre-judged anyone based on stereo-typing. However, whilst I still try to see the best in everyone, and believe that the majority of lawbreakers have redeeming qualities and characteristics, I think being engaged in law enforcement did stop me seeing life through rose-tinted glasses, and opened my eyes to what a cruel and wicked place the world can sometimes be. In that respect, I therefore acknowledge there are some people (thankfully a very small minority) who are evil to the point of being beyond redemption – and that is simply a fact of life you have to learn to accept.

****

As readers will have noted, I had some fun times and encountered a number of amusing events during my period of service. However, it's important to stress that none of my close colleagues were frivolous or flippant towards the job itself, and they worked tirelessly to perform this vital role to the best of their ability. It's of equal importance to also keep the fun aspect of the role very much in proportion, when compared to the vast amount of time spent devoted to the serious side of policing. In actual fact, when you consider that the fun elements I've referenced spanned more than 22 years, it's apparent that in reality the number of times they occurred was miniscule. Therefore, in no way did they detract from the many hours my colleagues dedicated to successfully undertaking essential police work, or undermine their devotion to duty as they strived to meet their obligations as public servants.

As already highlighted, I think sometimes having the capacity to make light of certain situations, by occasionally engaging in banter or harmless fun, helped many officers to cope more effectively with the stresses and strains of the job. Nonetheless, doing so came with a caveat as it was essential everyone knew where to draw the line and didn't cross any boundaries, which resulted in them indulging in gratuitous amusement at the expense of those who'd suffered personal misfortune or trauma. The vast majority of officers were discerning in their use of humour but, as indicated, there were occasions early on in my service when a few colleagues perhaps went a bit too far with some of their antics. However, during my latter days, there was a marked change in social attitudes when we entered another new dawn with more emphasis on political correctness – which meant that certain behaviours were no longer considered acceptable, nor tolerated. I'm not suggesting this was a bad thing as I would never advocate the exploitation of anyone experiencing adversity – but losing the fun element did mean that traditional ways of unwinding or letting your hair down were increasingly thwarted.

The overall picture I have painted about policing during the period I served is intended to be an honest account of how things were in a bygone era, and hopefully reflects the way things were done in those days, before certain behaviours and activities, once considered acceptable, were understandably consigned to the history books; so my amusing anecdotes should therefore be seen in that context.

Acknowledgements

This memoir is dedicated to all my former colleagues, from those at the top of the tree right down to everyone at the rock-face. It was an honour and a privilege to work alongside you in the battle to maintain law and order – so thank you for having me and for helping to create so many of my treasured memories.
In that regard my gratitude therefore also goes to Silver Crow for the significant part they played in helping me to achieve my goal in regard to writing this memoir.

****

A huge thank you to all my family and friends for the support you gave me whilst I was compiling my memoir, and also for being so patient and putting up with me throughout the five years it has taken me to complete this project. In particular my gratitude goes to my daughter Lily, my stepdaughter Amelia, my son-in-law Charlie, my step-niece Suzana, my friends Debs and Bex, and my mentors Gill and Brenda for all the help and guidance they've given me along the way. Without their input and advice I wouldn't have ended up giving this challenge my best shot, and I shall forever be grateful for their contributions. In that respect my gratitude therefore also goes to Silver Crow for the significant part they played in helping me to achieve my goal in regard to writing this memoir.